Religion
and
Mass Media

Religion
and
Mass Media

Audiences
and
Adaptations

Daniel A. Stout
Judith M. Buddenbaum

SAGE Publications
International Educational and Professional Publisher
Thousand Oaks London New Delhi

For information address:

 SAGE Publications, Inc.
2455 Teller Road
Thousand Oaks, California 91320
E-mail: order@sagepub.com

SAGE Publications Ltd.
6 Bonhill Street
London EC2A 4PU
United Kingdom

SAGE Publications India Pvt. Ltd.
M-32 Market
Greater Kailash I
New Delhi 110 048 India

Printed in the United States of America

Library of Congress Cataloging-in-Publication Data

Main entry under title:

Religion and mass media: Audiences and adaptations / editors, Daniel
  A. Stout, Judith M. Buddenbaum.
     p. cm.
  Includes bibliographical references.
  ISBN 0-8039-7173-7 (cloth: acid-free paper). — ISBN
0-8039-7174-5 (pbk.: acid-free paper)
     1. Mass media—Religious aspects—Christianity. 2. Mass media in
religion. I. Stout, Daniel A. II. Buddenbaum, Judith Mitchell,
1941- .
BV652.95.R43 1996
291.1′75—dc20   95-41786

This book is printed on acid-free paper.

96 97 98 99 10 9 8 7 6 5 4 3 2 1

Sage Production Editor: Astrid Virding
Sage Typesetter: Janelle LeMaster

Contents

PART I

The Current Status of Research
on Religion and Mass Media

Introduction

Toward a Synthesis of
Mass Communication Research
and the Sociology of Religion

DANIEL A. STOUT

JUDITH M. BUDDENBAUM

In his mystery novel, *The Name of the Rose*, Umberto Eco (1986) describes an argument between two 14th-century Catholic priests. At the core of the debate is the power of books and whether they are capable of spreading Satan's influence and ultimately destroying the church. Jorge, the venerable senior priest, contends that outside holy Scripture, books have the "power of a thousand scorpions" and should be kept out of the hands of the citizenry.

According to the story, only two priests are permitted to know the location of books once they are stored in a dark, cavernous library inside a Franciscan abbey. Opposing this fearful view of information, however, is William of Baskerville, who disagrees that the devil is in books. Meanings are in people, he argues, considering censorship the greater sin.

Although Eco's story is set in the 1300s, his descriptions of exhaustive efforts to restrict access to books remind the reader of issues that are relevant today. In recent years, religious leaders have become increasingly vocal about some of the content of television, movies, and other media. What do contemporary religious institutions teach their members about the appropriate role of mass media in religious life? Why are there often disagreements among church members about the nature of "media effects"? What is the relationship between religiosity and media-related behavior? How do audience members feel about the ways religion is presented in the news and entertainment media? These are some of the questions that frame the central issues in this volume.

Although Eco's book is fiction, the claim that church leaders often view new communication technologies with ambivalence is supported by historical evidence. Despite the fact that books, periodicals, radio, television, and computers are used by denominational structures to promote institutional religion, they also are frequently feared for their potentially harmful effects. For example, Pope Alexander VI taxed printing presses in 1501, predicting they would undermine faith in God (Pool, 1983). Similar concerns resurfaced in the early 19th century with the debut of the American novel as a literary form. Protestant and Catholic clergies often placed novels in the same category as alcohol and tobacco in describing their deleterious effects on Christian values (Douglas, 1988). Later, radio was criticized by citizens and church leaders who felt it had the power to control the minds of its listeners (Spigel, 1992; see also Chapter 6, this volume). More recently, groups such as Christian Leaders for Responsible Television and the Family Research Council have publicly denounced the Hollywood media industry for its alleged opposition to "family values" (see Hamilton & Rubin, 1992; Lacayo, 1995).

Churches are not the only ones to claim that mass media have a role in the erosion of religious values. Popular books such as Medved's (1992) *Hollywood vs. America* and Carter's (1993) *The Culture of Disbelief* have also added to public opinion about the perceived ability of media to trivialize and undermine religion. What appears to be missing from the public debate about media and religion, however, is any substantive information about what churchgoers themselves have to say about these issues. Perhaps even less is known about what major denominations teach their members about appropriate media use. The editors of this book take these omissions seriously in bringing together chapters that get beyond popular conjecture and casual assumptions about the effects of media on religious life. A number of research methods are applied as the contributors take a deeper, more thorough look at the question of how mass media play a role in religious communities.

This task is difficult to achieve given that the topic has received only superficial attention from scholars. Academic research on the subject of religion and media is scant at best, suffering from a lack of interdisciplinary study (see Chapter 2, this volume). There is considerable theoretical development in the sociology of religion, but little attention is paid to the role of mediated communication in these processes. Mass communication researchers, on the other hand, have created an academic literature about the nature of media effects yet rarely include religion in their discussions. This book represents one of the first attempts to promote interdisciplinary dialogue on the subject of religion and media.

Given the lack of scholarly research on the subject, this volume seeks to accomplish two things. First, it brings together chapters that, due to institutional divisions in the academy, might otherwise appear in a number of nonspecialized journals across a number of disparate fields of study. Second, unlike popular works on the topic, religious institutions and audiences are examined from a social science perspective. In other words, rather than trying to predict the effects of media on religious groups based on the analysis of message content alone, the editors have assembled a number of works that take a more scholarly and systematic approach to the study of religious institutions and audiences.

THE NEED FOR INTERDISCIPLINARY STUDY

The goal here is to achieve a creative synthesis of ideas between mass communication research and the sociology of religion. Chapter 2 makes the compelling argument that scholars in both areas have worked in relative isolation, with no clear bridge of understanding between them. This book represents an opportunity for the mass communication researcher to reflect more deeply on the phenomenon of "religiosity" and how it may expand knowledge about the nature of audiences. At the same time, it asks the sociologist of religion to ponder the question of how mass communication processes affect those social situations that are fundamental to the creation of religious worldviews. Although a few conferences and discussions on the subject have been held, there is growing sentiment that the research on religion and media is in need of an interdisciplinary synthesis of ideas.

What Sociology of Religion Has to Offer Mass Communication Research

Despite the fact that religion remains an important aspect of the U.S. social fabric, it is mentioned infrequently in studies of media audiences (see Chapter 2, this volume). Exceptions would include Hamilton and Rubin (1992) and Roberts (1983) who investigated the television-viewing habits of religious "conservatives and nonconservatives," thus recognizing, to a degree, the complex nature of religiosity. Besides these and perhaps a few others, however, communication researchers often describe religiosity using narrow, simplistic demographical measures that do not adequately reflect the role of religiosity in everyday life. When they do discuss religion, it is usually a secondary issue in a larger study on some other research topic. One questionnaire item inquiring about church membership or church attendance does not capture the full range of ways that religion plays a part in how individuals experience media. These narrow, superficial measures of religiosity ignore theoretical development that defines religiosity in a multidimensional way. Religion is manifested by behavior, belief, feeling, and social interaction (see review of research in Cornwall et al., 1986). Simply stated, mass communication researchers have only a limited knowledge of how religiosity defines audiences of mass media.

Research in the sociology of religion provides mass communication researchers with new insights about the nature of religiosity and how it might help orient the audience member to a particular worldview regarding media. For example, some sociologists recognize both personal and institutional modes of religiosity (Cornwall et al., 1986; Dittes, 1971; Lenski, 1963), a distinction rarely mentioned in mass communication research. Media scholars, because they tend to define religiosity in terms of institutional expectations (i.e., church attendance, official membership, etc.) only, often fail to inquire about an audience member's religious beliefs, behaviors, and feelings that do not require official membership in a particular religious group. That is, someone may believe in God, have personal prayers, give money to religious charities, and encourage others to believe in God, but if they do not attend a particular church, they are likely to be labeled "nonreligious" and, consequently, left out of religious media studies. This is done despite the fact that one's personal religiosity may be influential in how media are used.

There is a vast difference between the ways communication researchers and sociologists conceptualize the "religious" audience. In mass communication research, this audience is defined in terms of affiliations with institutions that have expectations about religious behavior and participation. This conceptualization, however, emphasizes only institutional dimensions and does not take into account the ways religion is manifested at the level of the audience member's *personal community*. Building on the work of Berger (1967), several argue that personal communities of family, friends, and coworkers create and sustain a religious worldview that is a more accurate predictor of behavior than are institutional sanctions (Fischer, 1982; Wellman, 1979). As researchers of mass communication examine these processes more closely, an expanded and more useful notion of religiosity may emerge. The chapters in this book may provide foundation-level data for this to occur.

What Mass Communication Research
Has to Offer the Sociology of Religion

If one accepts the basic assumptions of Berger (1967), Durkheim (1912), Park (1915), and Weber (1963), phenomena related to communication are key elements in the development of one's religiosity. Religious worldviews are created and sustained in ongoing social processes in which information is shared. In other words, an individual's information environment in which there is some degree of exposure to both religious and secular messages comprises a vital element of development. The impact of mass media in these processes, however, is only beginning to be addressed. Although mass media have been examined in terms of their cultivation of personal values (Gerbner & Gross, 1976), the social uses to which they are put (Katz, Blumler, & Gurevitch, 1974), their role in cultural processes (Carey, 1988), and their effects on general behavioral patterns in society (Meyrowitz, 1985; Postman, 1985), this work is rarely cited in the literature of the sociology of religion. Numerous opportunities exist, however, for new applications of these perspectives to the study of religious audiences.

One of the most intensely debated issues in the sociology of religion is the process of secularization in Western cultures (see discussions in Jary & Jary, 1991; Waxman, 1994). Yet although a small number of sociologists (see Chapter 2, this volume) have touched on mass communication issues, researchers have not adequately examined how media contribute to a religious institution's gain or loss of power in society. Today, religious institutions find themselves in an "information society," in which the exchange of messages through mediated communication is more frequent and more complex (Schement & Lievrouw, 1987; Straubhaar & LaRose, 1996; see also Chapter 18, this volume). This situation has contributed to popular assumptions that media are powerful agents of both good and evil, capable of impeding secularization on the one hand and accelerating it on the other hand. elevision offerings such as the *700 Club* and *VISN* are two examples of the belief that media can have a positive effect on one's spirituality, yet simultaneously, "unwholesome" media are criticized for having a secularizing influence on the audience (see Fore, 1987). Although the question of media effects has been addressed by mass communication researchers for almost a century, few sociologists have referenced this work in their contributions to the secularization debate.

TOWARD AN AUDIENCE-CENTERED
VIEW OF RELIGION AND MEDIA

For sociologists, a key question is how mass media help create the information environments in which a religious worldview is acquired. For researchers of mass communication, the primary issue is how religiosity contributes to interpretive processes. Both questions beg for an audience-centered approach to the study of religion and media. Therefore, this book is a departure from previous works that rely less on audience research than on descriptions of media content. Some of the contributing authors use quantitative methods to describe media behaviors among members of various religious groups, whereas others report qualitative analyses of the role of media in everyday life. Attitudes about how religion is reported in the press and how audience members describe conflicts associated with popular movies are also among the topics treated here. By shifting the unit of analysis to the audience members themselves, it is hoped that more cogent conclusions can be drawn about the effects of media in everyday social interactions within religious communities.

SCOPE AND ORGANIZATION
OF THE BOOK

Although there are many religions represented in the United States, this book is confined to a discussion of the relationship between various forms of Christianity and media use. In doing so, the reader is able to compare how denominational structures within the same religious tradition encourage a way of thinking about mass media in everyday life. Nevertheless, the contributors recognize the limitations of the work in covering the full range of issues related to religion and mass communication.

The contents of the book are organized into five parts. Part I includes this introduction as well as a literature review of relevant research on religion and media. This review (Chapter 2) provides the reader with a comprehensive summary of specific studies from a number of journals in the fields of communication and sociology. Chapter 2 also provides researchers, writers, and students with a much-needed reference source on what has been done in this important area of research as well as what is currently lacking.

Chapters in Part II describe what a number of religious institutions (i.e., Catholic, Fundamentalist, Mainline Protestant, Mormon, Evangelical, etc.) teach their members about media within the larger context of their religious doctrine. Questions of how religious institutions orient themselves to the world and how these orientations play out in terms of official statements and teachings about the media are addressed.

The remaining chapters are devoted to studies exploring the relationship between religion and mass media use. Part III reports research from general audiences not affiliated with one particular denomination. These chapters are empirical in nature. They also compare attitudes, behaviors, and feelings about the media across a number of religious communities. The data presented here speak to the question of how audience members behave relative to the media-given institutional directives.

The chapters in Part IV provide specific case studies of how a number of particular religious groups define the role of media in everyday life. Finally, the concluding chapter in Part V discusses the emerging information society and what it implies for religious institutions approaching the next century.

REFERENCES

Berger, P. (1967). *The sacred canopy: Elements of a sociological theory of religion.* Garden City, NY: Doubleday.

Carey, J. (1988). *Communication as culture.* Winchester, MA: Unwin Hyman.

Carter, S. L. (1993). *The culture of disbelief: How American law and politics trivialize religious devotion.* New York: Basic Books.

Cornwall, M., Albrecht, S., Cunningham, P. H., & Pitcher, B. L. (1986). The dimensions of religiosity: A conceptual model with an empirical test. *Review of Religious Research, 27*(3), 226-244.

Dittes, J. E. (1971). Two issues in measuring religion. In M. P. Strommen (Ed.), *Research on religious development* (pp. 79-106). New York: Hawthorne.

Douglas, A. (1988). *The feminization of American culture.* New York: Doubleday.

Durkheim, E. (1912). *The elementary forms of religious life.* London: Allen & Unwin.

Eco, U. (1986). *The name of the rose.* New York: Warner.

Fischer, C. S. (1982). *To dwell among friends: Personal networks in town and city.* Chicago: University of Chicago Press.

Fore, W. F. (1987). *Television and religion: The shaping of faith, values, and culture.* Minneapolis, MN: Augsburg.

Gerbner, G., & Gross, L. (1976). Living with television. *Journal of Communication, 26,* 173-199.

Hamilton, N. F., & Rubin, A. M. (1992). The influence of religiosity on television viewing. *Journalism Quarterly, 69,* 667-678.

Jary, D., & Jary, J. (1991). *The HarperCollins dictionary of sociology.* New York: Harper-Collins.

Katz, E., Blumler, J., & Gurevitch, M. (1974). Utilization of mass communication by the individual. In E. Katz, J. Blumler, & M. Gurevitch (Eds.), *The uses of mass communication: Current perspectives on gratifications research* (pp. 19-32). Beverly Hills, CA: Sage.

Lacayo, R. (1995, June 12). Violent reaction: Bob Dole's broadside against sex and violence in popular culture sets off a furious debate on responsibility. *Time,* pp. 25-30.

Lenski, G. (1963). *The religious factor: A sociologist's inquiry.* Garden City, NY: Anchor.

Medved, M. (1992). *Hollywood vs. America: Popular culture and the war on traditional values.* New York: HarperCollins.

Meyrowitz, J. (1985). *No sense of place.* New York: Oxford University Press.

Park, R. (1915). The city: Suggestions for the investigation of human behavior in the urban environment. *American Journal of Sociology, 20,* 577-612.

Pool, I. de Sola. (1983). *Technologies of freedom.* Cambridge, MA: Harvard University Press.

Postman, N. (1985). *Amusing ourselves to death: Public discourse in the age of show business.* New York: Viking.

Roberts, C. L. (1983). Attitudes and media use of the moral majority. *Journal of Broadcasting, 27,* 403-410.

Schement, J., & Lievrouw, L. (Eds.). (1987). *Competing visions, complex realities: Social aspects of the information society.* Norwood, NJ: Ablex.

Spigel, L. (1992). *Make room for TV: Television and the family ideal in postwar America.* Chicago: University of Chicago Press.

Straubhaar, J., & LaRose, R. (1996). *Communications media in the information society.* Belmont, CA: Wadsworth.

Waxman, C. (1994). Religious and ethnic patterns of American Jewish baby boomers. *Journal for the Scientific Study of Religion, 33,* 74-80.

Weber, M. (1963). *The sociology of religion.* Boston: Beacon.

Wellman, B. (1979). The community question: The intimate networks of East Yonkers. *American Journal of Sociology, 84,* 1201-1231.

2

Religion and Mass Media Use

A Review of the Mass Communication and Sociology Literature

JUDITH M. BUDDENBAUM
DANIEL A. STOUT

The United States has often been called "the nation with the soul of a church" because, as Mead (1967) explained in his classic essay by that name, certain core Christian beliefs form a "religion of the Republic." These beliefs support democratic government but also create among Americans a tendency to see their country as a "community of righteousness" and the "primary agent of God's meaningful activity in history" (pp. 280-281; see also Mead, 1975). There is, however, another sense in which "the nation with the soul of a church" is an apt description.

Surveys consistently show that the United States is by far the most religious of all advanced, industrial, democratic nations. To many outside observers, the religious commitment exhibited by Americans is the nation's most distinctive feature. More than 9 out of 10 Americans believe in God and in an afterlife; almost three fourths believe in life after death. Almost two thirds say that their religion is very important to them. More than half say they attend church regularly; about one fourth do so at least occasionally (Kosmin & Lachman, 1993, pp. 8-9; see also Gallup & Jones, 1989).

Because belief in God and an afterlife is widely shared, there is a certain universality to U.S. religiosity, but by the time of the Constitutional Convention, religious pluralism was the norm. Although 9 out of 10 Americans may believe in God and 6 out of 10 may go to church regularly, they do not go to the same church. As Mead (1967) points out, "Vis-à-vis each of the many conflicting religious sects, the new nation's central authority had to be neutral." Properly speaking, this neutrality really represents a "desectarianization of the civil authority" that is often mistaken for "secularization" (p. 269).

Still, there is a sense in which U.S. society is also very secular. Desectarianization forced at least minimal tolerance for alternative religious worldviews that both protected religion and limited its influence. Pluralism plus the forces of modernization "emancipated" people from "religious and metaphysical tutelage" so that many turned their "attention away from other worlds and toward this one" (Cox, 1965, p. 2). Although recent research suggests that Americans today are more religious than were their colonial forebears (Finke & Stark, 1992), they also have access to far more sources of information than the largely "religious and metaphysical tutelage" of earlier eras.

In the average U.S. home, the television set is turned on for at least 6 hours every day. Newspaper circulation is at an all-time high. The most popular magazines have circulations in the millions. Movies and video releases can gross upward of $20 million in a single week; records routinely go platinum.

The United States, then, is a media culture. Availability and consumption of mass media messages have increased and will, undoubtedly, continue to do so. Where once it was fashionable to see in that trend evidence of an inexorable march toward an entirely secular society and to speak knowingly of the "death of God" (Buchstein, 1972), today observers speak equally knowingly of religious revival. As Cox (1984) puts it,

> Rather than an age of rampant secularization and religious decline, it appears to be . . . an era of religious revival and the return of the sacral. No one talks much today about the long night of religion or the zero level of its influence. (p. 20)

Although most recent attention has focused on the influence of religion on politics, if the figures documenting the religiosity of U.S. people mean anything, religion should influence all aspects of daily life, including attention to the mass media. Therefore, this chapter reviews the existing studies in major communication and sociology journals as a way of documenting what is known and unknown about the relationship between these two major forces in people's lives. Such a review, we believe, can provide insight and also generate ideas for those who might not otherwise consider the implications of either religion or the mass media, whether their primary concerns are in communication, sociology, or some other area.

Both religion and the media can provide the narratives that define Americans as a distinctive people and that can influence individual opinions and behaviors. Religious leaders speak out regularly about the mass media. Whether church members pay attention to advice from their religious leaders about media use, however, is an open question. Searching the social science literature for evidence of religious influence on the audience for mass media is like looking for a needle in a haystack.

Studies of religious rhetoric and persuasive strategies abound. Research on the electronic church and its audience has proliferated. Studies of mass media attention to religion are also quite common. An examination of every issue of 17 top journals in mass communication and sociology[1] in which one would expect most such studies to be published, however, turned up only 59 articles since the end of World War II that provided any data on the relationship between religion and mass media use in the United States or Canada.[2]

RELIGION AND MASS MEDIA USE

Of the 59 studies identified for this chapter, 30 appeared in the communication literature and 29 in sociology journals. Very few from either field were really designed to examine the relationship between religion and mass media use. Reflecting their professional orientation, communication researchers sometimes used simple measures of religion to help explain mass media use and its consequences. Sociologists more often used simple measures of media use to explore correlates of religiosity.

Religion and Newspaper Use

Research indicates that people who attend worship services regularly are somewhat more likely to be newspaper readers than to be nonreaders (Sobal & Jackson-Beeck, 1981; Westley & Severin, 1964a). Those who read church newspapers are also significantly more likely than those who do not to use general circulation daily newspapers (McEwan & Hempel, 1977; Stamm & Weis, 1986).

There appear, however, to be some differences in attitudes toward newspapers and use of them across religious traditions. Westley and Severin (1964b), for example, found that about two fifths of all Catholics and just more than one third of the Protestants considered newspapers the most accurate and truthful news source. Most studies indicate that Catholics are slightly more likely than Protestants to be newspaper readers (Penrose, Weaver, Cole, & Shaw, 1974; Rigney & Hoffman, 1993; Westley & Severin, 1964a).

Although Roberts (1983) reported no difference in newspaper use among liberal Protestants, conservative Protestants, and the population as a whole, Rigney and Hoffman's (1993) more thorough examination did turn up religious differences. They also found that Catholics were more likely than non-Catholics to read newspapers, but religiously liberal Protestants were actually slightly more likely than Catholics to read newspapers. Both groups were significantly more likely to read newspapers than were fundamentalist Protestants. The small numbers in the sample made interpretations somewhat problematic, but Jews appeared to be the most likely to read newspapers; people from non-Judeo-Christian traditions and those unaffiliated with any religion were least likely to read.

Religion and Television Use

In general, people who do not watch television attend worship services less frequently than those who do watch (Tankard & Harris, 1980). Jackson-Beeck and Sobal (1980), however, found that those who attend worship services are somewhat less likely to be heavy television viewers, defined as watching more than 6 hours daily. Jackson-Beeck (1977) also found that nonviewers were significantly more likely than viewers to claim no religious preference. Similar proportions of Protestants were viewers and nonviewers, but Catholics were somewhat overrepresented among the viewers. More recently, Hamilton and Rubin (1992) found that television entertainment played a lesser role in the lives of conservative Protestants than it did in the lives of more liberal Christians. Stout (1994) found that attitudes about appropriate television viewing varied widely among devout Mormon women.

In the 1960s, at least, Protestants were slightly more likely than Catholics to consider television the most accurate and truthful news source (Westley & Severin, 1964b). Another study conducted almost a decade later showed that Latter-day Saint (Mormon) bishops were significantly more likely than rabbis to say that television overplays negative aspects of news. They also were significantly more likely than rabbis to consider the news media to be liberal and to consider Vice President Spiro Agnew's charge that the media are biased entirely justified (Duncan, 1972).

Religion and the Use of Other Media

According to a study by Westley and Severin (1964b), about one fifth of Catholics and of Protestants considered radio news best for accuracy and truthfulness. Similarly, Canadian Eskimos called radio their most important news source. The church ranked second. Television and newspapers ranked sixth and seventh out of 10 news sources in an Eskimo community with access to television, but newspapers ranked last as a news source in a similar community without access to television (Coldevin, 1976).

In another study from Canada, Fathi and Heath (1974) found that Catholic college students and those who attended church most often, regardless of their religious preference, were more likely than other students to listen to classical music or to both classical and popular music. Students with no religious preference and Protestants were more likely to listen only to popular music.

In the only study to mention magazine use, Swatos (1988) found that 45% of the conservative Christian antipornography activists he surveyed read religious magazines and 55% read secular ones. Of the secular magazines, *Reader's Digest, Good Housekeeping*, the weekly news magazines, and hobby magazines were mentioned most frequently.

Two additional studies combined use of multiple sources into composite measures to measure intellectualism. Wilensky (1964) found a standardization of culture via media exposure that cut across demographic categories, including religion, but also that exposure to "high-brow culture" as opposed to "poor television" entertainment was greatest among people with no religious preference. At the same time, exposure to high-brow culture was higher among Jews than Christians, among Catholics with four grandparents born in the United States than among Catholics with fewer U.S.-born grandparents, and among high-status Protestants with four or more U.S.-born grandparents than among other Protestants.

Nelsen (1973) also found generational differences among religions in intellectualism, as measured by a six-item scale that combined attending movies, plays, concerts, or the opera with reading quality books, elite newspapers, and magazines. In general, intellectualism was highest among Jews and higher among white Protestants than among Catholics. Controlling for religious group eliminated the relationship between intellectualism and worship attendance, but the generational effects remained.

EXPLAINING PATTERNS OF MEDIA USE

With the exception of the research by Duncan (1972), Nelsen (1973), and Rigney and Hoffman (1993), the studies cited in the preceding section treat religion simply as an incidental descriptor, but other studies have been developed within frameworks that provide explanations for the observed relationships between religion and the mass media. These frameworks can be classified as stemming from community integration, secularization, ideological, and psychological perspectives.

The Community Integration Perspective

Although most of the studies by communication researchers that were cited in the preceding sections were purely descriptive, the decision to include religion among the demographic variables most likely stems from the well-known research conducted by Janowitz (1952), Merton (1950), Park (1929), and other community integration theorists associated with the Chicago School of sociology.

According to this line of research, those who attend church are more integrated into a community than those who do not attend. Therefore, they have a greater need to know about their community and, consequently, are more likely than others to use local news media to learn about it. Media use also fosters community integration; those who subscribe to and use the media are more likely to become integrated into the community and active in its voluntary associations, including presumably local churches (Stamm, 1985, 1988).

Following the procedure developed by Janowitz (1952) in his work on people's participation in and identification with local facilities and institutions, most research in the community ties tradition measures integration by counting the total number of local memberships, including church membership. As a result, most studies do not make a clear case for the relationship between religion and media use. Only a few use church membership or religious activity as a separate measure of community ties.

In a study of the role of communication in people's readiness for change, Donohew (1967) found that church participants were integrated into their community. For them, readiness for change was somewhat more strongly related to use of news rather than nonnews content from both newspapers and television.

More recently, Finnegan and Viswanath (1988) found that church members were significantly more likely than nonmembers to read both the metropolitan daily newspaper and the community weekly and to have cable television in their home. Similarly, Neuwirth, Salmon, and Neff (1989) found that church membership loaded on community identity and localite indexes that, in turn, were positively related to use of local media, although the relationship was significant only for radio.

In the study that most explicitly examined the role of church ties, Stamm and Weis (1986) treated the Catholic Church as a local community in its own right. In support of the community ties hypothesis, they found that Catholics who felt close to their church, attended regularly, and were active on behalf of political issues of concern to the church were more likely than other Catholics to read a diocesan newspaper and also to subscribe to the local general circulation newspaper.

Although conceptually somewhat separate from the community ties research, a few studies have examined both church membership and media use to see how they, and other community activities, fit together to determine a lifestyle. In one study of this type, Havighurst and Feigenbaum (1959) used interview data in which Kansas City adults described their lives to place leisure activities into one of nine concentric circles representing leisure orientations. With circle one being the most home centered and circle nine representing the most organized community involvement, they placed church activity in circle four, along with attending movies and sporting events and union activity.

More recently, Schwartz (1980) found that members of a market segment he dubbed "progressive conservatives" placed newspapers in an "area of solid indifference" along with tennis, whereas "grim independents" considered newspapers even less important. The two groups could be distinguished by demographic characteristics and by their attitudes toward religion. Whereas progressive conservatives saw the church as playing a major role in their lives, grim independents attached little importance to religion.

Both the place of religious activity and of communication-related activities, however, may vary by life stage. Using cluster analysis to examine changes in behavior over time, Graney (1975) found that attending religious services often substituted for declines in telephone use and in reading, whereas increased television use substituted for decreases in church attendance that may occur with age or infirmity.

Secularization Theory

More common among sociologists of religion than among communication researchers, this perspective treats religion as part of an older, traditional way of life that will eventually decrease or disappear under the pressures of industrialization and modernization. In contrast to researchers in the community integration tradition who expect a positive and reciprocal relation between religiosity and use of news media, secularization theorists expect the relationship to be negative because the mass media are considered to be part of modern, secular society.

Whereas many community integration studies cite Merton's (1950) earlier work, studies in this vein usually cite his later contributions that introduced the localite-cosmopolite dichotomy (see Merton, 1957). Most of these studies use a scale consisting of four to six items, only one of which taps media use, to differentiate between the two orientations. A few studies using the single item ("Despite all the newspaper and TV coverage, national and international happenings rarely seem as interesting as events that occur in the local community in which one lives"), however, indicate that the localite orientation is related to religious activity (Roof & Hoge, 1980) and to conservative Christian beliefs (Roof, 1972, 1974). According to Roof and Hoge (1980), those different orientations create a cultural divide in the nation and in its churches. Consistent with that interpretation, Perry, Davis, Doyle, and Dyble (1980) found that both "churched" and "estranged" Protestants gave the localite response more often than did those with more minimal church ties.

Other secularization studies indicate that literacy and religiosity are positively correlated (Land, Dean, & Blau, 1991; Wuthnow, 1976a), but religious commitment tends to decline over time in those countries, including the United States, in which publication of religious books relative to secular ones has decreased (Wuthnow, 1976a, 1976b).

Similarly, studies of ethnic communities in the United States document differences in newspaper and television use and in worship attendance across generations and between communities that are, for the most part, consistent with secularization theory (Breton, 1964; Lauquier, 1961; Useem & Useem, 1945). Changes in both media use patterns and in religious activity reported in those studies, however, may have as much to do with linguistic facility as with secularization.

Ideological Frameworks

Many studies described under the secularization framework sometimes employ religious beliefs to explain attitudes toward the mass media and use of them, but studies using an ideological framework focus more closely on the place of religion in people's lives or on the beliefs themselves. Although researchers engaged in this kind of work need not assume a priori that religion and modernization as represented by the media are necessarily at odds, many do make that assumption.

Although the relationships appear to have changed somewhat over time and to be affected by demographics, including age and education, two studies indicate that both religious beliefs and levels of activity tend to depress support for expressive rights. In the first of those, Steiber (1980) found no relationship between tolerance for religious and political criticism. Although tolerance for both kinds of criticism increased between 1958 and 1972 in Detroit, in both periods both Protestants and Catholics were more tolerant of criticizing the president than of criticizing religion. Personal piety decreased tolerance for both kinds of criticism in all groups, but religious activity decreased religious tolerance only among black Protestants. For Catholics and for white Protestants, church activity was positively correlated with tolerance of religious criticism.

More recently, von Elten and Rimmer (1992) found education to be the strongest positive predictor of tolerance for freedom of speech and press even with controls for religious variables and for other demographics, but Christian orthodoxy was an equally strong negative predictor. Church attendance was a much weaker negative predictor.

Although those studies suggest that religiously inspired attitudes toward expressive freedom may have implications for media use, several ethnographies provide evidence that people use or refrain from using television according to the teachings of their church. Devout Old Order Amish and members of the Mennonite Church of God in Christ shunned radio, television, and other communication technologies, but other Mennonites and members of the Old German Baptist Brethren had a more relaxed attitude toward communication technologies. Unlike the others, the Old German Baptist Brethren church specifically permitted use of tape recorders and record players (Barclay, 1967).

In a related study, Bourgault (1985) found that members of one Pentecostal church in southeastern Ohio generally agreed that seeing movies, attending any public entertainment, and watching television were sinful. Some Wesleyans held similar views, but Presbyterians and Episcopalians did not consider any of those activities inherently wrong.

Psychological Perspectives

Studies of this type take into account motivations for media use or for religious behaviors. Rather than looking for simple and direct effects, researchers using this framework tend to examine complex systems of influence as they seek to explain the choices people make.

Loges and Ball-Rokeach (1993), for example, found that dependency relationships explain more variance in newspaper readerships than can be explained by demographics. According to their research, Catholicism was a significant predictor of using the newspaper for both self-understanding and social understanding, which, in turn, were significant predictors of readership.

Buddenbaum (1981) found that conservative Christians who watched religious television did not differ demographically from the general population of television viewers; however, the general television audience used television for entertainment and relaxation, whereas the conservative Christian subset who watched religious programs had media-related needs more in tune with intrinsically motivated church members.

Consistent with those findings, Hamilton and Rubin (1992) found that religious liberals used television as a source of information.

Conservative Christians' viewing patterns were more reactionary, marked by avoidance of certain content and use of other supportive programming for moral guidance. Similarly, McFarland and Warren (1992) found that, in general, Fundamentalists preferred to read supportive stories; however, those with a quest orientation toward religion were more likely to express a desire to read all kinds of content.

RELIGION AND MASS MEDIA CONTENT

Each of the frameworks for understanding the relationship between religion and media use carry with them implications for the kinds of media content religious people will find most attractive. Both the ideological and psychological perspectives suggest that religious people will be most attracted to content that is congruent with their value systems and needs. Research in both the community integration and secularization traditions suggests that content with a local angle may be most congruent.

Preferences

As might be expected, people who are active in a local church are more likely to read news about religion than those who are not active; however, conservative, God-oriented people preferred local content that mixed information with entertainment, whereas more highly educated "religious eggheads" preferred issue-oriented coverage exploring a variety of perspectives (Buddenbaum, 1982).

In a study of the effect of time constraints on media use, Grunig (1979) found that people who spend leisure time on religious activities preferred family-centered content, including news about child development and local schools, regardless of how much time they had available. Interest in nonlocal news, however, may be high when special circumstances make the news especially salient. Hammond and Mitchell (1965) found that parish ministers were twice as likely as campus pastors to be interested in news of their own denomination but only somewhat more likely to be interested in news of other denominations. Campus pastors were more likely than parish pastors to be interested in news of national and international affairs.

Other studies indicate that religious people, and especially Catholics, were more likely than others to know about Pope John Paul VI's 1967 encyclical concerning birth control, to consider it important, and to tell others about it (Adams, Mullen, & Wilson, 1969; Hanneman & Greenberg, 1973). Jews were more likely than non-Jewish white or black Americans to have substantive knowledge about specific events in Palestine and Israel (Gandy & El Waylly, 1985).

News preference may be affected by conditions that make particular subjects salient, but salience may also be affected by specific religious beliefs. Consistent with the common assumption that "dominion beliefs" may be one cause of environmental problems, Woodrum and Hoban (1994) found that those who believe God gave people the right to use nature for their own purposes were generally unconcerned about the environment. That kind of dominion belief, however, was essentially unrelated to the salience of religion, frequency of worship attendance, literal acceptance of the Genesis account of creation, or support for teaching creation science in schools. The only significant predictor was having little information about environmental issues from print, broadcast, and interpersonal sources.

Avoidances

Although there was no direct evidence in Woodrum and Hoban's (1994) research to suggest that people with dominion beliefs purposefully avoided information about environmental issues, other studies indicate that religiously active Christians who hold orthodox beliefs are more likely to avoid sexually explicit television entertainment programs than are those with less conservative religious beliefs (Hamilton & Rubin, 1992; Roberts, 1983).

When conservative Christians become involved in crusades against publications they consider pornographic, they may be taking their cues from their religious leaders because few of the participants have seen or read any of the material targeted by the protests (Swatos, 1988). That may not be true, however, for Catholics because within Catholicism elite opinions appear more mixed. Whereas half the nuns at a midwestern Jesuit seminary thought the Legion of Decency required obedience, just under one fourth of the priests and laity shared that view. Similarly, about half the priests and seminarians but only about one third of the nuns thought the *Index of Forbidden Books* should be eliminated (Wiley, 1967).

Although differences in attitude toward sexually explicit material cannot be explained by status differences among religious groups (Wood & Hughes, 1984), they may be related to beliefs about the consequences of this material. Both those they identified as feminists and as conservative Christians are equally opposed to pornography and want to see it legally restricted; however, their motives differed. Conservative Christians oppose it primarily because they see pornography leading to the breakdown of morals (Jelen, 1986). Like feminists for whom it is the primary motivation for wanting to see pornography banned, fundamentalist Christians are also more likely than Catholics, more liberal Protestants, and Jews to believe pornography encourages rape (Hertel & Hughes, 1987).

In general, people's attitudes toward sexually oriented material appear consistent with the teachings of their religious leaders. The effect of religious elites' opposition to violent entertainment on religious people's behavior, however, is less clear. One study found that for teenagers, church attendance was negatively correlated with exposure to violent television programs (Murray, Cole, & Fedler, 1970). A decade later, Roberts (1983) found no difference in the viewing of violent programs among conservative Protestant adults, more liberal Protestants, and the population as a whole, but more recently, Hamilton and Rubin (1992) found that conservative Christians were more likely than liberals to avoid violent television programs, although conservatives remained more concerned about sexual content than about violent programs.

Consistent with those findings, people with no religion, Catholics, and Protestants who did not describe themselves as born-again were three times as likely to have seen and liked *The Rocky Horror Picture Show* and at least twice as likely to have seen and enjoyed *The Exorcist* as were those Protestants who identified themselves as born-again (Bainbridge & Stark, 1981).

THE QUESTION OF EFFECTS

Although few of the studies cited in the previous sections use the kind of data or employ the kind of statistical analysis necessary to demonstrate a causal relationship, taken as a whole they suggest that religion does have some effect on the mass media people use, the way they use the media, and the content they prefer. But with the exception of research using the secularization framework that suggests that modernization, of which the proliferation of mass media is a part, may have an effect on religiosity, only a few studies have directly examined media effects on religious beliefs and behaviors.

Some research indicates that media coverage may lead people to attend religious crusades or rallies; however, the decision to accept a new religion depends more on people's preexisting religion and religious commitment, how much they already know about the new group, their motives for attending, and the persuasiveness of the program than on the nature of the media coverage (Catton, 1957; Stark & Bainbridge, 1980; Swatos, 1991).

Although media coverage may not persuade people to join a new religion, negative news probably can reduce support for a particular religion. After the PTL scandal, support for televangelists remained high among Fundamentalists who had traditionally supported televangelists, but respect also decreased in that group, particularly among those most exposed to secular media (Abelman, 1991; Houghland, Billings, & Wood, 1990).

CONCLUSION

Just as the number of studies in both sociology and communication has increased steadily during the past 50 years, the number providing some evidence of a relationship between religion and media use has increased from only a single study in the first decade after World War II to 13 between 1966 and 1975. Thereafter, the number leveled off at about two studies each year.

Despite increases in scholarly publishing over time, however, few researchers appear to have made any conscious effort to examine the relationship between religion and mass media use. Approximately four out of every five individual researchers or research groups whose work was examined in this chapter contributed only one study that included measures of both religion and mass media use. Seven individual researchers or research groups contributed two studies and one produced three. But like those who produced only a single study, about half included measures of religion or mass media use quite casually. Others contributing multiple studies used different theoretical perspectives or examined different religions, different media, or different relationships in their work.

For the most part, those who published in communication journals did not appear to read the sociology literature. Those who published in sociology journals seemed equally unfamiliar with media research. As a result, it is clear only that there are potentially important relationships between religion and media use, but the nature of those relationships is somewhat ambiguous. To the extent reasons for them are offered, the explanations appear rudimentary and sometimes contradictory.

In general, the available evidence indicates that people who attend church are more likely to use newspapers and watch television than those who do not attend. Jews appear more likely than Christians to use the mass media, or at least high-brow media. Catholics may or may not use mass media more than liberal Protestants, but both groups use them more than conservative Protestants or those who are unaffiliated with a religion.

In attending to the mass media, religious people appear to be more attracted to content that supports their beliefs than to content that may present a challenge, but that may be more true for conservative Christians than for other religious groups. Whereas conservative Protestants tend to be reactionary in their media use, avoiding especially sexually oriented content and even seeking to limit its availability to others, mainline Protestants are more supportive of expressive rights and more venturous in their media use. Special circumstances, however, including world events that are particularly relevant to a religious community, lifestyle, and stage of life, can affect content salience as well as use of specific media.

Just as religion has some effect on media use, the media appear to have effects on religion. By itself, mass media attention to a particular religion probably cannot lead people to join it, although the coverage may make people aware of other religions and their activities, induce some people to attend their events, and sometimes produce decreases in support for a religion or its leader. Consistent with that latter finding, availability and use are also linked to secularization.

Discrepant findings, as well as the apparent contradiction between studies linking religious identification and/or church attendance to use of the media and those seeing the media as linked to secularization, may be artifacts caused by using different research methodologies. Here, differences in conceptualization of mass media use as well as attention to quite different media or media content introduce ambiguities, but measurement of religion and religiosity appears to be the primary problem.

Church attendance taps only one form of religious commitment and may actually work against some religions and some very devout people if the highest level is "more than once a week." As a proxy for actual beliefs that might influence behaviors, the simple Protestant/Catholic/Jew trichotomy fails to distinguish among quite different strains within each tradition. For Christians, that problem can be partially alleviated by using measures of "Christian orthodoxy," but orthodoxy is most appropriate for assessing acceptance of conservative Christian teachings. Because of its emphasis on a literal interpretation of the Bible, using orthodoxy as a surrogate for religiosity makes little theological sense in other Christian traditions. It is even less appropriate in studies in which Jews may be included in the sample because orthodoxy measures also usually include a statement about the divinity of Jesus.

With the exception of one study that measured dominion beliefs, researchers do not appear to have considered the implications of religious beliefs other than those included in orthodoxy measures. The absence of sophisticated measures for what people who are not conservative Christians may be taught in their churches and may actually believe is probably responsible for many of the apparently contradictory findings. Their absence also contributes directly to problems in providing reasons for the findings.

Giving reasons requires having some explanatory framework, and that, in turn, requires careful explication of theory. Approximately one fourth of the existing studies are merely descriptive; one third might be classified as theory building. Of those that set out to test a theory, the focus was often on some proposition unrelated to the relationship between religion and mass media use. As a result, most provide little in the way of justification for use of particular measures or explanation for the reported relationships between religion and the media.

Better measures would strengthen work conducted within the ideological framework that seeks to link beliefs and behaviors. Better measures and more cross-fertilization across scholarly disciplines also could bring together the community integration framework, which was used most often either explicitly or implicitly by communication researchers, and the secularization framework, which informed much of the work published in sociology journals. This, in turn, might lead to better understanding of effects over time, such as those suggested by both frameworks.

Explanations for between-group differences could also benefit both from that kind of work and from more attention to the psychological frameworks, which to date appear to have been underutilized. Motivational theories, in particular, could greatly enhance understanding of within-group differences. Although "uses and gratifications" is one of the most commonly used approaches to understanding mass media use, there were only two studies in that vein that sought to examine what people want from the media. Another study used measures of "religion as quest" to examine information preferences and avoidances, but missing from the literature were studies exploring the effects on media use of associational versus communal attachments to a religious organization or of intrinsic and extrinsic motivations for religiosity.

The literature provides tantalizing glimpses of potentially important relationships between religion and mass media use. In reviewing the literature, however, one is struck more by what is not there than by what is. Surveys have been the method of choice; research employing experimental designs and ethnographic methodologies is quite rare. Use of multiple methods and multiple measures for key concepts is the exception rather than the rule. Theories of public opinion formation, including the agenda-setting tradition from mass communication, rational choice, cognitive processing, group dynamics, schema formation, social learning, socialization, developmental theories, and many more, could profitably be used to explore between-group and within-group differences.

Scattered studies, simple and simplistic measures, ambiguous and apparently contradictory findings, incomplete explanations, and a general lack of thoughtful and coherent explanations are common when new fields of social science inquiry open up. Although we believe the new research presented in this book will enhance understanding of the relationship between religion and mass media use, it cannot clear up or even avoid all of the problems identified in this examination of the existing literature. The possibilities for exploring the ways in which two major institutions may affect each other are virtually limitless. Providing a reasonably complete understanding will take time and much work. Given the importance of both religion and the mass media in U.S. society, however, the potential value of conducting research in this area seems well worth the effort.

NOTES

1. Mass communication journals examined for this study include *Communication, Communication Research, Critical Studies in Mass Communication, Human Communication Research, Journalism Monographs, Journalism Quarterly, Journal of Broadcasting and Electronic Media, Journal of Communication, Mass Comm Review,* and *Newspaper Research Journal.*

Sociology journals examined include the *American Journal of Sociology, American Sociological Review, Journal for the Scientific Study of Religion, Review of Religious Research, Social Compass, Social Forces,* and *Sociological Analysis.*

2. This total excludes studies in which a measure of religion or media use was embedded in a composite measure as well as those in which measures of religion and mass media use were related to some third variable if the data presentation made it impossible to determine with any certainty the relationship between religion and media. It also excludes a few studies, mostly ethnographies, conducted in Third World countries and a few that did not deal with Judeo-Christian religions.

For this study, the mass media are defined as newspapers, magazines, books, movies, videos, music, radio, and television that are intended for a large, diverse audience. With the exception of those that also included some information on the mass media audience, research on religious television was excluded both because it has been the subject of numerous other books and because we consider it a specialized genre akin to other religious media, which were also excluded.

REFERENCES

Abelman, R. (1991). Influence of news coverage of the "scandal" on PTL viewers. *Journalism Quarterly, 68,* 101-110.

Adams, J. B., Mullen, J. J., & Wilson, H. M. (1969). Diffusion of a "minor" foreign affairs news event. *Journalism Quarterly, 46,* 545-551.

Bainbridge, W. S., & Stark, R. (1981). The "consciousness reformation" reconsidered. *Journal for the Scientific Study of Religion, 20,* 1-16.

Barclay, H. B. (1967). The plain people of Oregon. *Review of Religious Research, 8,* 140-165.

Bourgault, L. M. (1985). The *PTL Club* and Protestant viewers: An ethnographic study. *Journal of Communication, 35,* 132-148.

Breton, R. (1964). Institutional completeness of ethnic communities and the personal relations of immigrants. *American Journal of Sociology, 70,* 193-205.

Buchstein, F. D. (1972). The role of the news media in the "death of God" controversy. *Journalism Quarterly, 49,* 79-85.

Buddenbaum, J. M. (1981). Characteristics and media-related needs of the audience for religious TV. *Journalism Quarterly, 58,* 266-272.

Buddenbaum, J. M. (1982). News about religion: A readership study. *Newspaper Research Journal, 3,* 7-17.

Catton, W. R., Jr. (1957). What kind of people does a religious cult attract? *American Sociological Review, 22,* 561-566.

Coldevin, G. O. (1976). Some effects of frontier television in a Canadian Eskimo community. *Journalism Quarterly, 53,* 34-39.

Cox, H. (1965). *The secular city.* New York: Macmillan.

Cox, H. (1984). *Religion in the secular city.* New York: Simon & Schuster.

Donohew, L. (1967). Communication and readiness for change in Appalachia. *Journalism Quarterly, 44,* 679-687.

Duncan, R. D. (1972). Agnew, clergymen, and the media. *Journalism Quarterly, 49,* 147-150.

Fathi, A., & Heath, C. L. (1974). Group influence, mass media, and musical taste among Canadian students. *Journalism Quarterly, 51,* 705-709.

Finke, R., & Stark, R. (1992). *The churching of America 1776-1990: Winners and losers in our religious economy.* New Brunswick, NJ: Rutgers University Press.

Finnegan, J. R., Jr., & Viswanath, K. (1988). Community ties and use of cable TV and newspapers in a midwest suburb. *Journalism Quarterly, 65,* 463-473.

Gallup, G., Jr., & Jones, S. (1989). *A hundred questions and answers: Religion in America.* Princeton, NJ: Princeton Religion Research Center.

Gandy, O. H., Jr., & El Waylly, M. (1985). The knowledge gap and foreign affairs: The Palestinian-Israeli conflict. *Journalism Quarterly, 62,* 777-783.

Graney, M. J. (1975). Communication uses and the social activity constant. *Communication Research, 2,* 347-367.

Grunig, J. E. (1979). Time budgets, level of involvement, and use of the mass media. *Journalism Quarterly, 56,* 248-261.

Hamilton, N. F., & Rubin, A. M. (1992). The influence of religiosity on television viewing. *Journalism Quarterly, 69,* 667-678.

Hammond, P. E., & Mitchell, R. M. (1965). Segmentation of radicalism: The case of the Protestant campus minister. *American Journal of Sociology, 71,* 133-143.

Hanneman, G. J., & Greenberg, B. S. (1973). Relevance and diffusion of news of major and minor events. *Journalism Quarterly, 50,* 433-437.

Havighurst, R. J., & Feigenbaum, K. (1959). Leisure and life-style. *American Journal of Sociology, 64,* 396-404.

Hertel, B. R., & Hughes, M. (1987). Religious affiliation, attendance, and support for "pro-family" issues in the United States. *Social Forces, 65,* 858-882.

Houghland, J. G., Jr., Billings, D. B., & Wood, J. R. (1990). The instability of support for television evangelists: Public reactions during a period of embarrassment. *Review of Religious Research, 32,* 56-64.

Jackson-Beeck, M. (1977). The non-viewers: Who are they? *Journal of Communication, 27,* 65-72.

Jackson-Beeck, M., & Sobal, J. (1980). The social world of heavy television viewers. *Journal of Broadcasting, 24,* 5-12.

Janowitz, M. (1952). *The community press in an urban setting.* Glencoe, IL: Free Press.

Jelen, T. G. (1986). Fundamentalism, feminism, and attitudes toward pornography. *Review of Religious Research, 28,* 97-103.

Kosmin, B. A., & Lachman, S. P. (1993). *One nation under God: Religion in contemporary American society.* New York: Harmony Books.

Land, K. C., Dean, G., & Blau, J. R. (1991). Religious pluralism and church membership: A spatial diffusion model. *American Sociological Review, 56,* 237-249.

Lauquier, H. C. (1961). Cultural change among three generations of Greeks. *American Catholic Sociological Review, 23,* 223-232.

Loges, W. E., & Ball-Rokeach, S. J. (1993). Dependency relations and newspaper readership. *Journalism Quarterly, 70,* 602-614.

McEwan, W. J., & Hempel, D. J. (1977). How information needs and effort affect channel choice. *Journalism Quarterly, 54,* 149-153.

McFarland, S. G., & Warren, J. C., Jr. (1992). Religious orientations and selective exposure among fundamentalist Christians. *Journal for the Scientific Study of Religion, 31,* 163-174.

Mead, S. E. (1967). The nation with the soul of a church. *Church History, 36,* 267-283.

Mead, S. E. (1975). *The nation with the soul of a church.* New York: Harper & Row.

Merton, R. K. (1950). Patterns of influence: A study of interpersonal influences and of communications behavior in a local community. In P. Lazarsfeld & F. Stanton (Eds.), *Communication research 1948-49* (pp. 180-219). New York: Harper & Row.

Merton, R. K. (1957). *Social theory and social structure.* Glencoe, IL: Free Press.

Murray, R. L., Cole, R. R., & Fedler, F. (1970). Teenagers and TV violence: How they rate and view it. *Journalism Quarterly, 47,* 247-255.

Nelsen, H. M. (1973). Intellectualism and religious attendance of metropolitan residents. *Journal for the Scientific Study of Religion, 12,* 285-296.

Neuwirth, K., Salmon, C. T., & Neff, M. (1989). Community orientation and media use. *Journalism Quarterly, 66,* 31-39.

Park, R. P. (1929). Urbanization as measured by newspaper circulation. *American Journal of Sociology, 34,* 60-79.

Penrose, J., Weaver, D. H., Cole, R. R., & Shaw, D. L. (1974). The newspaper reader 10 years later: A partial replication of Westley-Severin. *Journalism Quarterly, 51,* 631-638.

Perry, E. L., Davis, J. H., Doyle, R. T., & Dyble, J. E. (1980). Toward a typology of unchurched Protestants. *Review of Religious Research, 21,* 388-404.

Rigney, D., & Hoffman, T. J. (1993). Is American Catholicism anti-intellectual? *Journal for the Scientific Study of Religion, 32,* 211-222.

Roberts, C. L. (1983). Attitudes and media use of the Moral Majority. *Journal of Broadcasting, 27,* 403-410.

Roof, W. C. (1972). The local-cosmopolitan orientation and traditional religious commitment. *Sociological Analysis, 33,* 1-15.

Roof, W. C. (1974). Religious orthodoxy and minority prejudice: Causal relationship or reflection of localistic worldview? *American Journal of Sociology, 80,* 643-664.

Roof, W. C., & Hoge, D. R. (1980). Church involvement in America: Social factors affecting membership and participation. *Review of Religious Research, 21,* 405-426.

Schwartz, S. H. (1980). A general psychographic analysis of newspaper use and lifestyle. *Journalism Quarterly, 57,* 392-401.

Sobal, J., & Jackson-Beeck, M. (1981). Newspaper non-readers: A national profile. *Journalism Quarterly, 58,* 9-13.

Stamm, K. R. (1985). *Newspaper use and community ties: Toward a dynamic theory.* Norwood, NJ: Ablex.

Stamm, K. R. (1988). Community ties and media use. *Critical Studies in Mass Communication, 8,* 357-361.

Stamm, K. R., & Weis, R. (1986). The newspaper and community integration: A study of ties to a local church community. *Communication Research, 13,* 125-137.

Stark, R., & Bainbridge, W. S. (1980). Networks of faith: Interpersonal bonds and recruitment to cults and sects. *American Journal of Sociology, 85,* 1376-1395.

Steiber, S. R. (1980). The influence of the religious factor on civil and sacred tolerance, 1958-1971. *Social Forces, 58,* 811-832.

Stout, D. A. (1994). Resolving conflicts of worldviews: LDS women and television. *AMCAP Journal, 29*(1), 61-79.

Swatos, W. H., Jr. (1988). Picketing Satan enfleshed at 7-Eleven: A research note. *Review of Religious Research, 30,* 73-82.

Swatos, W. H., Jr. (1991). Getting the word around: A research note on communicating an evangelistic crusade. *Review of Religious Research, 33,* 176-185.

Tankard, J. W., Jr., & Harris, M. C. (1980). A discriminant analysis of television viewers and nonviewers. *Journal of Broadcasting, 24,* 399-409.

Useem, J., & Useem, R. H. (1945). Minority-group pattern in prairie society. *American Journal of Sociology, 50,* 377-385.

von Elten, K., & Rimmer, T. (1992). Television and newspaper reliance and tolerance for civil liberties. *Mass Comm Review, 19,* 27-35.

Westley, B. H., & Severin, W. J. (1964a). A profile of the daily newspaper non-reader. *Journalism Quarterly, 41,* 45-50.

Westley, B. H., & Severin, W. J. (1964b). Some correlates of media credibility. *Journalism Quarterly, 41,* 325-335.

Wilensky, H. L. (1964). Mass society and mass culture: Interdependence or independence? *American Sociological Review, 29,* 173-197.

Wiley, N. (1967). Religious and political liberalism among Catholics. *Sociological Analysis, 28,* 142-148.

Wood, M., & Hughes, M. (1984). The moral basis of moral reform: Status discontent vs. culture and socialization as explanations of anti-pornography social movement adherence. *American Sociological Review, 49,* 86-99.

Woodrum, E., & Hoban, T. (1994). Theology and religiosity effects on environmentalism. *Review of Religious Research, 35,* 193-206.

Wuthnow, R. (1976a). A longitudinal, cross-national indicator of societal religious commitment. *Journal for the Scientific Study of Religion, 16,* 87-99.

Wuthnow, R. (1976b). Recent pattern of secularization: A problem of generations? *American Sociological Review, 41,* 850-867.

PART II

Religious Beliefs
and Media Orientations

Institutional Perspectives

A s Alexis de Tocqueville (1889a) observed more than a century ago, the decision of the founding fathers to grant freedom to religion and to the press gave both greater influence in American life than might have occurred had they been linked more closely to government according to the European practice. In the United States, religion shapes the morals and manners of Americans (p. 307), but so, too, do the media (p. 185).

Therein lies the dilemma. Each religion believes it has the truth, but in a society in which none has an automatic claim to members and to money, all become voluntary associations—interest groups— competing with each other and with the surrounding society. Even as they need the mass media as a vehicle for promoting their truth and for the sense of legitimacy that attention from a supposedly neutral source can confer, they must constantly defend their truth against other truths conveyed via the mass media.

But only the media "can drop the same thought into a thousand minds at the same moment" (Tocqueville, 1889b, p. 102), and many of those thoughts run counter to the beliefs and behaviors that members of a particular religion consider appropriate. Therefore, every religion necessarily develops an attitude toward the media, both how to use it and how to defend against uses by others with differing visions of truth.

As a part of their truth, religions teach how people should understand God and also the surrounding society. The chapters in this part explore those teachings and their implications for mass media use as they are articulated by religious leaders and spelled out in official and quasi-official statements from religious institutions representing major traditions within Christianity.

In Chapter 3, Ted G. Jelen contrasts the Catholic position on intellectual freedom with the classic libertarian position. The church may no longer publish its *Index of Forbidden Books*, but Jelen argues, the church position on intellectual freedom has remained remarkably constant. Seeing truth as singular and knowable but recognizing limitations on human reason as a means of finding that truth, the Catholic position is that people require guidance if they are to resist the various temptations of the world. Therefore, the duty of the church is to provide that guidance by fulfilling its primary role of teacher.

Whereas the Catholic Church sees danger in an unfettered marketplace of ideas, mainline Protestants embrace that. As Judith M. Buddenbaum explains in Chapter 4, mainline Protestants can be highly critical of media fare, but for them, a marketplace of ideas is an absolute necessity in the quest for truth and the common good. Despite differences in theology, practice, and church polity, what unites mainline Protestants and sets them apart from others is the conviction that ultimate authority in spiritual and temporal matters, including message production and consumption, rests with the individual, for God has given people His word and blessed them with the gift of reason.

As Buddenbaum points out, mainline insistence that people must be free to interpret God's word for themselves leads naturally to tolerance for and use of even those messages that they find distasteful. Such an approach leaves them open to charges from outsiders that they reduce God's truth to subjective preferences. In contrast to mainline Protestants, more conservative Christians are often portrayed as upholding timeless standards based firmly on biblical teachings, but in Chapter 5, Quentin J. Schultze describes Evangelicals' attitudes toward the mass media as informed more by the surrounding culture and economics than by a coherent, well-developed theology. According to his analysis, the only distinctly religious current within Evangelicalism is the importance that Evangelicals attach to the biblical command to "make disciples of all nation . . . teaching them to obey everything I have commanded you." Because they see it as their duty to Christianize the world, they pin both their hopes and fears on the mass media, which they see simultaneously as an important tool for evangelism and as a threat to their values and beliefs. Whereas mainline Protestants give priority to the informational function, Evangelicals think in terms of spiritual persuasion.

Hopeful that media technologies can be used to influence the religious direction of the nation, Evangelicals seek to redeem the media through criticism, protests, and boycotts designed to eliminate content that might undermine people's faith in God and seduce them into immoral behavior. Fundamentalists sometimes join in those efforts, but they have less faith that media can be used for good. Often equating the media with a secular and inherently sinful world, they are more inclined to eliminate commercial mass media from their lives. Margaret Lamberts Bendroth discusses fundamentalist institutions and mass media in Chapter 6.

In its approach to the media, the Church of Jesus Christ of Latter-day Saints (Mormon) combines the Catholic teaching approach with Evangelical hopes and fears. In Chapter 7, Daniel A. Stout discusses the Mormon theology of the family and how it has contributed to teachings that encourage careful selectivity in using mass media. In recent years, the leaders of the Mormon church have made "media effects" a dominant issue in their religious teachings.

REFERENCES

Tocqueville, A. de. (1889a). *Democracy in America* (Vol. 1). (H. Reeve, Trans.). New York: Longman.
Tocqueville, A. de. (1889b). *Democracy in America* (Vol. 2). (H. Reeve, Trans.). New York: Longman.

3

Catholicism, Conscience, and Censorship

TED G. JELEN

For centuries, the Roman Catholic Church has taken a firm position on the issue of intellectual freedom. For much of its modern
history, the church has published an *Index of Forbidden Books* (*Index
Librorum Prohibitorum*) (see Betten, 1935; Burke, 1952), which was
generally proscribed reading for Roman Catholic laity. In the United
States, *censorship* (a term which Catholic leaders have not shrunk
from using) has been attempted by Catholic organizations, such as
the National Legion of Decency (movies) and the National Office for
Decent Literature (print).

Although the tactics of such groups have varied with the legal
climate, their general purpose has been to place certain information
media beyond the reach of the general public (Gardiner, 1958).

AUTHOR'S NOTE: I would like to thank Robert Preston and Fr. David Turner for
valuable comments and assistance.

Moreover, in the United States, the church has traditionally been accorded great deference by film producers in anticipation of Catholic reaction (Walsh, 1990; Wills, 1987). Furthermore, although American Catholics have recently been reluctant to accept church authority in many "private" matters (D'Antonio, Davidson, Hoge, & Wallace, 1989; McNamara, 1992), they still regard church attitudes toward literature as particularly salient (Jelen & Wilcox, 1990).

Superficially, the traditional Catholic position on intellectual freedom might appear to have changed in recent decades. Vatican II continued a trend by which the authority of the church had been de-emphasized and contracted (Burns, 1992). Indeed, the church ceased publication of the *Index of Forbidden Books* shortly after the Second Vatican Council in 1967 (Jelen & Wilcox, 1990). The current pontiff, however, has strongly reaffirmed the church's authority in a number of areas in which such authority had appeared to be more accommodating to individual preferences (John Paul II, 1993).

In this chapter, I hope to suggest that the Catholic position on intellectual freedom, and on media usage in general, has been characterized by impressive continuity. Although the style of presentation of the church's authority has certainly varied over time, the thrust of Catholic doctrine on intellectual freedom has been remarkably consistent. Through most of its history, the church's own sense of its role has been one of teaching. Although the church does retain its power to define right and wrong and good and evil, the primary emphasis of the Catholic position on intellectual freedom has been the development of well-formed individual consciences. Such authentically Christian consciences have always been the final authority in Catholic doctrine. Moreover, the development of such consciences is consistent with a plausible Catholic definition of human freedom.

The most compelling evidence for continuity in Catholic doctrine is the recent papal encyclical letter, *The Splendor of Truth* (John Paul II, 1993). In this ambitious work, Pope John Paul II seeks to reaffirm the church's moral teaching authority in the face of the challenges of modernity. Although the pontiff does not deal directly with questions of media use, he cogently restates the moral and, perhaps more important, the epistemological basis of traditional church teaching on issues of intellectual freedom. My purpose here is not teaching on issues of intellectual freedom. My purpose here is not to defend or to criticize the church's approach to issues of intellectual freedom but simply to present the church's position as clearly as possible.

THE CLASSICAL LIBERAL VIEWPOINT ON FREE EXPRESSION

Perhaps the Catholic position on intellectual freedom can best be understood by contrasting the church's position with the contemporary liberal perspective on free expression. Although applications of the principle of free expression have always been controversial, it seems fair to assert that the liberal viewpoint on media usage is one of virtually unlimited freedom to present ideas in public forums. Indeed, the cultural and legal presumption in favor of free expression has been so strong that it has been extremely difficult to regulate such "ideas" as obscenity and hate speech.

The liberal viewpoint can best be understood by examining the rationale presented by John Stuart Mill (1859/1956) in his classic work *On Liberty*. In it, Mill argues for virtually unlimited liberty of thought and expression and for a strong presumption against regulating individual behavior except in cases in which restriction is necessary to prevent harm to others. Although recent controversies over issues such as sexual harassment, pornography, and hate speech have illustrated that the notion of "harm" may not be as straightforward as Mill might have imagined, his work creates a strong presumption against restricting the actions of any person for her or his own good.

Such freedom is desirable from the standpoint of classical liberalism because liberals are ultimately agnostic on the question of truth (see especially Wills, 1970). Truth, for Mill, is in most important senses partial, individual, and necessarily incomplete. Human beings are constantly engaged in a search for truth (of which freedom of expression is an important tool) but will perhaps never know when truth has been attained. Indeed, rather than offering a substantive conception of truth, Mill offers a method by which truth can be understood to the best of our somewhat limited abilities. Consider Mill's rationale for freedom of expression in each of three cases:

1. If unconventional opinion proves to be correct, humanity has clearly gained from the expression of such opinions.
2. If an unconventional opinion proves false, society still gains because people come to understand their own, conventional opinions better by confrontation with opposing viewpoints.
3. An unconventional opinion may contain elements of truth by which more popularly held ideas may be modified without being abandoned.

This account of the benefits of free expression carries with it two important assumptions. First, people are thought to be competent to judge between opposing viewpoints. The ultimate test of the value of a viewpoint is its ability to persuade in a marketplace of ideas. False or harmful ideas will eventually die out as the result of the discourse of rational beings. Second, our approximations of truth may increase in quality as the beneficial effects of freedom of thought and action spread, but they can never be regarded as ultimately and finally true. For Mill, the search for truth is a process that will never, and can never, end (for an analysis of contradictions in classical liberal philosophy, see Bollinger, 1988).

Thus, we can improve our capacity for discerning progressively closer approximations of the truth by increasing the range of alternatives to which we are exposed. In *Utilitarianism*, Mill (1957) argues that two alternative beliefs and practices can only be evaluated by people "competently acquainted with both." From a liberal standpoint, one cannot competently choose between Christianity and Islam, for example, without thoroughly understanding the truth claims of both. Adherence to one religion while ignorant of the precepts of the other is simply the response of "habit," not of authentic human reason.

Two implications follow from this analysis. First, we increase our ability to make judgments about relative truth, utility, and so on to the extent that we expand the range of our experiences. Encounters with beliefs and practices that are ultimately judged as false, harmful, or pernicious have positive educative benefits. Second, because no person can ever exhaust the entire range of possible experiences, such judgments will necessarily be relative and tentative. Thus, all ideas are presumptively created equal (Wills, 1970); deeply held beliefs are, for most *public* purposes, merely "preferences" (Barry, 1990). In the final analysis, the *content* of truth claims in liberal societies must give way to the *process* by which approximations of truth are to be discovered.

THE CATHOLIC VIEWPOINT ON COMMUNICATIONS

In contrast to the classical liberal model, Catholic doctrine on proper use of communications media begins with the premise that objective truth exists and is accessible to humans. In the Augustinian framework, "natural law" is that portion of God's eternal law made available to humans through divine revelation and human reason (Gardiner, 1958; John Paul II, 1993). As creatures created in God's image, we are placed in charge of the earth and of ourselves. By making objective truth accessible to us, God calls us to participate in authentic human freedom. As John Paul II (1993) states,

> By forbidding man to "eat of the tree of the knowledge of good and evil," God makes it clear that man does not originally possess such "knowledge" as something properly his own, but only participates in it by the light of natural reason and of Divine Revelation, which manifest to him the requirements and the prompting of eternal wisdom. (p. 65)

It is important to take careful note of the dynamic by which truth in this religious sense comes to be apprehended. The ultimate appeal is to human reason, not the authority of Scripture. Although Scripture *is* an important source of Catholic religious thought, it is not generally regarded as a *final* authority, in part because it is incomplete. Scripture is a source of God's direct revelations to specific communities and must be understood in light of the faith experiences of those communities (see Jelen, 1993). When God chooses to reveal Himself directly, He speaks to people in their own idiom and in language that members of the community can understand. In contrast to the hermeneutics of evangelical Protestantism, the Catholic view is that specific scriptural revelations must be understood and evaluated in terms of their relevance for contemporary circumstances.

To illustrate, the dietary restrictions listed in the book of Leviticus might be quite reasonable advice for nomadic people, with primitive means of cooking and food preservation. Unless pork is handled very carefully, eating it can be a serious health hazard. Such a prohibition, however, may not make as much sense in contemporary industrialized societies, with their advanced means of climate control, refrigeration, and government inspections. The prohibition in Exodus on adultery, however, might still be regarded as binding today because the destructive consequences of sexual jealousy probably have not changed.

The comparison of kosher laws with the sixth commandment in the Catholic Bible serves to illustrate a serious tension in the use of reason to discern natural law. It might well be asked whether it is not a hazardous practice to allow humans to discern God's law for themselves, when humans are subject to temptations and possible distortions of reason. To stay with the example of adultery, is it not possible for individual people to rationalize acts of marital infidelity by appealing to contemporary circumstances?

This possibility of corrupt human reason raises the central tension within the Catholic natural law tradition: Our capacity for reason occasions the potential of genuine moral freedom, whereby the individual believer apprehends and internalizes the moral law and freely applies it to herself or himself (John Paul II, 1993). Conversely, the corrupt, carnal nature of humanity that is attributable to original sin allows human reason to be debased and directed away from its moral obligation to seek truth.

The combined spiritual/carnal nature of humanity poses tremendous opportunity as well as enormous risks. Understanding the Catholic position on censorship requires that attention be paid to both the potential and the temptations of human reason. John Paul II (1993) expresses this concern most clearly:

Man is constantly tempted to turn his gaze away from the living and true God in order to direct it toward idols (cf. 1 Thes. 1:9), exchanging "the truth about God for a lie" (Rom. 1:25). Man's capacity to know the truth is also darkened, and his will to submit to it is weakened. Thus, giving himself over to relativism and skepticism (cf. Jn. 18:38), he goes off in search of an illusory freedom apart from truth itself. (pp. 3-4)

As beings created in God's image, humans are given the responsibility for caring for the earth and for themselves (John Paul II, 1993). Because we are capable of caring for ourselves, we use reason to comprehend the natural law and to apply it to ourselves. The ability of humankind to submit to a law that is objective because it is God ordained but also self-prescribed is, from the standpoint of Catholic doctrine, the essence of human freedom. Such a conception of freedom, of course, closely resembles Isaiah Berlin's (1970) notion of "positive freedom," in which free persons are empowered to fulfill their "higher" natures. The gradual, continuous process by which the believer comes to understand and internalize natural law is to "free" himself or herself from the particular, the profane, and the mundane. Freedom, in this account, is the ability to do what one knows to be good.

Because there is only one truth in the Catholic account, how is submitting to that truth "liberating"? Even if one grants that such submission is in accordance with one's higher nature, does calling such submission freedom not involve a Rousseauian paradox of "forcing people to be free"? Children, for example, are not free to choose physical growth or nongrowth, even though most would regard growth as a natural process. Similarly, one might argue that obeying God's law may be desirable, but to term such action freedom is to be self-consciously ironic.

The answer is that people are not free to the extent that they innocently or deliberately reject God's higher law, because such rejection involves submission to other, inferior forces (Gardiner, 1958). That is, the individual who chooses not to follow the dictates of one's uncorrupted reason is most likely obeying the demands of appetite, pride, social pressure, or some other temptation. Authentic autonomy, in this view, is strictly illusory. The real choices, or "dimensions of variation" (Taylor, 1973), are adherence to divinely ordained natural law or obedience to some inferior temptation. To quote John Paul II (1993),

> Those who live "by the flesh" experience God's law as a burden, and indeed as a denial or at least a restriction of their own freedom. On the other hand, those who are impelled by love and "walk by the Spirit" (Gal. 5:16) and who desire to serve others, find in God's law the fundamental and necessary way in which to practice love as something freely chosen and freely lived out. Indeed, they feel an interior urge—a genuine "necessity" and no longer a form of coercion, not to stop at the minimum demands of the law, but to live them in their "fullness." . . . God's law does not reduce, much less do away with human freedom; rather it protects and promotes that freedom. (pp. 31, 57)

Thus, the possibility of choosing incorrectly between the sacred and the profane is what makes human freedom possible and what makes submission to God's law the fulfillment of human freedom. The risk in such an account is that humans will fall prey to various temptations and will deny their potential for freedom by yielding to other, temporal forces.

It is possible to divide human temptations into two general categories. The first might deal directly with carnal "appetites," such as greed, gluttony, lust, and so on. Anyone who has experienced uncontrollable hunger, lust, and so on is aware of the feeling of being "enslaved" by one's passions. A second type of temptation is more intellectual in nature. A belief in the sufficiency of our own mental or moral exertions, without the help of sanctifying grace, involves yielding to the temptation posed by the serpent when he said to Eve, "Ye shall be as gods" (Genesis 3:5, New Catholic Bible). An overconfident faith in the efficacy of undisciplined human reason might be regarded as a form of idolatry, in which the creation seeks to supplant the Creator. The sin of pride may ultimately be more pernicious than the mere indulgence of physical appetites, for a sense of moral self-sufficiency may undermine the "objective" basis for God-given morality. Indeed, both critics (Cadegan, 1987) and supporters (Betten, 1935; Gardiner, 1958) of Catholic censorship suggest that heresy, anticlericalism, and other doctrinal errors have been much more likely targets for Catholic condemnation than mundane materials such as obscenity. John Paul II (1993) poses the risk most starkly:

> [There is] *the risk of an alliance between democracy and ethical relativism,* which would remove any sure moral reference point from political and social life, and on a deeper level make the acknowledgment of truth impossible. (pp. 151-152)

The contrast between the temptation of pride and the classical liberal model of free expression could not be posed more directly. According to the standard defense of free speech and press, freedom from external constraints is desirable because people can be trusted to distinguish between better and worse alternatives. Indeed, the principal limitation on human reason is the artificial restriction of alternatives. Conversely, the Catholic position is that, although human reason (in conjunction with divine revelation) is ultimately the most reliable means of discerning truth, the mechanism is flawed and susceptible to temptations. Given the carnal and intellectual temptations to which humans are subject, it is by no means certain that truth will prevail in the marketplace of ideas.

Because of the limitations of human reason, the Catholic Church assumes its primary role as teacher. The faithful require guidance if they are to resist the various temptations offered by the world and continue to direct their attention to the discernment and actualization of God's law. The church derives its own sense of authority from Christ's charge to Peter:

> And I say also unto thee, that thou art Peter, and upon this rock I will build my church, and the gates of hell shall not prevail against it. And I will give unto thee the keys of the kingdom of heaven; and whatsoever thou shalt bind on earth shall be bound in heaven; and whatsoever thou shalt loose on earth shall be loosed in heaven. (Matthew 16:18-19, New Catholic Bible)

The importance of the church's *teaching* authority is paramount because of the necessary limitations on other aspects of the church's authority. Although the emphasis placed on the *Index of Forbidden Books* has varied historically, it was never considered remotely possible for the church to review all the published materials to which

Catholics might have access (Betten, 1935; Burke, 1952; Cadegan, 1987). If Catholics were permitted to read anything that did not appear in the *Index of Forbidden Books* or to view all films not condemned by the National Legion of Decency, these prohibitions would have little practical effect. Catholics would be free to consume the vast majority of harmful, pernicious, or dangerous publications because, inevitably, they would encounter arguments, books, films, and television programming for which the church provides no *specific* guidance. Like a concerned parent or teacher, the church can only hope laypeople internalize Catholic doctrine to the point that they will voluntarily reject communications that threaten their faith.

Even if more direct authority over the laity were desirable, such control would simply not be practical. As the pope describes the church's role, "In a positive way, the Church seeks, with great love, to help all the faithful to form a moral conscience which will make judgments and lead to decisions in accordance with the truth" (John Paul II, 1993, p. 130).

Thus, Catholic doctrine concerning use of communications media has consistently been directed at teaching the laity to recognize and resist the temptations offered by the secular world. Historically, the church has provided general guidance in the form of church dogma and more specific guidance through prohibitions and admonitions against certain books, films, and other communications. These specific recommendations, however, serve only as illustrations or examples of the type of material that Catholics are encouraged to avoid. The *primary* purpose of the church is to empower Catholics with individually well-formed consciences so they can make morally informed judgments about the type of communications to which they should expose themselves.

CONCLUSION

One point clearly deserves emphasis: The Roman Catholic Church is not committed to *intellectual freedom* as that term is conventionally understood. In contrast to the classical liberal model of free expression, Catholic doctrine regards human reason as readily corruptible and, therefore, a suspect, if necessary, means by which the faithful can discern truth. By virtue of its special status with Christ, the church seeks to provide guidance for people attempting to make intelligent and moral choices about the information and media to which they pay attention. Again, the primary function of the church is a *teaching* responsibility, through which people can come to internalize the norms of Catholic natural law doctrine and are thus able to apply God-ordained law to themselves. Despite a lack of recent examples of Catholic attempts to exert specific public authority over individual books, films, and programs, the church's commitment to guiding the consciences of Catholics has not changed.

Historically, of course, church guidance has often been presented in a rather authoritarian form. The *Index of Forbidden Books* as well as pronouncements from the National Legion of Decency and the National Office for Decent Literature have not typically been presented as suggestions. It is imperative, however, that the teaching function of such activities be recognized. More direct control of Catholic media usage would be impractical, and any attempt in that direction would ultimately be self-defeating. A church interested in providing access to salvation must, in the final analysis, depend on individual judgments made by individual believers. The most recent pronouncement by Pope John Paul II (1993) demonstrates that, now as ever, the primary business of Catholicism is the shaping and development of individual consciences. In so doing, the church seeks to maximize human freedom, understood as voluntary obedience to God's law as befitting creatures created in His image.

REFERENCES

Barry, B. (1990). How not to defend liberal institutions. *British Journal of Political Science, 20,* 1-14.

Berlin, I. (1970). Two concepts of liberty. In I. Berlin (Ed.), *Four essays on liberty* (pp. 118-172). New York: Oxford University Press.

Betten, F. S. (1935). *The Roman Index of Forbidden Books briefly explained.* Chicago: Loyola University Press.

Bollinger, L. C. (1988). *The tolerant society.* New York: Oxford University Press.

Burke, R. A. (1952). *What is the Index?* Milwaukee, WI: Bruce Publishing.

Burns, G. (1992). *The frontiers of Catholicism: The politics of ideology in a liberal world.* Berkeley: University of California Press.

Cadegan, U. M. (1987). *All good books are Catholic books: Literature, censorship, and the Americanization of Catholics, 1920-1960.* Unpublished doctoral dissertation, University of Pennsylvania.

D'Antonio, W., Davidson, J., Hoge, D., & Wallace, R. (1989). *American Catholic laity in a changing church.* Kansas City, MO: Sheed & Ward.

Gardiner, H. C. (1958). *Catholic viewpoint on censorship.* Garden City, NY: Hanover House.

Jelen, T. G. (1993). *The political world of the clergy.* Westport, CT: Praeger.

Jelen, T. G., & Wilcox, C. (1990). Denominational preference and the dimensions of political tolerance. *Sociological Analysis, 51,* 69-80.

John Paul II. (1993). *The splendor of truth.* Washington, DC: United States Catholic Conference.

McNamara, P. H. (1992). *Conscience first, tradition second: A study of young Catholics.* Albany: State University of New York Press.

Mill, J. S. (1956). *On liberty.* Indianapolis, IN: Bobbs-Merrill. (Originally published in 1859)

Mill, J. S. (1957). *Utilitarianism.* Indianapolis, IN: Bobbs-Merrill.

Taylor, C. (1973). Neutrality in political science. In A. Ryan (Ed.), *The philosophy of social explanation* (pp. 139-170). New York: Oxford University Press.

Walsh, F. R. (1990). "The Callahans and the Murphys" (MGM, 1927): A case study of Irish-American and Catholic church censorship. *Historical Journal of Film, Radio, and Television, 10,* 33-45.

Wills, G. (1970). *Nixon agonistes.* Boston: Houghton-Mifflin.

Wills, G. (1987). *Reagan's America: Innocents at home.* Garden City, NY: Doubleday.

4

Mainline Protestants and the Media

JUDITH M. BUDDENBAUM

When Martin Luther nailed his 95 theses to the church door in Wittenberg, he meant only to correct problems he perceived in Catholicism as it then existed. Instead, he broke its hegemony. By freeing the word of God from ecclesiastical control, Luther opened the way for religious diversity such that never again could a single church presume to speak for all Christians.

With at least 200 Christian churches in the United States today (Bedell, 1994), it is difficult to say with any authority, "This is what Christians believe." Doing that is especially difficult for the moderate to liberal Protestant churches that are often referred to collectively as mainline churches.

Some, such as the Lutherans, have a well-defined set of quite orthodox beliefs; others, such as the Quakers and Disciples of Christ, are essentially noncredal, insisting only that there is a God whose dealings with humankind are recorded in the Bible. Lutherans can trace their beliefs back to Luther, Presbyterians to Calvin and Knox, and the Methodists to Wesley. Although others have lineages that are less clear, all have been affected in one way or another by splits and mergers that affect both doctrine and church polity. All also incorporate at least some strains from more modern church leaders and theologians: Barth, Bonhoeffer, Buber, Bultmann, Gladden and Rauschenbusch, the Neibuhrs, Schleirmacher, Soderholm, and Tillich, to name just a few (Bainton, 1952; Curtis, 1970; Ferm, 1990; Forell, 1971; Gerrish, 1993; McGrath, 1993).

Although the mainline churches differ greatly in theology, practice, and church polity, what sets them apart from other Christian churches is their emphasis on the importance of the individual conscience and of human reason. Like Martin Luther, they would say,

> Unless I am convicted by Scripture and plain reason—I do not accept the authority of popes and councils, for they have contradicted each other—my conscience is captive to the Word of God. I cannot and I will not recant anything, for to go against conscience is neither right nor safe. (Bainton, 1952, p. 61)

Most also would add emphatically, however, that being "convicted by Scripture" and "captive to the Word of God" does not mean that the Bible is literally true. Some would even add that the Bible is not the sole source of God's word, for God can and does reveal Himself in other ways.

MAINLINE PROTESTANT CHURCHES AND THE MASS MEDIA

Mainline churches accept and embrace biblical interpretation and the higher criticism that more conservative Protestants reject. To mainline Protestants, properly understanding words in the Bible requires an examination of their context within the Bible itself and a sensitivity to the meaning they had for their original audience. Although God's message does not change because God does not change, generally accepted behaviors, including those associated with mass media use, do change over time as people use the best available scholarly methods in an effort to understand and apply God's message.

The beliefs that Christians can be recognized by their lifestyle and that society is perfectible led Calvinist Geneva to ban taverns, immodest dress, dancing, singing "indecent or irreligious" songs, and all books "considered wrong in religious tenets or tending toward immorality" (Bainton, 1952, pp. 118-119). In the United States, Calvin's teachings combined with Puritanism and then with the Methodist passion for perfectionism in ways that gave rise to the Comstock laws and that still find expression in crusades against pornography and other "immoral" or "unwholesome" media fare.

But whereas at the turn of the century mainline churches often led crusades to ban books, today, official pronouncements are more in line with Martin Luther's view:

> "I am persuaded that without knowledge of literature pure theology cannot at all endure, just as heretofore, when letters have declined and lain prostrate, theology, too has wretchedly fallen and lain prostrate. . . . Therefore I beg of you that at my request (if that has any weight) you will urge your young people to be diligent in the study of poetry and rhetoric." (quoted in Smith & Jacobs, 1918, p. 176)

Like other Christians, members of these churches are often appalled by and highly critical of what they see or read in mass media. Ultimately, however, most would agree with Luther that people need exposure to secular media even if the messages are sometimes at odds with church teachings. Therefore, their criticism of the media and their ways of dealing with perceived problems caused by media content differ markedly from both the Catholic and the conservative Protestant approaches.

Mainline Protestants reject the idea that the church is the final authority on religious truth. Members expect their leaders to teach and even to lead, but they see their leaders more as guides than arbiters because ultimate responsibility in matters of faith lies with each individual Christian. Therefore, religious leaders often disagree among themselves, and congregation members do not always agree with the clergy. Within each theological tradition, as well as within each denomination and congregation, there are some whose beliefs are more similar to those held by Evangelicals and Fundamentalists than to the positions associated with mainline Protestantism.

Some Christians believe news should be reported and interpreted in accord with their particular religiously inspired worldview; when it is not, they see the mass media as deliberately biased and anti-Christian (Olasky, 1988; Park, 1927). But mainline churches are more likely to complain primarily about what they perceive as inadequate and shallow coverage (Buddenbaum, 1990a, 1990b).

In entertainment fare, the mainline churches have been more inclined than other churches to express dismay over portrayals of violence than over sexual content. And where both the Catholic Church and church leaders aligned with the New Christian Right have used their teaching authority to warn their members to avoid entertainment that might lead them astray (Alley, 1990b), mainline churches prefer to identify the underlying causes of the problem and then work to expose and change what is wrong (Fore, 1990). Toward that end, the churches, both individually and collectively through their national and international organizations, advocate both education and structural change ("Believers Strive," 1994; Buddenbaum, 1981, 1984; Ferré, 1985; Fore, 1990; Hamelink, 1975; Lutheran World Federation, 1973; National Council of Churches, 1992, 1993; Soukup, 1993; World Council of Churches, 1968, 1983).

At the individual level, the primary problem, as these churches see it, is not so much that "bad content" exists and that people attend to it but that they do so uncritically and without taking personal responsibility. Therefore, they recommend that parents monitor media use by their children and take steps to protect them from content that may be too adult but also that they take the time to discuss media messages with their children. As an aid, they regularly call for media literacy programs that would help people learn to examine media messages in the light of their religious beliefs. They encourage congregations to provide opportunities for church members to come together to read, watch, and discuss popular books, television programs, and movies; mainline magazines carry book, television, and movie reviews that point out both strengths and weaknesses in popular entertainment fare.

At the societal level, again the problem is not so much that bad content exists but that shallow news, sex, and violence are overrepresented in the marketplace, whereas more thorough and thoughtful voices and other kinds of entertainment fare are virtually absent. To open up the channels of communication to more diverse viewpoints, they recommend steps to reduce commercial pressures that lead to an overabundance of easy-to-produce movies and television programs intended only to attract the largest possible audiences. The National Council of Churches (1993), for example, calls for direct church action through program development and investment strategies.

Church actions alone, however, may not be enough. Therefore, the council also calls for government leadership in developing broadcast standards, voluntary rating systems, and incentives that could offset the purely commercial support that produces pressures toward lowest-common-denominator fare. In general, these churches encourage change-oriented policy advocacy and involvement of the kind undertaken by the United Church of Christ in its lawsuit over inadequate and racially biased local news content that ultimately gave citizens standing in cases involving broadcast license renewals (*Office of Communication, United Church of Christ v. F.C.C.*, 1969).

These calls for more government involvement could be interpreted as calls for strict content controls, but that is not the aim of the mainline churches. Although their policy statements often couple freedom with responsibility, they advocate a true marketplace of ideas and support the First Amendment rights of those who own or communicate via the media. They caution against boycotts because boycotts harm those engaging in legal activities and do little to eliminate the message and nothing to address the root causes of the problem (Fore, 1990).

They abhor censorship, teaching that silencing even the most objectionable voices is inappropriate because "God seems to be astonishingly able to use 'blasphemers,' and even the Christian church for good. So that from the 'human side' it's sometimes difficult to distinguish God's so-called friends from God's so-called enemies" (Goetz, 1989, p. 255). Although there is a tendency for them to equate good content with good effects and bad content with bad effects, many see no real difference between high culture and popular entertainment. Both can seduce, but both can also reveal God (Alley, 1990a; VanTil, 1959). Both seduction and revelation can come in the same package as indicated by *Christian Century* reviews of two television programs that have generally been condemned by more conservative Christians.

In comparing her to Mary of the old *Mary Tyler Moore Show*, Rebeck (1989) notes that the *Murphy Brown* character is admirable because she has taken full responsibility for her alcoholism, overcome it, and moved on to be a respected professional instead of just a decorative accessory in the newsroom, even if "she is not necessarily a role model; she is sometimes too biting and makes her share of mistakes" (p. 950). And of *The Simpsons*, she says,

> This is no vapid, pristine Brady Bunch. . . . The Simpsons are a typical American family—typical in a way most family-based shows never acknowledge. Instead of presenting as normal some childhood traumas that most of us never face and then resolving them with presumptuous, simplistic parental advice, the Simpson children wrestle with problems like peer pressure and their own lack of self-understanding. . . . The Simpsons are not the ideal family. But they are not intended to be. . . . The Simpsons show us in a rather bald as well as witty way what it was . . . that made us brats as kids and neurotic as adults. (Rebeck, 1990, p. 622)

Of course, those programs are by no means the most offensive material available, but the same tendency to see good mixed with bad sometimes occurs even in discussions about pornography (see, e.g., Ross, 1990).

But even if good and bad content were completely separate so the bad could be eliminated without touching the good, censorship would be wrong because eliminating glimpses of evil would create an image of reality that is every bit as misleading as the one created by the present overemphasis on sex and violence. But more important, censorship deals only with eliminating the manifest content. It cannot address problems of misunderstanding, nor can it take into account motives, which also matter. As VanTil (1959) points out, the question for mainline Protestants is not whether the media or media use is sinful, for "a house or car, just as well as a horse or field, a radio or television set, a knife or a suit, may be used either in the service of God or the service of the prince of this world" (p. 197).

The proper question is whether all of these things are used "in the service of God."

From this perspective, watching even the most benign television program or reading a great book may be sinful if the activity is used as an escape, whereas watching a pornographic movie may be good if it is done to learn about the human condition and then to act in mitigating the forces that might lead people to engage in the portrayed behaviors. Similarly, mainline Protestants may praise a person who produces violent movies in an attempt to portray realistically the depths of human depravity (Fore, 1990) but condemn those who do it simply "as a cover for a quest for profit" (Alley, 1977; National Council of Churches, 1993).

CONCLUSION

Mainline Protestant churches call for more direct government action than has been common during the past decade and also support individual and collective action through lobbying and through investment strategies. They caution that the efforts should be aimed at expanding, not constricting, the marketplace. These churches support a marketplace of ideas as necessary in the quest for truth and the common good. Therefore, their basic approach to problems posed by the mass media is to deal with them through a kind of education that encourages both freedom and responsibility.

This approach flows naturally from core religious beliefs. Where some Christian churches encourage a dualistic worldview that makes sharp distinctions between the sacred and the profane, mainline churches consider "a religion that is restricted to the prayer-cell . . . a monstrosity" (VanTil, 1959, p. 44). For them, the involved life is preferable to withdrawal from the world.

Luther's doctrine of the two kingdoms contrasts sharply with the Calvinist view that Christians can and must create a Christian society as well as with Wesleyan teaching that people themselves can be made more perfect (Bainton, 1952; Buddenbaum, 1984; McGrath, 1993). But correctly understood, even Luther's more pessimistic worldview does not argue for withdrawal from the world.

Luther and Calvin taught that secular vocations are both a call from God and a call to service. According to Luther, Christians who have been justified by faith through God's grace have been blessed; their natural response, then, is to be a blessing to others by ministering to their spiritual and temporal needs (Bainton, 1952; Buddenbaum, 1984). From a Calvinist perspective, the "world which God loves and Christ saves" is the "workshop wherein the believer executes [God's] mandate" (VanTil, 1959, pp. 193-194). Like the Wesleyan teaching that man is evil but "can be rescued from his dire condition by the grace of God seconded by man's effort" (Lee, 1936, p. 320), these themes within mainline Protestantism argue for a kind of involvement typified by the social gospel movement (Curtis, 1970; Ferm, 1990).

But God-pleasing, effective involvement requires understanding the world. That requires information about the world, including its seamier side, as well as exposure to ideas that may be wrong but must be understood if they are to be combated. Churches and church members may disagree on the nature of the problem or on the proper solutions. But as with so much else in mainline religion, ultimate authority rests with the individual, for God has given people His Word and blessed them with the gift of reason. To many Christians, this approach "open[s] the floodgates of individualism" (Bainton, 1952, p. 44) in a way that reverses the natural order of things. Insisting that the Bible must be interpreted and that individual conscience and human reason are the guides reduces God's truth to subjective preferences and elevates the creature above the Creator, they might say.

Mainline Protestants, however, do not see it that way. They would agree that God is God and people are not. But they would add that God's truth and God's will are above and beyond the power of any person to comprehend in all its majesty. Therefore, pretending that one knows with certainty the mind of God is the height of arrogance and hypocrisy. It is no more subjective or dangerous to rely on individual conscience and reason than to vest authority in popes or church councils, which also err.

REFERENCES

Alley, R. S. (1977). *Television: Ethics for hire?* Nashville, TN: Abingdon.

Alley, R. S. (1990a). Television and public virtue. In J. P. Ferré (Ed.), *Channels of belief: Religion and American commercial television* (pp. 45-56). Ames: Iowa State University Press.

Alley, R. S. (1990b). Television, religion, and fundamentalist distortions. In R. Abelman & S. M. Hoover (Eds.), *Religious television: Controversies and conclusions* (pp. 265-273). Norwood, NJ: Ablex.

Bainton, R. H. (1952). *The Reformation of the sixteenth century.* Boston: Beacon.

Bedell, K. (Ed.). (1994). *Yearbook of American and Canadian churches.* Nashville, TN: Abingdon.

Believers strive to stem violence. (1994). *Christian Century, 111,* 69-70.

Buddenbaum, J. M. (1981). Media awareness/education programs: Analysis of an LWF survey. *LWF Documentation, 9.*

Buddenbaum, J. M. (1984). *Religion in the news: Factors associated with the selection of stories from an international religion news service by daily newspapers.* Unpublished doctoral dissertation, Indiana University, Bloomington.

Buddenbaum, J. M. (1990a). Network news coverage of religion. In J. P. Ferre' (Ed.), *Channels of belief: Religion and American commercial television* (pp. 57-78). Ames: Iowa State University Press.

Buddenbaum, J. M. (1990b). Religion news coverage in commercial network newscasts. In R. Abelman & S. M. Hoover (Eds.), *Religious television: Controversies and conclusions* (pp. 249-264). Norwood, NJ: Ablex.

Curtis, C. J. (1970). *Contemporary Christian thought.* New York: Bruce Publishing.

Ferm, D. W. (1990). *Contemporary American theologies: A critical survey.* San Francisco: Harper & Row.

Ferre', J. P. (1985). Religious perspectives on commercial television in the United States. *Critical Studies in Mass Communication, 2,* 290-294.

Fore, W. F. (1990). *Mythmakers: Gospel, culture and the media.* New York: Friendship Press.

Forell, G. W. (1971). *Christian social teachings.* Minneapolis, MN: Augsburg.

Gerrish, B. A. (1993). *Continuing the Reformation: Essays on modern religious thought.* Chicago: University of Chicago Press.

Goetz, R. (1989). On blasphemy: Advice for the Ayatollah. *Christian Century, 106,* 253-255.

Hamelink, C. (1975). *Perspectives on public communication.* Baarn, Holland: Ten Have.

Lee, U. (1936). *John Wesley and modern religion.* Nashville, TN: Cokesbury.

Lutheran World Federation. (1973). *Joint report of the task force on mass communication and the task force on public strategy.* Geneva: Author.

McGrath, A. E. (1993). *Reformation thought.* Oxford, UK: Basil Blackwell.

National Council of Churches. (1992). *Global communication for justice.* New York: Author.

National Council of Churches. (1993). *Violence in electronic media: A policy statement adopted by the General Board.* New York: Author.

Office of Communication, United Church of Christ v. F.C.C., 425 F.2d 543 (D.C. Cir. 1969).

Olasky, M. (1988). *Prodigal press*. Westchester, IL: Crossway.

Park, R. E. (1927). The yellow press. *Sociology and Social Research, 12,* 3-11.

Rebeck, V. A. (1989). From Mary to Murphy: Codependent no more. *Christian Century, 106,* 949-950.

Rebeck, V. A. (1990). Recognizing ourselves in the Simpsons. *Christian Century, 107,* 622.

Ross, M. E. (1990). Censorship or education? Feminist views on pornography. *Christian Century, 107,* 244-246.

Smith, P., & Jacobs, C. M. (Eds.). (1918). *Luther's correspondence* (Vol. 2). Philadelphia: United Publishing.

Soukup, P. A. (1993). Church documents and the media. In J. Coleman & M. Tomka (Eds.), *Mass media* (pp. 71-79). Maryknoll, NY: Orbis.

VanTil, J. R. (1959). *The Calvinist concept of culture*. Grand Rapids, MI: Baker Books.

World Council of Churches. (1968). *The church and the media of mass communication: Appendix XI. The Uppsala 68 report*. Geneva: Author.

World Council of Churches. (1983). *Gathered for life*. Geneva: Author.

5

Evangelicals' Uneasy Alliance
With the Media

QUENTIN J. SCHULTZE

E vangelicals have always interacted dynamically with the media and the broader culture. At times, they have seen the media as powerful vehicles for carrying out distinctly religious purposes, such as transmitting the faith to the unconverted (evangelism), educating and edifying evangelical believers, raising funds for domestic and international missionary work, and mobilizing Evangelicals for religiously inspired political action. At other times, Evangelicals have rejected the media as tools of the devil, restricting media use among members and firing salvos at moviemakers, rock music groups, TV producers, and other "worldly" people.

Indeed, Evangelicals' perspective on the media is best understood as the interplay between opposing views of culture—a majority view that optimistically believes the media can be used successfully to transform culture to the will of God and the opposing minority view that pessimistically identifies the media with apostate culture.

These opposing views represent both the range of popular evangelical sentiment and the spectrum of official positions taken by evangelical institutions. They also represent fractures and fissures within
Evangelicalism, which has never been known for its unanimity or
cohesion but instead for its competitive and individualistic spirit.
Finally, such opposing views reflect broadly American currents of
media criticism. This is why even some of the harshest Evangelical
media critics sometimes join with non-Evangelicals in a chorus of
media criticism aimed at issues such as television violence, pornography, and liberal news bias.

WHO ARE THE EVANGELICALS?

Evangelicals are not a coherent or unified movement of Christian
institutions. Rather, they are a "mosaic" (Marsden, 1980) of often
culturally diverse denominations, parachurch organizations, educational and theological institutions, media, independent local
churches, and the like. Perhaps the simplest way to define *Evangelicalism* is to say that it represents the most popular strains of conservative Protestantism—"conservative" not primarily in politics or
ideology but in religious faith and practice.

The most common conservative religious views among Evangelicals include the following: a more or less "literal" view of the Bible
as the divinely inspired Word of God; a strong belief in the need for
"personal, eternal salvation" from one's sins through faith in Christ;
an unwavering faith in the divinity of Christ and His real resurrec-
tion from the dead; and an emphasis on the importance of a spiritu-
ally transformed life (sanctification). Within this conservative
religious framework, however, Evangelicalism covers a remarkably
wide spectrum of individual groups and movements, from fundamentalist churches to conservatives within mainline Protestant denominations (Dayton, 1976; Harrell, 1981; Marsden, 1984).

This chapter focuses on what are sometimes called *neo-Evangeli-
cals* (Erickson, 1969; Marsden, 1987; Nash, 1963; Noll, 1986). They
are the Evangelicals who avoid the more reactionary and separatis-
tic Fundamentalism, who sometimes work ecumenically with other
religious groups, who are more open to intellectual life, and who

still hold strongly to evangelical tenets of Christianity. By and large, they represent the "center" of Evangelicalism, perhaps as many as 50 million Americans.

They include *neo-Pentecostals*, who believe in special manifestations of the Holy Spirit (e.g., speaking in tongues) but do not believe that such blessings are necessary for salvation. The Assemblies of God denomination now includes many such congregations, especially in suburban areas. It also includes many Protestants in the *charismatic* movement, which swept across many denominations in the 1980s. That movement was a kind of popular neo-Pentecostalism characterized by highly emotional and even ecstatic worship styles. In addition, this Evangelicalism includes various *confessional* denominations (e.g., the Presbyterian Church in America, the Orthodox Presbyterian Church, the Christian Reformed Church, and arguably some conservative Lutheran churches). It also includes many independent "community" churches and parachurch groups (e.g., most media evangelism organizations, such as the Billy Graham Evangelistic Association); Wesleyan churches, such as the Church of the Nazarene; "peace churches," such as the Mennonites and evangelical Quakers; southern denominations, such as Southern Baptists; and many black denominations and congregations.

COMMON HOPE

Despite these differences, Evangelicals have generally agreed on a few basic tenets about the media. First, *Evangelicals tend to see the principal function of the media as evangelism, or proclamation of the gospel.* It is not easy to overstate the significance of this perspective. Regardless of which evangelical group one examines, the defining mythos is nearly always the hopeful drive to convert lost souls. In other words, when Evangelicals think religiously about the media, they do not think primarily in terms of entertainment or information but in terms of spiritual persuasion. This persuasive priority derives directly from Evangelicals' theological convictions regarding the need for personal salvation. Because all people who do not believe personally that Christ died on the cross for them will be doomed to eternal death, it is incumbent on Evangelicals to share that gospel with all people as quickly and effectively as possible. Generally speaking, Evangelicals cite the "Great Commission": "Therefore go and make disciples of all nations, baptizing them in the name of the Father and of the Son and of the Holy Spirit, and teaching them to obey everything I have commanded you" (Matthew 28:19-20, NIV).

This Great Commission led Evangelicals to become leaders in the development of all major media in the United States. Evangelicals founded most of the early book publishing organizations in the early years of the colonies, resulting eventually in an enormous publishing industry in the 1990s represented by nondenominational names such as Logos, Word, and Zondervan (Ferre', 1990). Similarly, emphasis on the Great Commission led Evangelicals to champion mass printing and distribution in the United States in the 1830s, primarily via the Bible *tract*—short booklets or pamphlets designed to present the gospel of Christ quickly to individuals and households (Nord, 1984). Evangelical periodical publishing boomed in the late 1800s, until the daily newspaper and monthly consumer magazine began to whittle away at their circulations (Olasky, 1990). In the 1920s, Evangelicals dove into radio broadcasting even before the medium was fully developed (Schultze, 1988); more recently, broadcast television and cable TV have become the vehicles for their excursions into "electronic evangelism" (Schultze, 1991).

Influenced by this godly commission to convert the world to Christ, Evangelicals continue to invest heavily in media outreach programs even though there is very little evidence that mass media evangelism is actually very effective. Furthermore, many Evangelicals themselves admit that they either do not like evangelical media or they simply do not use them. Most evangelical media have notoriously small audiences made up largely of Evangelicals. Nevertheless, the evangelistic impulse guides much evangelical thought about the media at seminaries and in denominational offices. For instance, Richard Mouw (1994), president of Fuller Seminary, sees studying popular culture "as a good first step in *missiological* reflection" (p. 18). In his view, Evangelicals cannot evangelize the non-evangelical world unless they first understand the popular culture that saturates contemporary life. Therefore, he calls for studying popular culture as "a way of *gathering in* theological insights" (p. 18).

COMMON FEARS

Generally speaking, Evangelicals remain hopeful about the media as evangelistic enterprises. But they have not been so sanguine about the "secular" media. From the laity to denominational prelates and theologians, from popular evangelical celebrities and parachurch media watchdog groups to average congregants, Evangelicals have feared the media. This fear takes many forms, from knee-jerk salvos to carefully articulated criticism, but all of it seems to share the same overall theme: *The secular media threaten the values and beliefs of evangelical faith.*

Perhaps the most unusual but also the most compelling critique comes from theologians and intellectuals, who fear the media are popularizing and deluding the evangelical faith. Often the harshest criticisms of this type are reserved for television as the most influential mass medium (Muggeridge, 1977; Owens, 1980). Frequently, however, the critique extends to all media and to popular culture in general.

For example, highly respected evangelical theologian David F. Wells (1993), in his book *No Place for Truth*, largely rejects popular culture simply because it is popular and typically image oriented rather than print oriented. He laments that "populist tastes have now assumed the dominant place in American culture, because television has been able to purvey them so effectively and, in the process, to push other kinds of taste and ability to the cultural periphery" (p. 197). He goes on to suggest that evangelical religion is one of the "most obvious locations where popular culture . . . and the kind of discourse that goes with it, has now achieved a market dominance." He concludes that the major culprit in this watering down of faith and culture is television, which achieves its broad appeal by "thinning its substance" (p. 197).

In response to this pessimistic and elitist kind of critique, other evangelical theologians offer a more hopeful reading of the evangelical enterprise in contemporary culture. Mouw (1994), for example, suggests the "market orientation" in popular media is not all bad because Christ Himself "approached people in terms of the particularities of their context." He adds that "contemporary popular culture is a distorted version of something that God meant to be good. So we must 'undistort' it" (p. 16).

Wells's critique represents the high-brow evangelical rejection of popular culture, whereas Mouw's represents the more optimistic, missiologically oriented critique. On the more popular and less intellectual end of Evangelicalism, fears about the media range from seemingly paranoid conspiratorial theories to the typical complaints about the nefarious moral influences of various kinds of media content. In fact, there is no single, grassroots view of the media emanating from the evangelical trenches. Rather, there are various faddish critiques that ebb and flow with the rise and decline of parachurch leaders. It is not always clear if these leaders themselves completely believe what they say about the media, however, because Evangelicalism often uses hyperbole to communicate its religious messages and because such popular media criticism is often expressed in conjunction with fund-raising appeals. As a pamphlet produced by World Mission Teams (1987) suggested, Evangelicals often seem to be blessed with a "*tenth* gift of the Holy Spirit . . . the *Gift of Exaggeration.*"

Perhaps no evangelical media critic has received more publicity in the last decade than Methodist preacher Donald Wildmon, who formed the National Federation for Decency (NFD), the National Coalition for Better Television, and later the American Family Association as watchdog groups aimed at cleaning up media content by ridding it of the "big three"—sex, violence, and profanity. In the 1970s, he urged his own congregation to turn off their TV sets. Encouraged by the publicity his campaign received, he resigned his pastorate and started the NFD. Soon he was organizing national boycotts of offensive TV programs and their sponsors. In the mid-1980s, Wildmon and the National Association of Evangelicals, a coalition of evangelical groups and denominations, collaborated on a "Statement of Concern" that they submitted to 3,000 heads of a fairly wide range of Christian agencies and schools. The statement used ecumenical rhetoric (e.g., "Christians have no monopoly on virtue") to encourage people of all faiths to join together to combat immoral television programming and anti-Christian stereotyping in news and entertainment shows. Wildmon's efforts eventually extended to magazines (e.g., *Playboy*) and movies.

Wildmon entered the "culture war" from the evangelical camp, but he increasingly appealed to a broader range of people who shared his moral concern with the "great struggle ... going on inside our borders" (Fackler, 1990, p. 112). This kind of broad, moralistic media criticism is widely expressed by many evangelical para-church leaders. Probably the most influential of these is radio host and top-selling book author James Dobson, whose Focus on the Family ministry emphasizes "profamily" values, including conservative moral critiques of media content. Dobson's ministry is one of the few evangelical organizations to publish a newsletter for parents concerned about the impact of popular culture. Focus on the Family produced *Learn to Discern*, a hard-hitting, multimedia examination of the moral impact of the popular teen media, especially violent and lyrically explicit rock music, sexually oriented advertisements, and excessive television viewing. In the book based on the presentation, however, Focus on the Family's Youth Culture Specialist Bob DeMoss (1992) laid much of the blame on evangelical parents who refuse to believe there is a spiritual and moral problem in youth media.

Evangelicals' moral vision of the media is subtly but profoundly different than most criticisms leveled by mainline Protestant leaders. The major difference is captured nicely by Mouw (1994), who suggested that Christian conservatives criticize Las Vegas because of its gambling, booze, and promiscuity, whereas liberals blast the town's greed, bad taste, and sexism. In other words, Evangelicals almost invariably focus their cultural criticism on *personal* moral practices, whereas mainline groups usually emphasize social and aesthetic issues. Indeed, *this highly personalistic approach to morality is one of the distinguishing features of evangelical media criticism.*

In contrast to these moralistic critiques, the evangelical fringe has always been deeply suspicious of the ideological tenor of mainstream media. It is hard to get a handle on the more fundamentalistic fringe, however, because its media are not nearly so public and because its rhetoric is so dynamic. Fringe thought usually sees the media as part of a "liberal" conspiracy to corrupt the nation's values and even to undermine democracy. Parachurch leader Reverend Tim LaHaye (1984), for instance, wrote that Americans "are seeing the world through the eyes of liberal/humanists who consider religion to be irrelevant" (p. 46). He sees the media as part of a larger ideological conspiracy emanating from the former Soviet Union and resurrects some of the conspiracy theories popularized by the right-wing John Birch Society in the 1960s and 1970s. Similarly, the popular evangelical radio talk show host Marlin Maddoux (1990), who founded the U.S.A. Radio Network, says,

> There are extremely powerful people in America who have a very definite agenda that's not in the best interests of freedom. These are people who have enormous wealth and who exert immense influence on the government, on tax-exempt foundations, on the universities, on the news media, and on the entertainment industry.... A good deal of Wall Street money is involved in trade with the Soviets, in the control of the national media, and in the running of foreign affairs. (p. 171)

In other words, big business greed and communist ideology find common ground in media.

EVANGELICAL CULTURAL MOTIFS

Regardless of whether one looks at evangelical fears or hopes about the media, however, there are four recurring cultural motifs that seem to shape evangelical perceptions of the media. These beliefs run across the leadership and down through the laity. Interestingly enough, these motifs are deeply American, not just evangelical, suggesting that evangelical views of the media are significantly shaped by the surrounding culture (Schultze, 1990).

First, Evangelicals display a *remarkable disinterest in religious tradition*. This disinterest is undoubtedly the product partly of the high value Americans place on personal freedom. As a whole, Evangelicals do not look to the past to make sense of the present or future. In fact, often they do not know or care much about the history of Christianity or even of their own denominations or congregations. Instead, they are strongly future oriented, a trait Allan Nevins (1971) links to U.S. culture generally. As a result, Evangelicalism is prone to faddish cultural and media critique. One day it is a major boycott of an offensive television program and the next it is a wide-eyed march against a movie such as *The Last Temptation of Christ*, even if nearly all of the marchers have not seen it. Without a guiding tradition of articulate media criticism and theory, it is difficult for Evangelicals to get their theological bearings in the contemporary culture wars. As a result, most religious groups are more easily manipulated by "professional" media critics who claim to speak for Evangelicals.

Second, Evangelicals typically hold a *remarkably uncritical faith in media technology*. Although it is less common among evangelical intellectuals, it is a widely held belief that both increases evangelical criticism of the secular media and enhances commitment to evangelistic media. Like many Americans throughout the history of the nation, Evangelicals have equated technological progress with progress itself. Arguing that U.S. popular religion is really a syncretism of technology and Protestantism, David Himrod (1984) suggests that such syncretism is evident "when human inventions replace the Lord's creations as the symbols which bind the present to the biblical past" (p. 54). Evangelist William Foulkes (1937) wrote that "radio waves" might create another "Pentecost—a potential Pentecost at least" (p. 230). Similarly, in his book *The Electric Church*, former executive director of National Religious Broadcasters Ben Armstrong (1979) wrote that radio and television had "broken through the walls of tradition" and "restored conditions remarkably similar to the early church" (pp. 8-9). He even interpreted Revelation 14:6 ("And I saw another angel fly in the midst of heaven . . .") as a prophecy about satellites (pp. 172-173).

Third, Evangelicals usually *strive to popularize their culture*, creating an ironic affinity between secular media and evangelical culture. As historian Nathan Hatch (1989) has documented, the rapid popularization of Evangelicalism began in the early 19th century when numerous preachers and Bible teachers challenged the existing social and religious authority of college-trained clergy by creating emotionally stirring messages for popular audiences. They deintellectualized and dramatized their preaching, replacing the genteel language of educated clergy with vernacular speech. In short, Evangelicals became expert marketers of religion, as evidenced today in everything from the gospel music industry, a $300 million business (Romanowski, 1990, p. 144), to evangelical book publishing and broadcasting. As a result of this popularization, evangelical culture generally mirrors the secular culture that Evangelicals often criticize. Moreover, Evangelicals, except for the more separatistic Fundamentalists, tend to consume the same media as non-Evangelicals and to live more or less in the same wider culture. This sometimes leaves Evangelicals with very little room to create a distinctive critique of the media.

Fourth, *evangelical views of the media are greatly shaped by the U.S. spirit of individualism.* More than their mainline counterparts, Evangelicals are likely to follow the ideas expressed by particular personalities rather than the official media critiques offered by denominational leadership bodies. Evangelicalism is significantly organized around influential, charismatic individuals who have a talent for garnering audiences and developing media organizations, especially parachurch organizations. Evangelical book publishing, for instance, depends heavily on best-sellers by well-known Evangelicals, such as radio preacher Charles Swindoll, former televangelist and presidential aspirant M. G. "Pat" Robertson, psychologist-broadcaster James Dobson, and radio commentator, columnist, and prison ministry executive Charles Colson. Evangelical media criticism, in turn, depends significantly on the views of such talented evangelical communicators who use primarily evangelical media to criticize the mainstream media.

EVANGELICALS AS AMERICANS

There are very few distinctly religious currents in evangelical views of the media. Evangelicalism is greatly shaped by the cultural and economic currents that influence U.S. society. Evangelicals tend to "baptize" their fears about the media with popular theology, but their criticisms are often identical to the moral and ideological salvos emanating from many streams of U.S. life. This is precisely why even some of the most conservative Evangelicals, going into battle to "redeem" the media, will align themselves with Roman Catholics, mainline Protestants, and even Jews. Conservative Jewish movie critic Michael Medved (1992), for instance, became a darling of many evangelical groups in the mid-1990s when his book, *Holly-wood vs. America,* was published by media mogul Rupert Murdoch's HarperCollins, which also owns the evangelical Zondervan publishing house. The Reverend Jerry Falwell's Moral Majority and Wildmon's American Family Association have established similarly broad constituencies defined more by the militant style of criticism than by a distinctly evangelical remedy.

Perhaps the only distinctly evangelical view of the media is the hope that media technologies can be used to influence the *religious* direction of the nation. Evangelicals' emphasis on the Great Commission is the strongest version of that hope. Nevertheless, even this view of the media as God-ordained vehicles for evangelization is not wholly out of tune with U.S. culture. Popular evangelists of notable integrity such as Billy Graham find broad acceptance of their style and even of their substance. To the extent that their message seems to resonate with religiously "generic" values, such as honesty, fidelity, forgiveness, and love, even distinctly evangelical preachers garner support from many sectors of the religious community in the United States.

Perhaps the most significant thing that can be said about evangelical views of the media is that they are not easily controlled by denominational structures or even by local pastors. Evangelicalism in the United States is highly dynamic, tuned to popular voices of charismatic figures and charged by the ongoing culture wars created and maintained through the media. No religious institutions are going to be able to dictate to Evangelicals what to believe about the media. On the other hand, neither will Evangelicals be able to free themselves easily from the self-imposed media criticism of the popular evangelical marketplace.

REFERENCES

Armstrong, B. (1979). *The electric church.* Nashville, TN: Thomas Nelson.

Dayton, D. W. (1976). *Discovering an evangelical heritage.* New York: Harper & Row.

DeMoss, R. G., Jr. (1992). *Learn to discern.* Grand Rapids, MI: Zondervan.

Erickson, M. J. (1969). *The new evangelical theology.* London: Marshall, Morgan, and Scott.

Fackler, M. (1990). Religious watchdog groups and prime-time programming. In J. P. Ferre' (Ed.), *Channels of belief: Religion and American commercial television* (pp. 99-116). Ames: Iowa State University Press.

Ferre', J. P. (1990). Searching for the Great Commission: Evangelical book publishing since the 1970s. In Q. J. Schultze (Ed.), *American Evangelicals and the mass media: Perspectives on the relationship between American Evangelicals and the mass media* (pp. 99-118). Grand Rapids, MI: Academie.

Foulkes, W. H. (1937). Radio evangelism. In J. M. Bader (Ed.), *The message and the method of the new evangelism* (pp. 228-233). New York: Round Table.

Harrell, D. E. (Ed.). (1981). *Varieties of southern Evangelicalism*. Macon, GA: Mercer University Press.

Hatch, N. O. (1989). *The democratization of American Christianity*. New Haven, CT: Yale University Press.

Himrod, D. K. (1984). The syncretism of technology and Protestantism: An American popular religion. *Explor, 7*, 49-60.

LaHaye, T. (1984). *The hidden censors*. Old Tappan, NJ: Fleming H. Revell.

Maddoux, M. (1990). *Free speech or propaganda: How the media distort the truth*. Nashville, TN: Thomas Nelson.

Marsden, G. M. (1980). *Fundamentalism and American culture*. New York: Oxford University Press.

Marsden, G. M. (Ed.). (1984). *Evangelicalism and modern America*. Grand Rapids, MI: Eerdmans.

Marsden, G. M. (1987). *Reforming fundamentalism: Fuller Seminary and the new Evangelicalism*. Grand Rapids, MI: Eerdmans.

Medved, M. (1992). *Hollywood vs. America: Popular culture and the war on traditional values*. New York: HarperCollins.

Mouw, R. M. (1994). *Consulting the faithful: What Christian intellectuals can learn from popular culture*. Grand Rapids, MI: Eerdmans.

Muggeridge, M. (1977). *Christ and the media*. Grand Rapids, MI: Eerdmans.

Nash, R. H. (1963). *The new Evangelicalism*. Grand Rapids, MI: Zondervan.

Nevins, A. (1971). The tradition of the future. In T. E. Kakonis & J. C. Wilcox (Eds.), *Now and tomorrow* (pp. 396-404). Lexington, MA: D.C. Heath.

Noll, M. (1986). *Between faith and criticism: Evangelicals, scholarship, and the Bible in America*. San Francisco: Harper & Row.

Nord, D. P. (1984). The evangelical origins of mass media in America. *Journalism Monographs, 88*.

Olasky, M. (1990). Democracy and the secularization of the American press. In Q. J. Schultze (Ed.), *American Evangelicals and the mass media: Perspectives on the relationship between American Evangelicals and the mass media* (pp. 47-68). Grand Rapids, MI: Academie.

Owens, V. S. (1980). *The total image, or, selling Jesus in the modern age*. Grand Rapids, MI: Eerdmans.

Romanowski, W. D. (1990). Contemporary Christian music: the business of music ministry. In Q. J. Schultze (Ed.), *American Evangelicals and the mass media: Perspectives on the relationship between American Evangelicals and the mass media* (pp. 143-169). Grand Rapids, MI: Academie.

Schultze, Q. J. (1988). Evangelical radio and the rise of the electronic church. *Journal of Broadcasting and Electronic Media, 32*, 289-306.

Schultze, Q. J. (1990). Keeping the faith: American Evangelicals and the mass media. In Q. J. Schultze (Ed.), *American Evangelicals and the mass media: Perspectives on the relationship between American Evangelicals and the mass media* (pp. 23-46). Grand Rapids, MI: Academie.

Schultze, Q. J. (1991). *Televangelism and American culture: The business of popular religion.* Grand Rapids, MI: Baker Books.

Wells, D. F. (1993). *No place for truth, or, whatever happened to evangelical theology.* Grand Rapids, MI: Eerdmans.

World Mission Teams. (1987). *Status report on the Great Commission.* St. Petersburg, FL: Author.

6

Fundamentalism
and the Media, 1930-1990

MARGARET LAMBERTS BENDROTH

" To me, the radio is the most wonderful invention ever conceived by the human brain" (p. 70), Reverend I. M. Hargett (1930), pastor of Tulsa, Oklahoma's Million Dollar Methodist Church, declared. "How unbelievable it is to think of the air around us being continually filled with human voices, some talking, some preaching, some lecturing, some singing" (p. 70). In his brief address at the Winona Lake Bible Conference in 1930, Hargett enthusiastically mined radio technology for spiritual truths. God answered prayer, he imagined, through a divine sending station "working perfectly thousands of years before Marconi was born" (p. 71). Humans, too, had sending stations: "Abraham, thousands of years before the American continent was dreamed of," set up on the plains of Haran and "got a message across to God" (p. 71). "Martin Luther, intrepid reformer, tuned in at Wittenberg" and "John Wesley set up a radio station in the Holy Club at Oxford and heard a call from God to evangelize the British Isles" (p. 72).[1]

Hargett's unbridled enthusiasm for radio was typical of midcentury fundamentalists—although he perhaps stands alone in interpretive ingenuity. Radio was nothing less than a miraculous gift, bestowed by God to speed the progress of worldwide evangelization. "Until the 20th century it had been technologically impossible for the Church to reach every person in the world with the gospel," radio evangelist Barry Siedell (1971) wrote. "Today it is possible" (p. 19).

It is, of course, hard to gauge such enthusiasm without a brief digression on the nature of 20th-century U.S. fundamentalism. In the United States, the movement is only about a century old, arising out of the spiritual crisis of the late 19th century and emerging as a distinct body within evangelical Protestantism during the acrimonious theological controversies of the 1920s (Marsden, 1980). In the aftermath of those battles, religious liberals were quick to proclaim victory; however, the story was far from over. In the midcentury decades, fundamentalists who left their mainline denominations quietly prospered, creating scores of parachurch and missionary organizations dedicated to evangelism (Carpenter, 1980, 1984). Indeed, it is this side of fundamentalism—its innovative, entrepreneurial spirit in the service of worldwide conversion—that goes farthest to explain the movement's ready acceptance of secular media, such as radio and, to a certain extent, television.

Midcentury fundamentalism is clearly a significant precursor of contemporary evangelical attitudes toward the media; however, it would be unwise to draw a direct line to the present, for reasons that should emerge more clearly as this chapter progresses. Although fundamentalists have done much to shape the ethos of contemporary religious conservatism, they hardly stand for the phenomenon as a whole. They are, for example, distinct from modern-day evangelicals by virtue of their dispensational theology and uncompromising separatism—it is perhaps best to think of them as a subgroup within the larger evangelical mosaic (see Dayton & Johnston, 1991; Marsden, 1984).

Beyond that, the picture grows even more complicated. Although opposition to "modernism" is considered a hallmark of fundamentalist theology, most fundamentalists were—and are—not against modernity in every instance. Resistance to worldliness did not require physical isolation from the world; in fact, throughout the 1930s and 1940s, many fundamentalists stayed in mainline churches, hoping to purify them from within (Hamilton, 1994). Nor was their separatism necessarily reactionary and simplistic, a fact well illustrated in their uses of radio and television. From the mid-1920s through the 1950s, the movement's leaders worked hard to develop a consistent, biblically based rationale for proper Christian uses of media technology. The reasons why they were so uniformly enthusiastic about radio and so mixed and uncertain about television are complicated; however, the fact of the problem itself reveals ways in which conservative religious communities attempt to navigate their constituents through uncharted and often threatening waters.

When fundamentalists encountered radio in the 1920s, the first philosophical hurdle they had to overcome was its potential for entertainment. Although they were heirs to the great tradition of urban revivalism, with its penchant for drama and spectacle, 20th-century fundamentalists tended to be suspicious of prideful display that elevated the self. They were men and women armed with a serious purpose: to produce Bible scholars, evangelists, and working Christians who were willing to do battle with the world, the flesh, and the devil. Typical of this attitude is a *Sunday School Times* editorial against "So-Called Humor in the Pulpit," warning the faithful not to be "carried away by the modern tendency to want to have every serious truth sugar-coated" by witty sermon stories ("So-Called Humor," 1954, p. 941).

Most often, however, fundamentalists opposed Hollywood movies. In a pamphlet titled *What Is Wrong With the Movies*, evangelist John R. Rice (1938) characterized them as an "unmitigated curse . . . the feeder of lust, the perverter of morals, the tool of greed, the school of crime, the betrayer of innocence" (p. 9). Although, as this quotation suggests, Rice's analysis was wide ranging, it boiled down to a single principle: Movie-style entertainment was antithetical to true Christianity. "Can one inflame the imagination, arouse sex passion, and fill the mind with lewd pictures and be just as good and pure in heart as before? Certainly not," he declared (p. 102). "I do not know one active, successful soul-winner . . . who frequently attends picture shows" (p. 107).[2]

Prohibitions on moviegoing were relatively easy for fundamentalist parents and clergy to defend as well as to enforce; radio, however, was laden with ambiguities. To be sure, some fundamentalists opposed radio listening because, as they argued, it was the medium of the devil, the "prince of the power of the air." Others objected on more traditional grounds, that the radio "might well be called the helpmeet of the movie, the 'lust of the ear,' " for "it places religion on an equal basis with mere entertainment" (Loveless, 1946, pp. 15-16).[3]

But radio's defenders easily produced counterarguments. Radio was an undeniably useful tool for evangelism, Moody Bible Institute broadcasting instructor Wendell P. Loveless (1946) argued. "The one who is awake to his responsibilities and opportunities as an ambassador for Christ will be quick to employ every legitimate means of conveying the good news to a sinful and dying world" (p. 17). Thus, Loveless pointed out, "The history of spiritual movements throughout the Dispensation of the Church reveals that the best known and most up-to-date methods and instruments have been used to bring people under the sound of the gospel" (p. 17).

Radio proved immediately adaptable to foreign missionary work. In 1930, two enterprising missionaries, Reuben Larson and Clarence W. Jones, procured a broadcasting license from the government of Ecuador, built a 200-watt transmitter, and established HCJB, the first radio station in the country. The *Voice of the Andes* eventually transmitted gospel radio across the entire Western hemisphere (Cook, 1961; Hill, 1983; Jones, 1946).

Reaching U.S. audiences raised another, even more difficult, set of problems for fundamentalist broadcasters. They worried that secular radio listeners were more casual and indifferent, inured to the wonders of modern technology. "It is so easy for the indifferent worldling to turn the dial to another program," one editorial complained, "or to get up and walk away. If the old-time evangelist needed power for his work, how much more must the radio messenger of God's grace lean on the supernatural!" ("The Radio," 1937, p. 55).

Fundamentalists soon realized that radio format demanded a new, more informal style of evangelistic preaching. Wendell Loveless (1946) instructed his Moody students to avoid a "preachy" or "oratorical" tone. "People want the voice on the air to talk to them," he reminded, "not shout at them." The goal was to capture the listeners' interest first and then to introduce the gospel. Thus, Loveless argued, even gospel radio programs needed to have "entertainment value," a quality he carefully differentiated from mere "amusement." "A radio audience may be amused for a half hour without the accomplishment of anything instructive," he explained. "But the gospel broadcaster, who properly employs entertainment factors, has held the interest of his listening audience and has rendered a constructive service" (Loveless, 1946, pp. 21-25, 46-47).

The other objection to radio was that it was too impersonal a medium to communicate spiritual truths. Broadcasters who could not see their audience, the reasoning went, would be flat and ineffective preachers. Thus, when Moody Bible Institute began its own radio station in 1926 (WMBI), programmers made systematic efforts to overcome this handicap. The cast of one program that was specifically designed for elderly and bedridden "shut-ins" took prayer requests over the telephone and periodically visited listeners in their homes. A friendly young woman, Aunt Teresa, hosted the KYB (Know Your Bible) club for children. In 1930, the institute hosted a 2-day rally for some 4,000 radio listeners, treating them to personal tours, musical presentations, and appearances by popular broadcasting figures. Radio programs themselves also regularly featured accounts of personal conversions resulting from radio listening, and by 1930, WMBI received over 20,000 letters a year (Kadley, 1952; Runyan, 1930; "Visits to Shut-Ins," 1927).

If numbers are any indication, fundamentalist radio was a considerable success. A study of Chicago radio programming, published in 1942, found that 61% of the city's religious programs were sponsored by fundamentalist organizations—a figure that did not even include those broadcast over WMBI (Parker & Eastman, 1942). fundamentalist Bible teachers, such as Walter L. Wilson, proved durable and popular; well-known preachers, such as Donald Grey Barnhouse and Charles Fuller, reached national audiences on CBS and the Mutual Network. Fuller's warm, folksy *Old Fashioned Revival Hour* proved immensely popular; a series of mass meetings held in 1938 attracted crowds as large as 40,000, not to mention millions of others listening in by radio (Wright, 1988).

But there was always competition. By the early 1930s, radio had entered its "establishment era," characterized by increasing government supervision and network control of the airwaves. This development had immediate implications for fundamentalist broadcasters hoping to garner national audiences. In 1929, the Federal Radio Commission (later the FCC) mandated a certain amount of free airtime to noncommercial public service organizations, a category that included religious programming. As a minority Protestant voice, fundamentalists were at a direct disadvantage; the Federal Council of Churches, dominated by mainline Protestants, allocated the free airtime for its own constituents and, in fact, persuaded the networks not even to sell airtime to fundamentalist programs (Ellens, 1974; Finke & Stark, 1992).[4]

Lack of public access encouraged a certain amount of creativity, but in the long run the quality of fundamentalist radio declined. Forced to survive on listener donations, broadcasters issued ever more insistent appeals for contributions. Programming became increasingly personality oriented and repetitious, largely because a simple preaching format was the least expensive to produce. Some stations such as WMBI and KEYD in Minneapolis did not even bother to compete nationally but chose to serve a loyal but generally uncritical constituency of fundamentalist listeners (Christianson, 1949).[5] In 1949, William Ward Ayer, pastor of New York's Calvary Baptist Church, singled out a radio preacher as a particularly bad example of the cultural naïveté of his fellow fundamentalists: "He was using the same oratorical method the popular evangelist at the turn of the century used, ringing all the changes in a heightened flowery style, with much repetition, heroics and dramatics," Ayer (1949) complained. "His mode was what the world calls 'hammy' " (p. 331).

Ayer was not the only one who worried about broadcasting standards. The National Religious Broadcasters was formed in 1944 as an arm of the National Association of Evangelicals (which was formed in 1942) to both defend and to monitor its fundamentalist constituency. Its constitution included a "Code of Ethics," which outlined clear professional standards in programming content and financial accountability ("Code of Ethics," 1949, p. 7). By that time, however, fundamentalists had far less power to engage the world on their own terms; indeed, the lines that separated godly from ungodly became increasingly vague and ambiguous in the years after World War II. Although many conservative Christians eschewed all types of secular entertainment, others, equally devout, busily appropriated film media for evangelistic purposes. Some of these movies were simply documentaries of missionary endeavors; others, such as those produced by the Billy Graham Evangelistic Association, were full-fledged dramatizations of spiritual truths (Martin, 1991).

The advent of television complicated things still further, although, as with radio, many fundamentalists were initially cautious. Television airtime was prohibitively expensive and its public service allotments were controlled by mainline Protestants. Moreover, in the early years of television, when few Americans had sets of their own, many watched in bars and taverns.

Still worse, television-style entertainment was laden with moral ambiguities. "Often, while viewing a dramatic presentation," a New Jersey woman confessed in 1954, "the thought came, 'How is this any different from attending a movie or the theater?' " (Smith, 1954, p. 236). Fundamentalist viewers also found themselves assaulted with advertisements for alcohol and tobacco, featuring seductive starlets and movie stars.

Put simply, television was worldly. As a Florida pastor observed wryly, "The boast of one network is that it 'brings the world right into your home.' Who wants the world as we know it in our homes?" (Battles, 1955, p. 942). Indeed, television hit on every aspect of worldliness, defined by Moody Bible Institute president William Culbertson as "pleasure—the lust of the flesh, . . . possessions—the lust of the eye," and "pride—the honor and praise of men" (Culbertson, 1953, p. 865).

By the 1950s, fundamentalist ranks had split between old-fashioned separatists and a more world-affirming neo-evangelical movement led by men such as Billy Graham, himself a pioneer in religious television. Neo-evangelists saw far more possibilities than problems in the new medium; for one thing, it had the same evangelistic potential as radio, if not more. "We must not make the same mistake we made with the movies," Theodore Elsner, president of the National Religious Broadcasters, urged its members. "We should have stepped into this field in the very beginning, and prepared Christian films for the proclamation of the gospel. Ultimately, television will enter most of our homes. This is certainly a real challenge!" (Elsner, 1949, p. 8). Fuller Seminary professor Edward Carnell agreed that the evangelistic potential of television far outweighed its dangers. "TV, while it may threaten to convert every home into a theater, can also turn every parlor into a church," he reminded, urging religious telecasters to "be courageous, remembering that by overtaking man in his solitude TV enjoys an access into hearts which the organized church does not" (Carnell, 1950, p. 89).

In the 1950s, fundamentalist and evangelical periodicals tried to offer guidelines about safe television viewing. Predictably, little consensus emerged. A *Moody Monthly* reader poll, conducted in 1954, found a bewildering range of attitudes, from innocent pleasure ("TV is kept in place in our home because we genuinely want to please the Lord Jesus"; Hitt, 1954, p. 11) to sour contempt ("It would take the cost of only two TV sets to set up a mission station in the Philippine Islands"; Hitt, 1954, p. 11) (see also "What Have," 1953). Very few participants in the discussion were willing to turn off the set for good; most enjoined an open, yet carefully vigilant, approach.

The poll also suggests that fundamentalist viewers were beginning a conversation about television, especially as it affected children, that many nonfundamentalist parents and critics have joined more recently. Almost all poll respondents limited their children's viewing, though few did it successfully. "I'm sure that TV is all right if it's controlled," a mother of young children wrote, "but how many people control it?" (Hitt, 1954, p. 13). More than anything else, fundamentalist parents recognized that television promised an unprecedented challenge to their moral authority. "It should be evident by now," as one mother concluded, "that Christians are going to have to work harder than the forces of the world if they are to combat evil and keep it out of their homes" (Matson, 1949, pp. 634-635).

From here, the story becomes more familiar. Initially, fundamentalists and evangelicals were far less successful in television and found most frequently on small, local community access television stations. In these settings, conservative religious broadcasters learned cheap and efficient means of production, including national syndication. In 1960, when the Federal Communications Commission ruled that stations were no longer obligated to provide free airtime to religious groups, mainline Protestant programming dropped dramatically. Evangelicals and fundamentalists began their upward trajectory in commercial broadcasting, especially in cable networks, that resulted in the televangelism empires of the present day.

It is worth pointing out, however, that only a minority of the so-called televangelists were fundamentalists. Charismatic and Pentecostal preachers, with a tradition of showmanship that reached back several generations, translated far better on the screen than their more sober, straight-laced fundamentalist cousins (see Harrell, 1985). Jerry Falwell's *Old-Time Gospel Hour* was an unadorned rendering of the Sunday morning service at Thomas Road Baptist Church. "The choir behind him sang traditional Baptist hymns," Francis Fitzgerald (1986) writes, "and he, strong-jawed and portly of figure, wearing a thick three-piece black suit, looked every inch the Baptist preacher of the pretelevision era" (p. 128). Although the program contained a few televangelism standards—women with *"Charlie's Angels* hairdos" and men with "television-era poufs"—its main purpose was to edify, not to entertain (Fitzgerald, 1986, p. 128).

Seen in a larger historical perspective, Falwell's program suggests a fair degree of consistency in fundamentalist uses of television. It is unabashedly evangelistic and only entertaining enough to gain a hearing, unlike the larger world of televangelism, which tried and true fundamentalists scorn for its worldly values. "While I thank God for the opportunity of preaching the gospel through the medium of television," Michigan pastor Truman Dollar (1986) wrote in Falwell's *Fundamentalist Journal,* "I realize that we must be careful not to degenerate into the 'entertainment mentality' of the world. . . . What we see in the world, we often see in the church the next year. The atmosphere reflects an audience that says, 'Entertain me' " (p. 74). Like an old-time fundamentalist, Dollar reminded his readers that "we live in a complex world of serious spiritual problems. Religious entertainment simply is not enough. Let us practice some discipline. It is not as much fun, but it is more helpful!" (p. 74).

As this brief historical sketch illustrates, fundamentalism was, and is far more than a simple reaction to modernity. One of its primary purposes was to provide a cultural roadmap for Christians who wished to maintain a supernaturalistic faith in an increasingly materialistic culture. Fundamentalism helped its adherents to negotiate, rather than to avoid or ignore, worldly temptations. The biggest problem, perhaps, was not that task itself but the nature of those temptations, now no longer simple twists in the road but rather huge and impenetrable obstacles in the path.

NOTES

1. For a similar message, see Bowden (1926).
2. For a brief list of objections to movies, see Stroh (1921).
3. See also the equivocal editorial in *Moody Bible Institute Monthly* ("Radio," 1926).
4. See also "A Radio Conspiracy" (1946).
5. Despite the article's title ("KEYD to Christless Homes"), it describes a station format with very little appeal to non-fundamentalists.

REFERENCES

A radio conspiracy. (1946, April 15). *United Evangelical Action*, p. 24.
Ayer, W. W. (1949). How wise are Fundamentalists? *Moody Monthly, 49*, 331-332.
Battles, R. W. (1955). What about television? *Sunday School Times, 26*, 941-942.
Bowden, W. S. (1926). God's radio. *Moody Bible Institute Monthly, 26*, 416-417.
Carnell, E. (1950). *Television: Servant or master?* Grand Rapids, MI: Eerdmans.
Carpenter, J. (1980). Fundamentalist institutions and the rise of evangelical Protestantism. *Church History, 49*, 62-75.
Carpenter, J. (1984). From Fundamentalism to the new evangelical coalition. In G. Marsden (Ed.), *Evangelicalism and modern America* (pp. 3-16). Grand Rapids, MI: Eerdmans.
Christianson, S. (1949). KEYD to Christless homes. *Moody Monthly, 49*, 470-471.
Code of ethics. (1949, March). *United Evangelical Action*, p. 7.
Cook, F. S. (1961). *Seeds in the wind*. Miami, FL: World Radio Missionary Fellowship.
Culbertson, W. (1953). Why shouldn't I? *Moody Monthly, 53*, 865-867.
Dayton, D., & Johnston, R. (1991). *The variety of American Evangelicalism*. Downers Grove, IL: InterVarsity Press.
Dollar, T. (1986). Entertainment or enlightenment? *Fundamentalist Journal, 5*, 74.
Ellens, J. H. (1974). *Models of religious broadcasting*. Grand Rapids, MI: Eerdmans.
Elsner, T. (1949, March). NAE radio commission. *United Evangelical Action*, pp. 6, 8.

Finke, R., & Stark, R. (1992). *The churching of America: Winners and losers in our religious economy.* New Brunswick, NJ: Rutgers University Press.

Fitzgerald, F. (1986). *Cities on a hill: A journey through contemporary American cultures.* New York: Simon & Schuster.

Hamilton, M. S. (1994). *The fundamentalist Harvard: Wheaton College and the continuing vitality of American Evangelicalism, 1919-1965.* Unpublished doctoral dissertation, University of Notre Dame.

Hargett, I. M. (1930). God and radio. *Winona Echoes,* pp. 70-72.

Harrell, D. E. (1985). *Oral Roberts: An American life.* New York: Harper & Row.

Hill, G. (Ed.). (1983). *Airwaves to the soul: Influence and growth of religious broadcasting in America.* Saratoga, CA: R&E Publishers.

Hitt, R. T. (1954). Giant in the parlor. *Moody Monthly, 54,* 11-13, 47-49.

Jones, C. (1946). *Radio: The new missionary.* Chicago: Moody.

Kadley, J. (1952). Twenty-five wonderful years. *Moody Bible Institute Monthly, 52,* 390-392, 428.

Loveless, W. P. (1946). *Manual of gospel broadcasting.* Chicago: Moody.

Marsden, G. (1980). *Fundamentalism and American culture: The shaping of twentieth-century Evangelicalism.* New York: Oxford University Press.

Marsden, G. (1984). The evangelical denomination. In G. Marsden (Ed.), *Evangelicalism and modern America* (pp. vii-xvi). Grand Rapids, MI: Eerdmans.

Martin, W. (1991). *A prophet with honor: The Billy Graham story.* New York: William Morrow.

Matson, V. (1949). What shall we do with television? *Moody Monthly, 49,* 633-634, 672-673.

Parker E. C., & Eastman, F. (1942). Religion on the air in Chicago. In G. H. Hill (Ed.), *Airwaves to the soul: Influence and growth of religious broadcasting in America* (pp. 93-105). Saratoga, CA: R&E Publishers.

Radio. (1926, February). *Moody Bible Institute Monthly, 26,* 309.

Rice, J. R. (1938). *What is wrong with the movies?* (12th ed.). Grand Rapids, MI: Eerdmans.

Runyan, W. M. (1930). Something new in radio. *Moody Bible Institute Monthly, 30,* 589.

Siedell, B. (1971). *Gospel radio: A twentieth-century tool for a twentieth-century challenge.* Lincoln, NE: Back to the Bible Publications.

Smith, E. M. (1954). One Christian and television. *Sunday School Times, 20,* 236-237.

So-called humor in the pulpit. (1954, November 13). *Sunday School Times, 96,* 941.

Stroh, G. (1921). Practical and perplexing questions. *Moody Bible Institute Monthly, 21,* 272.

The radio and soul-winning. (1937). *Moody Bible Institute Monthly, 38,* 55.

Visits to shut-ins by Moody radio workers: Told by one of them. (1927). *Moody Bible Institute Monthly, 27,* 439.

What have you learned about living with TV. (1953, September). *Moody Monthly, 54,* 19-20.

Wright, E. C. (1988). *The old fashioned revival hour and the broadcasters.* New York: Garland.

7

Protecting the Family

Mormon Teachings About Mass Media

DANIEL A. STOUT

The relationship between mainstream Christianity and mass media is inherently "paradoxical" (Hitchcock, 1988). The dilemma results from the fact that church leaders often associate mass media with "the world," which they alternately condemn (as in the case of television violence) and embrace (when media teach religious values). This paradox is reflected in the instruction members of the Church of Jesus Christ of Latter-day Saints, more commonly referred to as Mormons, receive from the pulpit. On the one hand, communication technologies are considered tools for family enjoyment and edification. Elder[1] Gordon B. Hinckley (1975) of the Quorum of Twelve Apostles[2] states,

> Let there be good magazines about the house, those which are produced by the Church and by others, which will stimulate their thoughts to ennobling concepts. Let them read a good family newspa-

per that they may know what is going on in the world. . . . When there is a good show in town, go to the theater as a family. Your patronage will give encouragement to those who wish to produce this type of entertainment. And use that most remarkable of all tools of communication, television, to enrich their lives. (p. 39)

On the other hand, church leaders have recently stepped up their criticism of much of what they see on television, in movies, and in popular magazines. "We are at war," asserts Elder M. Russell Ballard (1995), also a Mormon apostle. "In the media today, . . . Lucifer's influence has a far more dominant influence than has the Lord's" (p. 2). As these warnings increase, the time may be right to examine specific Mormon teachings about mass media in greater depth.

According to Mormon belief, a prophet named Joseph Smith received a series of heavenly visions during the early 19th century (Church of Jesus Christ of Latter-day Saints, 1981). He founded a Christian church that would eventually settle in Utah and, from there, expand into a worldwide denomination of 8.8 million members (Church of Jesus Christ of Latter-day Saints, 1995). Mormonism embraces the concept of modern-day revelation through a hierarchy of priesthood leaders. Since the time of Joseph Smith, a prophet and 12 apostles have guided the church, communicating the Lord's message to the people. Twice a year in General Conference,[3] the prophet, apostles, and other general authorities[4] instruct members on how to resist temptations associated with modern times. Recently, leaders have exhorted members to protect their families from the potentially harmful effects of mass media. As they grow in numbers, Mormons are often encouraged to use television, movies, and other media in ways consistent with their religious goals.

The Mormon Church is expanding at a rapid pace (Heaton, 1992; Stark, 1994). As leaders strive to preserve the church's conservative religious core, worldwide growth presents new challenges. Although a few scholars have written about changing demographics (Goodman & Heaton, 1986; Heaton, Goodman, & Holman, 1994), the struggle between Mormon identity and assimilation (Mauss, 1994), and cultural tensions surrounding the church's recent globalization (Young, 1994), few have addressed the issue of mass media in church expansion. How religious communities grow and assimilate, however, has much to do with the quantity and types of information available. Television, radio, printed media, and computer technologies expose religious audiences to secular culture in new ways. Given this situation, social scientists may want to further investigate how religious institutions teach members selectivity regarding mass media. Such teachings are likely to impact the nature and scope of the information spheres of the congregation.

Although the Mormon Church owns a number of commercial television and radio stations, newspapers, and other media vehicles,[5] it is often critical of how these media are used in the larger society. Expectations about appropriate media use have risen, and church magazines often contain guidelines for developing critical media skills. This chapter describes what the Mormon Church teaches about "media effects" and how these teachings have evolved in recent years.

The first section explains some of the theological foundations of Mormon teachings about media. Then, three ways Mormons are instructed about proper media use are discussed. The chapter concludes with some of the sociological implications of these approaches. This analysis is based primarily on a review of General Conference addresses and articles published in the *Improvement Era* and *Ensign* since 1897. These are official publications of the Mormon Church and their articles by general authorities are considered modern-day Scriptures and guides for living. They contain official announcements as well as directives from the apostles of the church.[6] The *Index to Periodicals of the Church of Jesus Christ of Latter-day Saints* assisted in the identification of articles addressing topics such as "books," "mass media," "moving pictures," "television," and "radio." A smaller number of nonconference talks and articles on the subject of media effects are also summarized here.

MORMON THEOLOGY OF THE FAMILY
AND THE MEDIA PARADOX

The family is the sine qua non of Mormon theology. For Mormons, the family is eternal, and through obedience to God's laws, families live together in the hereafter. Their ordinance of eternal marriage reflects this concept. The eternal nature of the family is also emphasized in the genealogies kept by members, so that ordinances (e.g., baptism, eternal marriage) can be conducted vicariously on behalf of ancestors who may not have embraced the gospel during their mortal lives. These strong commitments to family life are at the core of church leaders' praise and criticism of mass media, which they feel have the power to both strengthen or destroy the traditional family unit. Recent criticisms of media by apostles represent a benevolent effort to protect the family from what is considered a deterioration of values in the U.S. home. Much of contemporary mass media, however, are undermining these commitments to home and family, according to church leaders. In General Conference addresses, the media are often associated with rising teenage pregnancy, divorce, and drug use. In a churchwide address, Spencer W. Kimball (1978), then president of the church, conveyed the strong belief that mass media erode the family: "Never before have there been so many insidious influences threatening the family as today, around the world. Many of these influences come right into the home—through television, radio, magazines, newspapers, and other forms of literature" (p. 45). Using even stronger language, Elder Ezra Taft Benson (1982) declared that media attempt to "restructure the family along the lines of humanistic values" (p. 59). "Images of the family" as depicted in television and film, he argues, "portray a philosophy contrary to the commandments of God" (p. 59).

These views give rise to three main strategies in Mormon teachings about media effects. First, various types of media (i.e., soap operas, talk shows, R-rated movies, etc.) have been discouraged in church talks and articles. Second, entire General Conference addresses have been devoted to the question of media effects. This has occurred more frequently in the past 25 years. Third, specific guidelines or recommendations for appropriate media use are suggested. In recent years, these recommendations have shifted from artistically and intellectually grounded criteria to a rules-based approach focusing almost exclusively on the avoidance of media depictions considered inconsistent with church teachings (e.g., violence, sexual intimacy, etc.).

WARNINGS ABOUT SPECIFIC
CATEGORIES OF MEDIA CONTENT

Soon after settling in Utah in 1847, church leaders began warning members about various categories of art and media. Brigham Young, for example, praised the theater for its potential in communicating religious principles but admonished members to avoid tragedies, which instilled fear in "our women and children" (Young, 1977, pp. 243-244). Since that time, recommendations against broad categories of media have been a consistent strategy of church leaders. In 1898, "dime-novels" were discouraged ("Book Companions," 1898), and in 1918, jazz was compared to the orgies of Rome (Hicks, 1989). Later, Elder S. Dilworth Young (1955) asserted that comic books did "untold evil" to the family, able to "stultify . . . desire to learn good literature" (p. 428).

Since the 1970s, condemnations by church authorities of various categories of media have become even more common. Advertising, soap operas, daytime talk shows, and R-rated movies have all been singled out in church publications and in General Conferences. Criticism of advertising focuses on the perception that media entice members to buy things they do not need and promote hedonistic values. In a 1964 General Conference address, Sterling W. Sill (1964) stated, "We employ some of our best advertising brains and use our finest communication media to persuade ourselves and others to take a greater part in the very evils that God has specifically forbidden" (p. 110).

Church leaders also express the fear that advertising encourages young people to "drink and to smoke" (McKay, 1965), which are prohibited by the church's health code. Leaders have been particularly critical of advertisements promoting "cigarettes, beer, and other vices" (Asay, 1992, p. 40; Perry, 1993).

Soap operas and talk shows have also recently come under attack. Elder Neal A. Maxwell (1993) of the Quorum of Twelve Apostles warns the membership against both in a General Conference talk:

> Instead of being communicating neighbors, we are flooded with talk shows, some of which feature not real conversation but exhibitionism and verbal voyeurism among virtual strangers.

We are lathered with soap operas in need of nothing so much as soap—for the scrubbing of themselves! (p. 77)

Also, the 1991 article "TV Free: Giving Up the Daytime Habit" was published in *Ensign* magazine, discouraging Mormon women from watching soap operas (Strong-Thacker, 1991). The article relates the experiences of a woman who, by giving up daytime television, makes better use of her time and achieves a higher level of spirituality.

No classification of media, however, has drawn more criticism from the church hierarchy than R-rated movies. Since the introduction of ratings by the movie industry in the 1970s, many leaders have embraced this system as the line of demarcation between appropriate and inappropriate films. R-rated movies have become synonymous with "unclean" media in the official discourse about media. Elder H. Burke Peterson (1993), Emeritus General Authority, asserts that R-rated movies "are produced by Satanic influences" (p. 43). Teenagers avoiding R-rated movies are held up as role models in talks by church officials: "You know it isn't hard to recognize a real warrior for the Priesthood. . . . He is the one who says no when others say yes to movies on Sunday, to R- or X-rated shows at any time" (Peterson, 1974, p. 68).

Given the frequency with which church leaders condemn R-rated movies, it has become a common standard for judging media among Mormons. In a talk that is often cited as the definitive criterion for determining appropriate movies, President Ezra Taft Benson (1986) admonishes, "Don't see R-rated movies or vulgar videos or participate in any entertainment that is immoral, suggestive, or pornographic" (p. 45). In the 1970s, the Mormon-owned *Deseret News* refused advertisements for R-rated movies, and only edited versions of R-rated films are permitted on the Brigham Young University (BYU) campus.[7] This policy became controversial when university officials refused to show *Schindler's List,* Stephen Spielberg's critically acclaimed film about the Holocaust (Robinson, 1994; Waite, 1994). The R rating was the key criterion in deciding not to show it, despite the film's moral theme and historical contribution.[8]

MEDIA EFFECTS AS A PRIMARY THEME
IN CHURCH TEACHINGS ABOUT MEDIA

Although Mormon leaders have always warned members about the effects of mass media, the topic has become a dominant theme in recent General Conference talks and church magazine articles. Since 1970, members have been advised about the effects of rock music, the appropriate use of television, and criteria for selecting movies.

One example is a General Conference address by Elder Boyd K. Packer (1974) of the Quorum of Twelve Apostles titled "Inspiring Music—Worthy Thoughts." The main thrust of the address is the deleterious effects of "hard rock" music:

> One of the signs of apostasy in the Christian churches today is the willingness of their ministers to compromise and introduce into what had been, theretofore, the most sacred religious meetings the music of the hard rock culture. Such music has little virtue and it is repellent to the Spirit of God. (p. 25)

Elder Packer goes on to say that hard rock music is like pornography and has the power to "dull the spiritual sensitivity of men" (p. 25). Later in the talk, he tells young people to go through their record albums "and set aside those records that promote the so-called new morality, the drug, or the hard rock culture" (p. 27).

Echoing these points is Elder M. Russell Ballard (1989) in a General Conference address devoted exclusively to the effects of television. Whereas a number of leaders have mentioned the harmful effects of television as a sidelight, this is perhaps the first General Conference sermon dedicated completely to educating members about the harmful effects of television programs and movies. Although the talk begins with an acknowledgment of "the many benefits" of television, it quickly turns to the effects of immoral mediated messages: "Unfortunately, however, far too much programming is not wholesome. . . . Therefore, I express a word of warning and caution about such programming" (p. 78). Citing various psychological studies, television is considered the primary cause of declining creativity among children, decreasing sympathy for suffering, poor time management, and a growing inability to "learn from reality" (p. 79). Elder Ballard closes his remarks by exhorting members to "limit television to a maximum of two hours a day of carefully selected programs" (p. 80) and promises that, by doing so, significant changes will be realized.

A third example is a lesson fully devoted to "The Powerful Influence of the Media" in *Come Unto Me: Relief Society Personal Study Guide*, which contains the required topics for Sunday meetings of the church's women's organization. Each week, millions of Mormon women assemble in meeting houses to participate in these lessons, which are planned and approved by church leaders. The lesson begins with a list of harmful effects of media, which include "learning to be violent, to think that immorality is normal and good, to expect instant solutions to problems, to want something for nothing, and to believe in unrealistic situations and incorrect values" (Church of Jesus Christ of Latter-day Saints, 1991, p. 195). Several admonitions are given to Mormon women, including the need to help children interpret what they see on television and to avoid placing televisions in bedrooms,[9] because they "shorten sleeping time and may cause mental and physical stimulation that make sleep difficult or impossible" (p. 197).

THE USE OF "GUIDELINES" IN
MORMON TEACHINGS ABOUT MEDIA

For more than 100 years, guidelines for appropriate media use have been available to Mormons in church publications. When general authorities give biannual addresses, lists of suggestions for achieving a gospel-centered approach to media use are often provided. Sometimes these guidelines include criteria for analyzing inspiring art and literature, and sometimes they simply suggest how families can avoid undesirable media content that is violent or sexually explicit.

In 1903, two talks published in the *Improvement Era* tell Mormon readers "what elements constitute a good book" ("Books," 1903,

p. 199). They should "be thought-producing" (p. 199), "stimulate and awaken good and noble feelings" ("What Books," 1903, p. 291), and "open up to you realms of pure thought" (p. 291). Readers are encouraged to use book reviews and the American Library Association Catalogue in choosing "the best books"—those that will expose members to the "broad culture" ("Books," 1903, p. 200). By 1932, reviews of current movies, which evaluated films based on plot development, casting, and photography, were being published in the *Improvement Era* ("Motion Pictures," 1932).

An "outline for analysis" given to members in a 1934 issue of the *Improvement Era* encourages the use of literary criticism in evaluating movies. This outline asks readers to consider character development, plot, and theme analysis in making choices. Another series of articles ran in 1948, "emphasizing a few of the important questions to raise in rating movies" (Josephson, 1948, p. 30), which include "plot, characterization, theme, message, comedy, tragedy, and trueness-to-life or verisimilitude" (p. 30). Mormons must become "more intelligent critics" of media, according to the article, which defines criticism as the "art of judging . . . works of art and literature" (p. 31).

Guidelines based on artistic criteria, however, have appeared less frequently in church publications in the past 25 years. Several leaders reacted strongly to the so-called new morality of the 1970s, expressing disdain for rock music, popular movies, and television programs assumed to be in conflict with religious values.

Ezra Taft Benson (1988), then an apostle, was especially vocal in expressing disdain for the mass media of the 1970s:

> Now, what of the entertainment that is available to our young people today? Are you being undermined right in your homes through television, radio, slick magazines, and rock music records? Much of the rock music is purposely designed to push immorality, narcotics, revolution, atheism, and nihilism through language that often carries a double meaning and with which many parents are not familiar. (p. 322)

The rock opera *Jesus Christ Superstar* was officially banned from church-sponsored activities (see Hicks, 1989; *Priesthood Bulletin,*

1971), and the Woodstock Music Festival and subsequent movie were "a gigantic manifestation of a sick nation," according to Benson (1988, p. 325).

Since then, church recommendations about media use have been more rigidly tied to religious principles and standards than to the intellectual frameworks that characterized earlier articles on media. In the last two decades, a number of articles have appeared in the church's *Ensign* magazine, each with lists of points to consider when viewing television and movies. One such article asks members, "Are principles contrary to the gospel taught in this program? Do the characters dress immodestly or behave immorally? Would we feel comfortable during the entire program if the Savior was watching with us?" (Tucker, 1988, p. 21).

In 1987, a list of recommendations for television was published, which warned against using television as a baby-sitter, watching sports excessively, and watching programs "that promote immorality or violence" ("Helping Children Understand," 1987, pp. 58-59). Three years later, the church offered 10 ways to "make sure television's influence on your family is a positive one":

1. Apply "selective viewing" (turning the set off when the preplanned program is over)
2. Limit the amount of time watching television
3. Turn off "objectionable" programs
4. Watch "wholesome" and "educational" programs only
5. Discuss programs with children
6. Teach children critical viewing skills
7. Turn off programs that reflect values inconsistent with church teachings
8. Turn off programs that are violent
9. Use TV as a springboard for reading
10. Develop a personal perspective about TV ("Making the Most," 1990, pp. 70-71)

Articles advocating this type of rules-based approach to media use continue to appear on a regular basis both in official church publications and in General Conference talks. "Can I Watch a Movie?" appeared in a 1991 issue of *Ensign*, pointing out several "methods to determine the content of a movie" before seeing it (Schaefermeyer, 1991, p. 32). Speaking in General Conference, Elder H. Burke Peterson (1993) encouraged young people to think about the effects of media, pray for guidance, and "walk away from" R-rated films (p. 43).

SUMMARY AND DISCUSSION

Mormon leaders embrace a powerful model of mass communication that is reflected both in how the church uses media for religious purposes as well as in public warnings about their deleterious effects on the family. Mormons are expected to have critical media skills based on religious beliefs and commitment to the family. Latter-day Saints are encouraged to use commercial television, radio, newspapers, and other communication technologies for information and entertainment. Media selectivity, however, has been a dominant theme in church sermons, publications, and Sunday lessons. Advice about appropriate media use is offered frequently, assertively, and at times quite specifically, as with the admonition not to view any R-rated movies.

Basic to Mormon theology is latter-day revelation, which Mormons seek from church publications for advice about how to live in troubled times. Since the days of the early church, the effects of media has been an important topic, but in the past 25 years, warnings about the evil nature of some movies, television programs, and other media offerings reflect a growing sense of urgency. Where media issues were once a secondary topic in many church talks and articles, entire General Conference addresses are devoted to topics as specific as "The Effects of Television." Recommendations are made about which classifications of media are desirable and which are not. Although Mormonism has always had a strong tradition in the arts, intellectual criteria for media criticism are stressed less than rules-based approaches, which are designed to protect the family from the harmful influences of media. The decision not to show the recent film *Schindler's List* on the BYU campus illustrates the emphasis on rules-specific guidelines over artistic criteria.

Mauss (1994) contends that as the church expands, there is a "growing trend at the grass-roots level toward a fundamentalist religious posture both in life-style and in scriptural interpretation" (p. 34). Teachings about media effects appear to support this conclusion. As church leaders continue to perceive societal threats to the family, they are likely to advocate didactic approaches to media education over those that emphasize interpretation and analysis. This situation raises a number of questions for future research: What impact will the more didactic approach to media literacy have on Mormons' view of art in general? What critical media skills do Mormons actually apply in everyday life? How obedient are church members to the admonitions of their leaders?

These questions remind social scientists of the need to broaden knowledge about the Mormon audience. Although this chapter provides some insights about church teachings, the question of the actual role of mass media in Mormon life cannot be fully understood without additional attention to how Mormons themselves describe their experiences with mass communication.[10]

NOTES

1. "Elder" is the title given to men holding the Melchizedek, or higher, priesthood in the Mormon Church.

2. The Quorum of Twelve Apostles is the governing body of the Mormon Church. Members consider the apostles to be mouthpieces of the Lord and look to these leaders for divine guidance.

3. General Conference is an extremely important event for Mormons. Church leaders give "talks" that contain modern-day revelation, and the conferences are broadcast via satellite to church meeting houses throughout the world. Members are also encouraged to obtain published copies of these addresses.

4. Numbered with the Quorum of Twelve Apostles are additional church leaders designated as "general authorities," who also address the worldwide church in General Conference.

5. Among the Mormon Church's media holdings are 16 radio stations, 3 television stations, a major market newspaper, a book publishing house, a motion picture studio, and a number of church magazines. For a more detailed discussion on Mormon media ownership, see Gottlieb and Wiley (1984) and "Money in Media" (1991), an article published in the *Arizona Republic*.

6. Iannaccone and Miles (1994) argue that these publications reflect the church's position on many subjects. One important feature in *Ensign* is "The First Presidency

Message," which members are encouraged to read each month. Priesthood holders in local congregations are asked to visit homes of church members to share this message as part of the "Home Teaching Program."

7. The university banned edited versions of R-rated movies from the Varsity Theater in January of 1995 (Sanderson, 1995). Explaining the decision, Rush Sumpter of BYU's Student Leadership Development Services stated, "A handful of people have complained that prophets and brethren say it's wrong to see rated-R movies. We don't want to offend those few" (Sanderson, 1995, p. 1). In July, however, officials reversed their decision, responding to strong student support for the movies (Broadbent, 1995).

8. BYU officials would not allow *Schindler's List* to be shown on campus unless Amblin Entertainment permitted an edited version. When the request was denied, the decision was made not to show it. A campuswide debate ensued, with the school newspaper, the *Daily Universe*, running several letters for and against the decision. In a campus lecture, Gerald R. Molen, the film's executive producer who is also a Mormon, encouraged BYU students to see it.

9. In a popular book in the Mormon community titled *Why Do Good People See Bad Movies?* Wright (1993) argues that survey data show a direct correlation between "youth with televisions in their bedrooms" and "sexually permissive" behavior (p. 6). This book is often quoted by church leaders in sermons on media effects.

10. The author would like to thank Bryce Rytting who read an earlier version of this chapter and made valuable comments.

REFERENCES

Asay, C. E. (1992, May). Be men! *Ensign,* pp. 40-42.

Ballard, M. R. (1989, May). The effects of television. *Ensign,* pp. 78-81.

Ballard, M. R. (1995, April). *God's purpose for the artist in the gospel plan.* Address given at the dedication of the Tuacahn Arts Center, St. George, UT.

Benson, E. T. (1982, November). Fundamentals of enduring family relationships. *Ensign,* pp. 59-61.

Benson, E. T. (1986, May). To the youth of the noble birthright. *Ensign,* pp. 43-46.

Benson, E. T. (1988). *The teachings of Ezra Taft Benson.* Salt Lake City, UT: Bookcraft.

Book companions. (1898, December). *Improvement Era,* pp. 138-143.

Books: Their choice, use, and value. (1903, January). *Improvement Era, 6,* 198-204.

Broadbent, R. (1995, July 18). Varsity Theater to resume showing edited R-rated movies. *Daily Universe,* p. 1.

Church of Jesus Christ of Latter-day Saints. (1981). *The doctrine and covenants.* Salt Lake City, UT: Author.

Church of Jesus Christ of Latter-day Saints. (1991). The powerful influence of the media. In *Come unto me: Relief society personal study guide 3* (pp. 194-199). Salt Lake City, UT: Author.

Church of Jesus Christ of Latter-day Saints. (1995). *LDS information in the Internet.* Salt Lake City: Author.

Goodman, K. L., & Heaton, T. B. (1986). LDS church members in the U.S. and Canada. *AMCAP Journal, 12*(1), 88-107.

Gottlieb, R., & Wiley, P. (1984). *America's saints: The rise of Mormon power.* New York: Harcourt Brace Jovanovich.

Heaton, T. B. (1992). Vital statistics. In D. H. Ludlow (Ed.), *Encyclopedia of Mormonism* (Vol. 4, pp. 1518-1537). New York: Macmillan.

Heaton, T. B., Goodman, K. L., & Holman, T. B. (1994). In search of a peculiar people: Are Mormon families really different? In M. Cornwall, T. B. Heaton, & L. A. Young (Eds.), *Contemporary Mormonism: Social science perspectives* (pp. 87-117). Chicago: University of Illinois Press.

Helping children understand the media's influence. (1987, January). *Ensign,* pp. 56-59.

Hicks, M. (1989). *Mormonism and music.* Chicago: University of Chicago Press.

Hinckley, G. B. (1975, November). Opposing evil. *Ensign,* pp. 38-40.

Hitchcock, J. (1988). We speak what we do know: Religion and mass communication. In R. W. Budd & B. D. Ruben (Eds.), *Beyond media: New approaches to mass communication* (pp. 178-193). New Brunswick, NJ: Transaction Books.

Iannaccone, L. R., & Miles, C. A. (1994). Dealing with social change: The Mormon Church's response to change in women's roles. In M. Cornwall, T. B. Heaton, and L. A. Young (Eds.), *Contemporary Mormonism: Social science perspectives* (pp. 265-286). Chicago: University of Illinois Press.

Josephson, M. C. (1948, January). And so the movies! *Improvement Era,* pp. 25-31.

Kimball, S. W. (1978, May). Strengthening the family: The basic unit of the church. *Ensign,* pp. 45-48.

Making the most of TV. (1990, October). *Ensign,* pp. 70-71.

Mauss, A. (1994). Refuge and retrenchment: The Mormon quest for identity. In M. Cornwall, T. B. Heaton, & L. A. Young (Eds.), *Contemporary Mormonism: Social science perspectives* (pp. 24-42). Chicago: University of Illinois Press.

Maxwell, N. A. (1993, May). Behold the enemy is combined (D&C 38:12), *Ensign,* pp. 76-79.

McKay, D. O. (1965, October). President David O. McKay. *Official Report of the Annual General Conference,* pp. 144-146.

Money in media. (1991, July 3). *Arizona Republic,* pp. A1, A9.

Motion pictures. (1932, March). *Improvement Era,* pp. 297-298.

Packer, B. K. (1974, January). Inspiring music—worthy thoughts. *Ensign,* pp. 26-28.

Perry, L. T. (1993, November). Choose the right. *Ensign,* pp. 66-68.

Peterson, H. B. (1974, November). As a beacon on a hill. *Ensign,* pp. 68-70.

Peterson, H. B. (1993, November). Touch not the evil gift, nor the unclean thing. *Ensign,* pp. 42-44.

Priesthood bulletin. (1971, August). [Official publication of the Church of Jesus Christ of Latter-Day Saints].

Robinson, R. (1994, September 28). *Schindler's List* pulled from Varsity Theater schedule, editing difficulties blamed. *Daily Universe,* p. 1.

Sanderson, E. (1995, January 31). R-rated films cut from Varsity film schedule. *Daily Universe,* p. 1.

Schaefermeyer, W. A. (1991, December). Can I watch a movie? *Ensign,* pp. 29-32.

Sill, S. W. (1964, October). Elder Sterling W. Sill. *Official Report of the Annual General Conference,* pp. 110-113.

Stark, R. (1994). Modernization and Mormon growth: The secularization thesis revisited. In M. Cornwall, T. B. Heaton, & L. A. Young (Eds.), *Contemporary Mormonism: Social science perspectives* (pp. 13-23). Chicago: University of Illinois Press.

Strong-Thacker, K. (1991, July). TV free: Giving up the daytime habit. *Ensign*, pp. 29-31.

Tucker, L. A. (1988, February). What's on TV tonight? *Ensign*, pp. 18-22.

Waite, J. (1994, October 7). R-ratings steal the show. *Daily Universe*, p. 4.

What books to read. (1903, January). *Improvement Era, 6*, 290-294.

Wright, R. (1993). *Why do good people see bad movies? The impact of R-rated movies.* National Family Institute.

Young, B. (1977). *Discourses of Brigham Young* (J. A. Widstoe, Ed.). Salt Lake City, UT: Deseret.

Young, L. A. (1994). Confronting turbulent environments: Issues in the organizational growth and globalization of Mormonism. In M. Cornwall, T. B. Heaton, & L. A. Young (Eds.), *Contemporary Mormonism: Social science perspectives* (pp. 43-63). Chicago: University of Illinois Press.

Young, S. D. (1955, June). Joys of childhood. *Improvement Era*, pp. 428-429.

PART III

The Role of Religiosity
in Mass Media Use

Comparative Studies of Audience Behavior

Seeing certain beliefs that are widely shared across Judeo-Christian traditions, both Tocqueville (1889) and Mead (1967, 1975) concluded that religion is the unifying force that gives shape to U.S. morals and mores. Both also note, however, that the First Amendment guarantee of religious freedom inevitably meant pluralism and denominationalism.

Without automatic claims to legitimacy, churches were forced to compete with each other for members and for money. And as so often is true for manufacturers seeking to market quite similar products, churches frequently emphasize their distinctive beliefs. But in religion, those particularistic beliefs are deeply held and certainly as central to the faith as any that may be shared with other religions. It is those distinctive elements that create each religious tradition's understanding of a proper relationship to God and to the world.

Lying within those different understandings are the seeds of what Hunter (1990) describes as a culture war. According to his analysis, the struggle to define the United States and U.S. culture inevitably

becomes a battle "to control the 'instrumentality' of reality definition . . . the businesses and industries of public information, art, and
entertainment" (p. 226). Although Hunter sees the battle as one
between the forces of religion and secularism, conflict is just as likely
to stem from different religiously inspired worldviews (Wuthnow,
1989).

As the chapters in Part III point out, some religious traditions
teach shunning the world; others would accept, understand, or
engage it. Some teach that people need protection from, or at least
warnings about, mass media content that presents a contrary reality
that could lead them away from true and correct beliefs and behaviors. Others see problematic content as something more akin to a
prophetic pronouncement through which members can learn about
God and about the world.

Beliefs carry with them implications for how one should behave.
Long before the notion of culture wars became firmly embedded in
popular discourse, Martin Marty (1976) noted that U.S. religion has
long been " 'balkanized' in territories and denominations" (p. 12).
Calling the United States "a nation of behavers," he sought to "map"
U.S. religion using the relationship between beliefs and behaviors
as his guide. The chapters in this part perform a similar kind of
cartography. These chapters look to audience members themselves
to learn more about orientations toward the mass media across
religious traditions.

Chapter 8 picks up on Hunter's (1990) observation that the culture
war points to "a struggle over the meaning of 'speech' or the meaning of 'expression' that the First Amendment is supposed to protect"
(p. 226). Using a variety of religious measures to explore the link
between religion and support for civil liberties, Tony Rimmer's
careful statistical analysis of national survey data indicates that
religiosity is related to intolerance, but there are important differences by religious affiliation that are remarkably consistent with the
official institutional positions described in Part II. His finding that
Jews tend to be the most tolerant and conservative Protestants the
least tolerant sets the groundwork for subsequent chapters exploring religious differences in media use.

Judith M. Buddenbaum presents evidence in Chapter 9 of healthy
skepticism about newspapers but also widespread use of them for

political information that cuts across religious lines. At the same time, differences in newspaper subscribing provide some evidence that conservative Protestants tend to shun worldly influences as leaders of those traditions often recommend they do. Extending the analysis to include measures tapping styles of attachment teases out differences within each tradition.

Just as those findings call into question the assumption within the community ties literature that church membership is a form of community integration, the findings presented in Chapter 10 question whether religiosity is always related to a localite orientation. Using national and local survey data, Judith M. Buddenbaum and Stewart M. Hoover found that readership and satisfaction with religion news coverage lag behind public ratings of the importance of religion news. Mismatches between story preference and perceptions of how religion news is covered apparently account for the differences, especially for conservative Protestants who are more likely than mainline Protestants or Catholics to prefer localite coverage.

Themes from the preceding chapters come together in Thomas R. Lindlof's study in Chapter 11 of public reaction to the controversial motion picture, *The Last Temptation of Christ*. This film was met in the United States by public protests, criticism, and boycott attempts unprecedented in recent history for a media product. Lindlof discusses how this film enables us to see how audiences define their identities in local terms. It addresses the question of how cultural products provoke individuals to participate in protest efforts and appeal to certain standards of conduct and interpretation.

REFERENCES

Hunter, J. D. (1990). *Culture wars: The struggle to define America*. New York: Basic Books.

Marty, M. E. (1976). *A nation of behavers*. Chicago: University of Chicago Press.

Mead, S. E. (1967). The nation with the soul of a church. *Church History, 36*, 262-283.

Mead, S. E. (1975). *The nation with the soul of a church*. New York: Harper & Row.

Tocqueville, A. de. (1889). *Democracy in America* (Vols. 1-2). (H. Reeve, Trans.). New York: Longmans, Green.

Wuthnow, R. (1989). *The struggle for America's soul: Evangelicals, liberals, and secularism*. Grand Rapids, MI: Eerdmans.

Religion, Mass Media, and Tolerance for Civil Liberties

TONY RIMMER

When people are asked about their support for civil liberties, public opinion researchers have found widespread support for the general idea, but when pushed with specific hypothetical situations, survey respondents often qualify their support.

My general goal here is to consider religion, mass media, and tolerance for civil liberties. I am particularly interested in the role of religion in shaping attitudes toward First Amendment freedoms. This interest finds its focus in the First Amendment liberties of speech, press, and (religious) assembly. In developing my under-

AUTHOR'S NOTE: The author wishes to acknowledge earlier work by Karen von Elten, a former graduate student in the Department of Communications at California State University, Fullerton. Karen did much of the theoretical work reported here for her master's thesis. Thanks also go to the Times Mirror Corporation and to the Gallup Organization for making these data available. All conclusions derived from the data reflect the author's analyses and interpretation.

standing of this focus, I will attempt to clarify whether these liberties work together or are at odds with each other. Religion, some would have us believe, may not be a promoter of its fellow First Amendment travelers of free speech and press (see, e.g., Allport & Ross, 1967).

I executed this study by first developing a general model explaining tolerance and then applying it to some specific instances involving speech and press. In the process, I bring to bear diverse perspectives on religion and mass media. For religion, I consider a variety of indicators—denomination, evangelical tendency, church attendance, perceptions of how religious people perceive themselves to be, and how religious I judge them to be. For media, I explore perceptions of the press as an institution, people's impressions of press "stars," and how people perceive and use media for news and information.

In short, I have definitions to suit most seasons and persons. They cover the gamut of substantive, functional, and symbolic definitions (Roberts, 1984). I expect that these diverse perspectives will enhance understanding of how religion and mass media contribute to tolerance for civil liberties.

WHAT IS TOLERANCE AND HOW IS IT ASSOCIATED WITH RELIGION?

In their review of the concept, von Elten and Rimmer (1992) noted that tolerance is not just a lack of prejudice. Rather, a "tolerant person may disapprove of, or even abhor, the values and beliefs of certain individuals or groups while respecting their rights to express those opinions and beliefs" (p. 27). In accord with that definition, I define tolerance as occurring when a person supports the constitutionally guaranteed civil liberties of individuals or groups, whether or not he or she approves of them (Corbett, 1982; Nunn, Crockett, & Williams, 1978).

Research has identified three key variables associated with tolerance —education (Nunn et al., 1978; Stouffer, 1963), age (Nunn et al., 1978; Robinson, 1970; Stouffer, 1963), and religion (Allport, 1966;

Allport & Ross, 1967; Henley & Pincus, 1978; McClosky & Brill, 1983). Current events and the present political climate are also presumed to play a role. Because mass media report on such things, von Elten and Rimmer (1992) found an association (albeit a weak one) between mass media and tolerance. Education's association with tolerant attitudes is presumed to operate through the cognitive sophistication that higher education brings (Bobo & Licari, 1989). Research suggests that age is a negative predictor—older people are more likely to report less tolerant attitudes (Nunn et al., 1978; Stouffer, 1963) and to approve of the use of force by police to put down political demonstrations (Robinson, 1970). Religion, whether measured as a behavior (e.g., church attendance and participation in religious activities) or an attitude (e.g., perceptions of self as religious, religiosity), also has been found to show a negative relationship with tolerant attitudes (Allport, 1966; Allport & Ross, 1967; Corbett, 1982; McClosky & Brill, 1983; Nunn et al., 1978). This relationship varies depending on the dimensions of religiosity being considered, less so on how prejudice is defined (Cygnar, Jacobson, & Noel, 1977).

In a secondary analysis of data from a national public opinion poll with 4,200 respondents, von Elten and Rimmer (1992) found support for the assertions identified in the literature. Their regression model incorporating education, age, religion, and media reliance accounted for 22% of the variance in their tolerance measure. Education and newspaper reliance were significant, positive predictors of tolerance; religiosity, church attendance, and age were significant, negative predictors.

For this chapter, I revisited the same data set in an attempt to elaborate on the role of religion (beyond religiosity and church attendance) and media in tolerance and to further develop the von Elten and Rimmer (1992) model. In particular, I wanted to incorporate ideology into the model to accommodate an argument that religiosity as we had earlier measured it taps only conservative Christian beliefs that are part of a worldview that also includes a respondent's political ideology (J. Buddenbaum, personal communication, August 10, 1994). Not surprisingly, the findings here are in line with von Elten and Rimmer's earlier work, but there are some impressive and intriguing new insights. Impressive in that a slightly less parsimonious model was found to account for 33% of the variance in the system, whereas the original model accounted for 22% of the variance. Intriguing in that some additional variables added to the model here raised new questions requiring interpretation. I find here that religion plays various roles depending on how the concept is operationalized (what is "religion"?) and the context in which its role is assessed (what am I measuring religion against?).

In general, however, religion has a negative relationship with tolerance for civil liberties. The more religious one is, the less tolerance one shows. Underlying this assertion are two key variables—education and ideology. Education and a liberal personal ideology appear to promote tolerance, whereas a conservative ideology is negatively related with tolerance. Religion, I conclude, is inherently conservative. The news medium one relies on (TV, newspapers, radio) makes a significant, though minor, contribution. News media might best be seen as indicators of education, meaning that newspaper and radio news reliance is associated with higher levels of education and TV news reliance is associated with lower levels of education.

I now explore these various dimensions of religion, media, and tolerance. First, I describe the data being analyzed and how I identified and developed particular measures. Next, I report on my tolerance measures. I then consider my various measures of religion and media use and their respective bivariate relationships with tolerance. Finally, I bring media and religion together in a multivariate model that considers their relationship with tolerance, both for civil liberties in general and for some more specific speech and press issues.

THE DATA

The data considered here are a nationwide probability sample (stratified by community size) of face-to-face interviews with 4,244 respondents (Ornstein, Kohut, & McCarthy, 1988) collected April 25, 1987, through May 10, 1987, by the Gallup organization for the Times Mirror Company. Blacks (n = 755) were oversampled.

The period that these data were collected in needs to be kept in mind, particularly because evidence (and common sense?) suggests that tolerance is to some extent a child of its times—it depends on the political climate. This surely applies in media-financed public opinion polling insofar as question topics (and perhaps even wording) likely will reflect the salience and valence of current issues. Data were gathered in the early phases of a presidential election campaign to assess the mood of the U.S. electorate going into the 1988 elections. Interviewees presumably thought they were responding to a political survey and answered accordingly. We are faced, then, with two problems typical of secondary analysis: The data may be dated, and the orientation of respondents to the questions might have some unknown impact on my findings. The reader should exercise caution, then, in generalizing from these data to other times and contexts. But the reader should revel, too, in these large-scale, rich, and carefully collected data.

THE MEASURES

Tolerance

Twenty-four survey questions asked for responses associated with tolerance and civil liberties. They included, for example, agree-disagree questions such as "Books that contain dangerous ideas should be banned from public school libraries" and "The police should be allowed to search the houses of known drug dealers without a court order." These questions were tested with factor analysis (principal components, varimax rotation) to see if some underlying structures might describe a tolerance construct. Nine variables accounting for 21% of the variance in the system were combined to create a normally distributed, 28-point scale with standard deviation of 5.6 (Cronbach's alpha for reliability = 0.81). This "Tolerance for Civil Liberties" index served as the primary dependent measure.

Six agree-disagree questions addressing specific First Amendment speech and press concerns were also identified for subsequent analysis. They addressed issues such as tolerance regarding the expression of ideas in speech and in books, national security interests versus press freedom, government censorship, and tolerance for X-rated books and movies.

Religion

The data are rich in religion measures. Respondents reported their religion (Protestant, Roman Catholic, Jewish, Greek and Russian Orthodox, and Mormon); evangelical tendency ("Would you describe yourself as a 'born-again' or evangelical Christian?"); church attendance ("Do you go to church/synagogue every week, almost every week, once or twice a month, . . .?" etc.); and how religious they perceived themselves to be ("To what extent do you consider yourself to be a religious person?").

I added to this complement of religion questions by developing a "religiosity" construct. In contrast to how religious respondents perceived themselves to be, this religiosity index measured how religious I judged them to be. Five statements calling for agreement-disagreement (e.g., "Prayer is an important part of my daily life" and "I never doubt the existence of God") were developed through factor and reliability analysis into an additive index we call "Religiosity." The 16-point index was reliable (Cronbach's alpha = .89) but had a severe negative skew.[1]

This religiosity measure appears to be more consistent with the "intrinsic" rather than "extrinsic" religious orientation described by Allport and Ross (1967). An intrinsically oriented person "lives" his or her religion whereas the extrinsically oriented person "uses" his or her religion. Allport and Ross argued that extrinsically oriented persons are more likely to be prejudiced than are intrinsically oriented persons.

Alienation

Because Allport and his associates have identified a generally negative relationship between religion and tolerance, I wondered whether alienation might play a role in promoting prejudice. Perhaps those who are alienated might be drawn to religion to satisfy a need for belonging. Similar arguments, which draw on the ideas of Durkheim and Merton, have been made for an inverse relationship between anomie and religion; however, findings have been inconsistent (see, e.g., Carr & Hauser, 1976).

Anomie refers to a feeling of frustration when rules are unclear, whereas alienation is the frustration that can occur when the rules are clear but the individual feels left out. I use the term *alienation*, then, in a constructive sense as a motivator in one's search for identity and belonging. Hamilton and Rubin's (1992) exploration of the TV-viewing motivations and preferences of religious conservatives suggests a role for alienation, and Wilson and Miller's (1968) study of "Fear, Anxiety, and Religiousness" further endorses the idea. Alienation, then, might be an explanatory variable of tolerance.

Factor and reliability testing of a battery of questions identified two dimensions involving economic and political alienation, which were then developed as additive indexes. Reliability was weak for the five-question economic alienation index (Cronbach's alpha = .5) and unreliable for the political alienation index. These weak reliabilities suggest that my approach to assessing the role of alienation would probably not be successful. Perhaps if I had looked at political efficacy ("how much does my vote count?" [Newhagen, 1994]) rather than political alienation, I might have had more success with scale reliability. This approach seemed to be moving me away from the central task so it was not pursued further.

A second more subtle dimension of alienation might be a respondent's general confidence in public figures and institutions, particularly those associated with the constructs we are considering here—religion and media. Therefore, an index was developed that finished up as a three-question additive index I called "TV Stars" (Cronbach's alpha = .5), tapping respondents' opinions of three TV practitioners—news anchor Dan Rather, TV interviewer Barbara Walters, and talk-show host Oprah Winfrey. Attempts to develop an index of "Religious Stars" were not successful. Estimations of Billy Graham allied him with the TV Stars index (at some cost to that index's reliability, which meant we left him off), whereas assessments of Jerry Falwell, Jesse Jackson, Martin Luther King, and Pope John Paul were (predictably?) inconsistent with each other.

Ideology

I introduced the idea earlier that ideology might underlie much of tolerance and religion such that it should also be controlled for. Ideology involved two dimensions. First was "personal ideology," a 7-point scale ranging from *conservative* through *lean toward conservative* to *lean toward liberal* and, finally, *liberal*. The scale was scored conservative-low and liberal-high because I assumed that a liberal personal ideology would be positively correlated with tolerance. The second ideology dimension considered whether a respondent reported being a born-again or evangelical Christian. The assumption was that being born-again in the terms of this public opinion poll would indicate conservative tendencies.

Media

For media, we explored perceptions of the press as an institution, people's impressions of the institution's stars (the TV Stars index already noted), and how people perceive and use media as sources of news and information. The latter questions involved newspapers, television news, and radio news.

RELIGION AND TOLERANCE

What are the relationships among the various religion measures and tolerance? Correlations among the variables measured at the interval level show a consistent pattern of negative relationships between the religion variables and tolerance.

In general, the more religious people are, the less tolerant they are. This can be seen for "frequency of church attendance," "perception of self as religious," and particularly for religiosity. TV news use is weakly and negatively associated with tolerance and positively associated with the religion variables; newspaper use is weakly but positively associated with tolerance and negatively associated with religiosity (see Table 8.1).

These correlations are somewhat more revealing when broken out by religious denomination. Figure 8.1 is a composite line graph of

Table 8.1 Zero Order Pearson Correlations of Tolerance and Religion
Measures ($n = 2,700$)

	Tolerance	Religiosity	Church Attendance	Perception of Self as Religious
Religiosity	−.49**[a]			
Church attendance	−.22**	.41**		
Perception of self as religious	−.30**	.60**	.55**	
Education	.42**	−.24**	ns	ns
Age	−.18**	.09**	.14**	.12**
Ideology (liberal hi)	.29**	−.15**	−.13**	−.16**
Alienation (economic)	.24**	−.21**	ns	ns
Assessment of TV stars	ns	.13**	ns	ns
Newspaper use	.07**	−.05**	ns	ns
TV news use	−.10**	.07**	.04**	.06**

a. Cube transform of religiosity ($r = -.46$** for religiosity in its original, negatively skewed distribution form).
**$p < .001$; ns = no significance.

group medians that explores tolerance by frequency of church attendance by the religious denominations nominated by respondents—Protestant, Catholic, Orthodox, Jewish, Mormon, "other religion," and "no religion." It shows that those reporting low and high frequencies of church attendance tend to show higher levels of tolerance than do those reporting moderate levels of church attendance.

Although a pattern of negative relationships is consistent across each of the denominations, the relationship between church attendance and tolerance for all respondents is curvilinear. This finding is masked by the linear assumption of the Pearson correlation given in Table 8.1, but graphing the relationship supports Allport and Ross's (1967) finding that the relationship between church attendance and tolerance is curvilinear. We should note, however, that the overall curvilinear relationship may be powered by those reporting no religious affiliation.

Religiosity showed a consistent negative relationship with tolerance across all religious denominations. A display of side-by-side boxplots of tolerance by religious denomination revealed differences in centers across denominations. The boxes in Figure 8.2 indicate the middle 50% of the data, the "whiskers" reaching up and down from each box indicate where data were defined as "outliers"

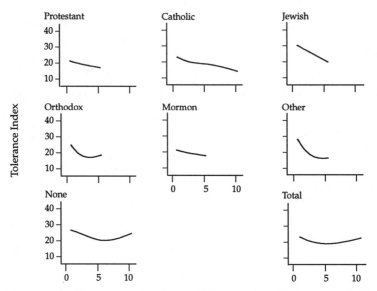

Figure 8.1. Composite Graph of Tolerance by Frequency of Church Attendance by Religious Preference

(the "circles" above the Protestant and Catholic boxplots), and the line across the centers of each box indicates the median for each group. From this figure, it can be seen that the Christian denominations generally show low tolerance scores, whereas Jewish respondents and those not reporting a religious affiliation show higher tolerance scores.

MEDIA AND TOLERANCE

What of media use and tolerance? Figure 8.3 is a two-way boxplot display of "medium relied on for national news" and tolerance with the width of each boxplot scaled to show group size. From this figure, it can be seen that newspaper and radio reliers tend to show the same patterns of response, both in terms of center and of spread. TV news reliers, however, show a different pattern in their relationship with tolerance. Their center is significantly less than that for newspaper and radio reliers, and their spread is quite different. They show much less variance in their response set for tolerance.

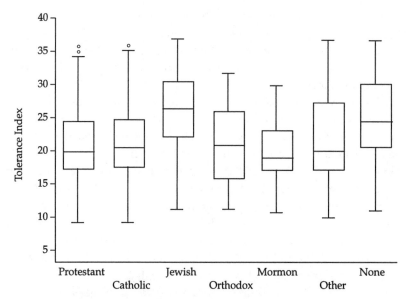

Figure 8.2. Two-Way Boxplots of Tolerance by Religious Denomination

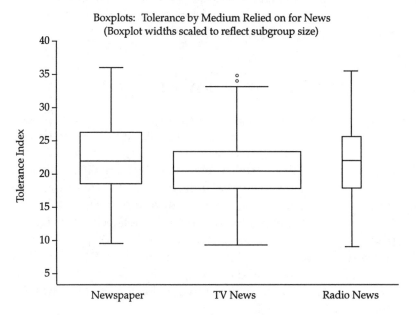

Figure 8.3. Two-Way Boxplots of Tolerance by News Media Reliance

Apart from a few outliers at the high tolerance end, TV reliers appear to be more consistent in their tolerance scores. They are more like each other on tolerance. Newspaper and radio reliers show more variation among themselves, and the patterns for these two media are similar.

The suspicion is that Simpson's Paradox is at play here. Simpson's Paradox proposes that either the magnitude or the direction of a relationship between two variables is influenced by the presence of a third factor (Pagano & Gauvreau, 1993). It is the classic "third-variable" problem. If this third factor really does confound the relationship between the first two variables, failing to control for its impact will make the magnitude of the association appear greater than it actually is. In my case, education might be this third variable. The literature asserts a role for education, and we have a moderate positive correlation ($r = .42, p < .001$) between education and tolerance. The higher one's education, the more tolerant one is of others' civil liberties. Our medium reliance measures may merely be a mask for education, in the sense that TV reliers tend to be less well educated and newspaper reliers tend to be better educated (Rimmer & Weaver, 1987). I might now add radio news reliers as being better educated than TV news reliers.

PERSONAL IDEOLOGY AND TOLERANCE

But there is a second phenomenon I suspect might also be playing a third-variable role—that of ideology. First, there is personal ideology. The more conservative a person reports they are, the less tolerant they are likely to be. Conversely, the more liberal they are, the more tolerant they will be. Indeed, Table 8.1 shows this to be the case. Personal ideology is positively associated with tolerance ($r = .29, p < .001$) and negatively and weakly related with religiosity ($r = -.15, p < .001$), frequency of church attendance ($r = -.13, p < .001$), and perception of self as religious ($r = -.16, p < .001$). The more liberal respondents report themselves to be, the more tolerant they are. The more religious they report themselves to be, the less tolerance they show.

A second ideology dimension showed up in this analysis in the form of evangelical tendency, whether a person reports they are a born-again or evangelical Christian. These born-again Christians were older (t = 4.96, df = 2,341, p < .001), less well educated (t = 8.23, df = 3,939, p < .001), and more conservative (t = 7.22, df = 3,945, p < .001) than those who said they were not born-again. The born-again were less tolerant (t = 17.86, df = 2,029, p < .001) and scored higher on my religiosity scale (M-W's U = 760774, p < .001) than did their counterparts.

Each of these two ideology dimensions might be unique to public opinion polls, such as I have here. The questions being asked are time-dependent, often addressing issues that are in the news at the time. So, they have salience for respondents, but respondents might often break out in their responses along ideology lines. It would seem important, then, to control for ideology. We do this for personal ideology, alienation, and whether a respondent reports they are born-again.

THE MULTIVARIATE RELATIONSHIP AMONG RELIGION, NEWS MEDIA, AND TOLERANCE

Von Elten and Rimmer's (1992) five-variable regression model accounted for 22% of the variance in their system. Their variables were education, age, religiosity, church attendance, and media reliance. In this section, I report on a new regression model describing the multivariate complex predicting tolerance in my variables of interest and then apply its explanatory variables to five specific First Amendment speech and press issues. This new model includes some variables that would appear to have theoretical interest for my analysis, but in the interest of parsimony, I impose a minimum regression coefficient cutoff (accept if beta > .1). In effect, I am arbitrarily imposing my general model on respondent replies to five specific First Amendment issue questions. What I lose in question-by-question flexibility, I hope I make up for with consistency across questions.

My new model accounted for 33% of the variation in my tolerance measure, even with the beta coefficient cutoff standard of 0.1 imposed.[2] The model consisted of seven variables, three of which were common to the von Elten and Rimmer (1992) model. The three were religiosity, education, and a now expanded media reliance measure. Age and frequency of church attendance were no longer significant predictors. New to the model are ideology, alienation, and confidence in politics. Whether a respondent was born-again or evangelical was a significant predictor, but it was eliminated because it did not meet the .1 beta coefficient criteria.

Although the variance accounted for by the model has shown a statistically significant increase of some 11% (see Table 8.2), claims for the model have to be more modest. I have addressed a criticism of the earlier model by controlling for ideology, and the ideology controls are useful. Personal ideology was a significant predictor of tolerance, but being born-again or evangelical was not. Alienation and political confidence also make a contribution, and I interpret their roles in the context of ideology. The substantive variables of religiosity and education retain their explanatory power, though religiosity (beta = $-.32$, $p < .001$) now plays a larger predictive role than does education (beta = $.27$, $p < .001$). In the system of controls offered here, religiosity is a strong negative predictor of tolerance and education is a positive predictor. No other religion variables met the model's criteria. But apart from age and church attendance dropping out of the model, all I appear to have effected is some fine-tuning of the earlier model. The R-square increases associated with each of the additional variables are not substantial, though they are statistically significant.

News media play a significant, albeit weak, role in predicting tolerance. TV news reliance is an inverse predictor and newspaper and radio news reliance are positive predictors of tolerance. I had speculated that education might explain news media relationships with tolerance, but the relationships now being reported were obtained even after education was controlled for. These news media influences, nevertheless, are slight. Media exposure measures showed no significance. What little media influence was found came from fuzzier reliance measures.

Table 8.2 Stepwise Multiple Regression Models for Tolerance and for Particular Speech and Press Issues (coefficients are standardized beta weights; $n = 4,244$)

Predictors	Beta Weight (R-Square Change) Tolerance Index	Tolerance for X-Rated Publications	Tolerance for Library Books/Ideas	Tolerance for Communist Speech	Tolerance Government Censor News	Tolerance Press Freedom
Religiosity[a]	-.32** (.18**)	.20**	-.28**	-.10**	-.16**	ns
Education	.27** (.09**)	ns	.27**	.19**	.17**	-.05**
Ideology	.15** (.03**)	-.09**	.07**	.05**	.12**	-.07**
Alienation[b]	.13** (.02**)	.03*	.15**	.12**	.07**	.10**
Political confidence[c]	.12** (.01**)	-.07**	.06**	ns	.06**	-.12**
Newspaper relier[d]	.18** (.003**)	ns	.17**	.12**	.19**	ns
TV news relier[d]	-.14** (.002**)	ns	-.14**	-.10**	-.16**	ns
Adjusted R-square	33%	6%	26%	10%	11%	4%

a. Cube transform of religiosity.
b. Alienation ("economic" rather than "political").
c. Confidence in politics (personalities rather than institutions).
d. Dummy coded.
*$p < .05$; **$p < .001$; ns = no significance.

At the same time, the model has some utility in explaining five separate speech and press issues. As Table 8.2 shows, the variance accounted for varies substantially across the issues—much more than expected. It ranges from a high of 26% with regard to opposition to banning from school libraries books that contain dangerous ideas to a low of 4% regarding tolerance for press freedom to report matters involving national security. The way tolerance is defined is evidently an important issue.

The adjusted R-squares indicate that the model works best in predicting opposition to banning books in school libraries. It is moderately successful in predicting opposition to government censorship of news involving national security and tolerance for communist and Ku Klux Klan speech in a community. The betas show a significant role for the news media in predicting tolerance for each of these three issues.

DISCUSSION

Religiosity does account for a substantial amount of the variation in tolerance for others' civil liberties, and this held for the general question as well as for most of the specific speech and press issues studied here. The diversity in variance accounted for across these speech and press issues suggests that the way tolerance or prejudice is defined is important. These two findings are contrary to those of Cygnar et al. (1977). Furthermore, the religiosity construct used here was more intrinsic than extrinsic. Allport and Ross (1967) predicted that extrinsic constructs would account for even more variation in prejudice than would intrinsic measures of religiosity.

Religion's role in tolerance for others' civil liberties was generally a negative one. Regardless how it was measured, the more religious one is, the more intolerant one is of others' civil liberties. The phenomenon was informed here by one's ideology and, to a lesser degree, by alienation. The more conservative a person reported they were, the less tolerant they appeared to be. Education was a significant, positive predictor of tolerance, but its impact here came in second to religiosity. Those who reported they relied on TV for their news about the world were relatively intolerant, whereas those who reported they were newspaper or radio news reliers were more likely to be tolerant. Age did not play a role. This was surprising, given the support for it in the literature.

Although religiosity and education appear to play substantial roles in promoting tolerance for others' civil liberties, the news media's role is one of slight and fuzzy influence. Presumably news media can reinforce existing attitudes regarding tolerance as already defined by one's religion, education, and ideology. There is scant evidence here that news media can innovate or even initiate tolerant attitudes for other people's civil liberties.

NOTES

1. The skew of the Religiosity index (skew coefficient = –1.2) was so severe that even a cube power transform was not able to bring it to normality. The transform did move the distribution closer to normality. Because attempts to reexpress the index were not entirely successful, I usually report it as developed rather than as transformed. This has the advantage of avoiding problems in interpreting data elevated to the third power! We do run the transformed distribution in the final regression runs. Readers should note, however, that the Religiosity index does not meet the normality assumptions for regression analysis. Therefore, its multivariate contribution may be inflated.

2. Regression diagnostics showed no substantial multicollinearity, with the exception of newspaper and TV news reliance. As might be expected, these two dummy-coded categories showed relatively higher tolerance and lower variance inflation factors, suggesting they were correlated with each other. Plots showed the residuals to be randomly distributed. This analysis was executed in SPSS/PC+. A final diagnostic check run in Stata found the model accounting for 44% of the variance in tolerance! I report this in passing for the prestige possibilities it might gain for the model, but I elected to go with the more conservative 33% obtained with SPSS/PC+. The substantial discrepancy between the two software packages is an issue for another study.

REFERENCES

Allport, G. (1966). The religious context of prejudice. *Journal for the Scientific Study of Religion, 5*, 447-457.

Allport, G., & Ross, J. M. (1967). Personal religious orientation and prejudice. *Journal of Personality and Social Psychology, 5*, 432-443.

Bobo, L., & Licari, F. C. (1989). Education and political tolerance: Testing the effects of cognitive sophistication and target group affect. *Public Opinion Quarterly, 53,* 285-309.

Carr, L. G., & Hauser, W. J. (1976). Anomie and religiosity: An empirical re-examination. *Journal for the Scientific Study of Religion, 15,* 69-74.

Corbett, M. (1982). *Political tolerance in America: Freedom and equity in public attitudes.* New York: Longman.

Cygnar, T. E., Jacobson, C. K., & Noel, D. L. (1977). Religiosity and prejudice: An interdimensional analysis. *Journal for the Scientific Study of Religion, 16,* 183-191.

Hamilton, N. F., & Rubin, A. M. (1992). The influence of religiosity on television viewing. *Journalism Quarterly, 69,* 667-678.

Henley, N. M., & Pincus, F. (1978). Interrelationship of sexist, racist and antihomosexual attitudes. *Psychological Reports, 42,* 83-90.

McClosky, H., & Brill, A. (1983). *Dimensions of tolerance: What Americans believe about civil liberties.* New York: Russell Sage.

Newhagen, J. E. (1994). Self-efficacy and call-in political television show use. *Communication Research, 21,* 366-379.

Nunn, C. Z., Crockett, H. J., & Williams, J. A. (1978). *Tolerance for nonconformity.* San Francisco: Jossey-Bass.

Ornstein, N., Kohut, A., & McCarthy, L. (1988). *The people, the press, and politics: The Times Mirror study of the American electorate.* New York: Addison-Wesley.

Pagano, M., & Gauvreau, K. (1993). *Principles of biostatistics.* Belmont, CA: Duxbury.

Rimmer, T., & Weaver, D. (1987). Different questions, different answers? Media use and media credibility. *Journalism Quarterly, 64,* 28-36.

Roberts, K. A. (1984). *Religion in sociological perspective.* Homewood, IL: Dorsey.

Robinson, J. P. (1970). Public reaction to political protest: Chicago, 1968. *Public Opinion Quarterly, 34,* 1-9.

Stouffer, S. A. (1963). *Communism, conformity and civil liberties.* Gloucester, MA: Peter Smith.

von Elten, K., & Rimmer, T. (1992). Television and newspaper reliance and tolerance for civil liberties. *Mass Comm Review, 19,* 27-35.

Wilson, W., & Miller, H. L. (1968). Fear, anxiety, and religiousness. *Journal for the Scientific Study of Religion, 7,* 111.

9

The Role of Religion in Newspaper Trust, Subscribing, and Use for Political Information

JUDITH M. BUDDENBAUM

B uilding on work by Janowitz (1952), Merton (1950), and Park (1929, 1978), studies cast in the community ties tradition commonly use worship attendance as a measure of community integration. According to this line of work, those who attend church are more integrated into a community than those who do not attend. Therefore, they have a greater need to know about their community and are more likely than others to subscribe to and use local news media to learn about it (Stamm, 1985, 1988; Stamm & Fortini-Campbell, 1983). Using worship attendance as a measure of community integration, however, rests on the implicit assumption that church mem-

AUTHOR'S NOTE: The author thanks the Center for Middletown Studies at Ball State University and the Ball Brothers Foundation, both of Muncie, Indiana, for funding this research.

bership is the functional equivalent of membership in any other local organization. That assumption gains some credence from research indicating that both worship attendance and membership in other groups are positively correlated with subscribing to newspapers (Finnegan & Viswanath, 1988; Janowitz, 1952; Merton, 1950; Neuwirth, Salmon, & Neff, 1989; Stamm, 1985; Stamm & Fortini-Campbell, 1983). At the same time, there is little reason to believe that the relationship will hold true for all religious traditions or for all members of any particular tradition.

In his classic work on prejudice, Allport (1954) points out that religion can be a way of retreating from the world. Indeed, Lenski (1963) found that kind of withdrawal from the world more common among those whose church involvement is communal, measured by the degree to which primary relations are limited to persons within the church, rather than associational, measured by frequency of attendance at corporate worship.

Because using religion as a shield against the world was also more common among those holding orthodox Christian beliefs, those with lower socioeconomic status, and those who perceived themselves to be the target of religious or ethnic prejudice, Lenski found it more often among Catholics than among white Protestants. More recently, however, Stamm and Weis (1986) found that Catholics who felt close to their church, attended regularly, read a diocesan newspaper, and were active on behalf of political issues important to the church were more likely to subscribe to the local general circulation newspaper and be involved in other community activities than were less active Catholics. Thus, Lenski's (1963) findings were probably more related to the status of Catholics in the United States 35 years ago than to anything inherent in the Catholic tradition.

By the mid-1980s, anti-Catholicism had declined whereas Catholic socioeconomic status had improved to the point at which Catholics were as likely to be highly educated and have a high household income as mainline Protestants (Roof & McKinney, 1987, pp. 172-173). Like mainline Protestant theology, Catholic teachings encourage social awareness and activity on behalf of both church members and nonmembers. And like mainline Protestants, their religious beliefs are not as orthodox as those of conservative Protestants, who are much more likely to ascribe to a literal interpretation of the Bible. In contrast to the universalist orientation of Catholic and mainline churches, conservative Protestantism tends to foster a more dualistic worldview that encourages withdrawal from the world and its temptations (Driedger, Currie, & Linden, 1983; Hart, 1992, pp. 43-81; Skillen, 1990).

Underscoring that worldview, conservative Protestant leaders have repeatedly linked the mass media to a secular humanist plot to destroy religion (Alley, 1990; Fackler, 1990; Heinz, 1983; Hunter, 1991; Liebman, 1983; Podesta & Kurtzke, 1990). Therefore, one might expect religion to be related to community integration and thus to newspaper trust, subscribing, and use for Catholics and for mainline Protestants but not for conservative Protestants.

That is what data from an October 1992 telephone survey of a random sample of 987 Middletown residents indicate for political uses of the media, where worldview is likely to have a greater impact than it would on other motives for subscribing to and using local newspapers.

RELIGION AND TRUST
IN NEWSPAPERS

As expected, respondents who considered themselves born-again and those who held orthodox beliefs were significantly more likely than others to distrust newspapers. The relationship was stronger for belief in an inerrant Bible, which is a hallmark of conservative Protestantism, than for other components of the orthodoxy measure.[1] Belief in the divinity of Jesus, that He will return to earth, and that miracles really happened and still happen today is common across all Christian traditions, although the second coming and the reality of miracles are usually more salient to conservative Protestants than to Catholics and more liberal Protestants.

Comparisons across five Christian traditions[2] indicate that trust was highest among Catholics and lowest among Fundamentalists and Evangelicals, although differences among groups were not statistically significant (see Table 9.1).

Table 9.1 Trust in Newspapers as a Source of Political Information,
by Religious Tradition (in percentages)

	Trustworthiness			
Religious Tradition	Not at All	Not Very	Somewhat	Very
Pentecostal (n = 61)	1.6	13.1	68.9	16.4
Fundamentalist (n = 35)	6.7	16.3	69.6	7.4
Evangelical (n = 57)	8.8	24.6	57.9	8.8
Mainline (n = 422)	5.0	18.0	64.0	13.0
Roman Catholic (n = 88)	4.5	15.9	62.5	17.0

NOTE: χ^2 = 13.03, df = 12, p = ns.

RELIGION AND
NEWSPAPER SUBSCRIBING

As might be expected on the basis of warnings about the mass media from conservative Christian leaders, Fundamentalists who distrusted newspapers for political information subscribed to significantly fewer local newspapers than did members of mainline Protestant churches (χ^2 = 39.07, df = 8, p < .001). Almost two thirds of the mainline Protestants who considered newspapers not very or not at all trustworthy subscribed to one of the local newspapers and almost one fifth subscribed to both, but more than half of the Fundamentalists did not subscribe to any paper. Although Pentecostals were more likely than other conservative Protestants to subscribe to at least one paper, two fifths of the Pentecostals did not subscribe to any paper; fewer than 10% subscribed to both. About 5% of the Evangelicals and almost 15% of the Catholics subscribed to both papers.

Because newspaper subscribing and use are generally higher among older people and those with higher incomes and education (Weaver & Buddenbaum, 1980), those findings might simply reflect the demographic characteristics of conservative Protestants as compared to more liberal Protestants and Roman Catholics. Examining the relationship between religion and subscribing for each of the five Christian traditions while controlling for age, education, and household income, however, showed that conservative Protestant subscribers were less likely to have strong church ties than were nonsubscribers. Mainline Protestant and Roman Catholic subscribers were more likely than nonsubscribers to have strong church ties (see Table 9.2).

Although Pentecostals were somewhat more likely to trust newspapers as a source of political information and subscribe to them than other conservative Christians, it was those Pentecostals who considered their religion relatively unimportant, did not share Pentecostal beliefs, and had only loose ties to the church who were most likely to subscribe. In contrast to the teachings of their churches, Pentecostal subscribers did not consider the Bible to be the inerrant word of God. Neither did they describe themselves as either charismatic or born-again. Although the subscribers had both associational and communal ties to a local church, not having church friends was most strongly related to subscribing. Not being a church leader was almost as strongly related.

Similar relationships between subscribing and the various measures of religiosity occurred for Evangelicals and for other Fundamentalists, except that among the other Fundamentalists being charismatic was related to subscribing. But unlike the Pentecostal churches, the conservative Baptist churches with which most of the other Fundamentalists surveyed for this study are affiliated do not emphasize gifts of the Spirit. Most discourage speaking in tongues.

In contrast to the conservative Protestants, total newspaper subscribing was correlated with having church ties for both mainline Protestants and Roman Catholics. In those churches, subscribers were more likely than nonsubscribers to consider their religion important. Because Catholic and most liberal Protestant churches encourage the beliefs included in the orthodoxy measure with the exception of the literal interpretation of Scripture, the weak positive relation between subscribing and orthodoxy suggests subscribers may accept their churches' teachings. Similarly, the negative relationship between subscribing and being born-again reflects the lack of emphasis that being born-again receives in mainline and Catholic churches. Although the relationship between subscribing and being charismatic is surprising, the positive correlations probably stem from the large interdenominational charismatic community in Middletown.

Table 9.2 Religious Ties and Total Newspaper Subscribing: Partial Correlations, Controlling for Age, Education, and Household Income

	Religious Tradition				
Tie	Pentecostal (n = 61)	Fundamentalist (n = 35)	Evangelical (n = 57)	Mainline (n = 422)	Roman Catholic (n = 88)
Salience	-.101	-.151	-.078	.031	.165
Beliefs					
Orthodoxy	-.270*	-.079	-.083	.023	.041
Born-again	-.286**	-.079	-.077	-.016	-.243*
Charismatic	-.150	.052	-.034	.089	-.064
Associational Ties					
Attend	-.010	-.106	-.159	.131*	.157
Leadership	-.283*	-.189*	.003	.177***	-.013
Activity	-.279	-.088	-.075	.156**	.219*
Communal Ties					
Friends	-.489****	-.139	-.087	.089	-.001
See people	.159	-.070	.223	-.078	-.041

$*p < .1$; $**p < .05$; $***p < .01$; $****p < .001$.

Unlike conservative Protestants, both mainline Protestant and Roman Catholic subscribers had associational ties to their church. Mainline Protestants also had church friends, but that communal tie probably did not reflect the kind of withdrawal from the world that it may represent in conservative churches. Having church friends but not going to church primarily to see them suggests a more internalized motivation for religiosity than that suggested by not having friends at church but attending services to see people.

RELIGION AND NEWSPAPER
USE FOR POLITICAL INFORMATION

Probably because the measure of newspaper use for political information tapped relative amounts instead of frequency of reading or time spent with newspapers, reported levels of use were quite similar across religious traditions.

Although all conservative Christians were somewhat less likely to report heavy use of newspapers for political information than mainline Protestants and Catholics, the difference was most pronounced for Evangelicals. About one third of the Catholics and mainline Protestants reported heavy newspaper use; only half as many Evangelicals were heavy users. As might be expected, however, use within each tradition was significantly higher among those who found newspapers at least somewhat trustworthy and subscribed to them than among those who did not trust newspapers ($r = .20, p < .001$) or subscribe to them ($r = .45, p < .001$).

As was true for subscribing, it was those Pentecostals and other Fundamentalists who were less tightly tied to their church who were most likely to use newspapers for political information. For Evangelicals, mainline Protestants, and Catholics, however, the findings were more mixed (see Table 9.3).

Pentecostals who used the local newspapers for political information were significantly more likely than nonusers to consider their religion unimportant, to say that they were not charismatic, to have few church friends, and to be inactive in the church. A similar absence of church ties was found among other Fundamentalists who used the newspapers heavily for political information. Probably

Table 9.3 Religious Ties and Newspaper Use for Political Information: Partial Correlations, Controlling for Age, Education, and Household Income

	Religious Tradition				
Tie	Pentecostal (n = 61)	Fundamentalist (n = 35)	Evangelical (n = 57)	Mainline (n = 422)	Roman Catholic (n = 88)
Salience	-.489****	-.016	.196	-.031	-.073
Beliefs					
Orthodoxy	-.208	-.130	.150	-.044	-.096
Born-again	-.191	-.081	.017	-.096	-.268**
Charismatic	-.243*	-.007	-.060	.037	-.012
Associational Ties					
Attend	-.091	-.029	.065	.116*	.003
Leadership	-.255*	-.114	.201	-.030	-.163
Activity	-.299**	-.055	.182	.030	.035
Communal Ties					
Friends	-.404***	.003	-.097	-.088	-.003
See people	-.149	.021	-.011	.070	-.060

*p < .1; **p < .05; ***p < .01; ****p < .001.

because of their small numbers in the sample, however, the relationships were not statistically significant.

Although Evangelicals with strong church ties tended not to subscribe to newspapers, use of them for political information was highest among those for whom religion was important, who shared their churches' teachings, and who had strong associational ties to the church. Those results appear paradoxical, but closer examination indicates that this group was divided into two camps, one typified by Reformed Presbyterian and Southern Baptist churches that encouraged redeeming the world through evangelism but not shunning involvement in it and another typified by a very large evangelical and charismatic congregation whose members were encouraged to trust and use information from the American Family Association and the Rutherford Institute instead of from the mass media. These charismatic Evangelicals plus a few from other evangelical churches account for the subscribing pattern. The Reformed Presbyterians, Southern Baptists, and a few others explain the use.

Among mainline Protestants and Roman Catholics, some church ties were related to newspaper use; others were not. Those who attended church regularly but who did not have leadership roles, who considered their religion very important, or who had church friends were the most likely to use the local newspapers for political information. In these traditions, it may be that church leaders' information needs were not completely satisfied by the relatively small local papers. Data from the same survey show that mainline Protestants and Catholics were significantly more likely than conservative Protestants to use an elite newspaper for political information ($\chi^2 = 24.47$, $df = 12$, $p < .05$).

CONCLUSION

In contrast to the traditional community ties literature that assumes that both church attendance and newspaper subscribing and use are marks of integration into a community, survey data from Middletown suggest that, in some cases, ties to a church may represent isolation from the community. The fact that other researchers have consistently found links between church activity and newspaper subscribing and use stems from the fact that they measured level of worship attendance without taking into account the kind of church attended. Therefore, their findings reflect the fact that in most communities mainline Protestants and Catholics outnumber members of conservative Protestant churches.

These findings from Middletown indicate that ties to a local church most likely represent the kind of community integration that leads to newspaper subscribing and use only for mainline Protestants and Catholics. Although the findings were somewhat mixed for Evangelicals, among Pentecostals, and other Fundamentalists, it was those who identified with a church but did not take their religion seriously, share its beliefs, or participate in church life who were most likely to subscribe to and use local newspapers for political information. That those who subscribed to and used the local papers had few church friends but went to church to see other people suggests that for them newspapers may in some way help compensate for being a member of but not really a part of a religious community.

NOTES

1. The orthodoxy measure combined Likert items positing the reality of miracles, Jesus' imminent return to earth, and a literally true, inerrant Bible (Cronbach's alpha = .8).

2. Respondents were placed in one of five Christian traditions on the basis of their answer to a question asking which local church they attended most often. For the most part, churches were categorized along denominational lines using research by Smith (1990) as a guide, but some were placed in a different category because of their distinctive characteristics.

Traditions include the following:

Pentecostal (orthodox/fundamentalist, charismatic): Apostolic, Assembly of God, Church of God—Full Gospel, Church of God—Mountain Assembly, Church of God in Christ, FourSquare Gospel, Full Gospel, Pentecostal, and some independent congregations

Other Fundamentalist (orthodox/fundamentalist, not charismatic): Church of Christ, Church of Christ in Christian Union, Church of God, Church of God —Anderson, Nazarene, Independent, National, Separate and United Baptist, Seventh-day Adventist, and some independent congregations

Evangelical (conservative, born-again, may or may not be charismatic): Bible Holiness, Brethren, Presbyterian—PCA, Southern Baptist, nondenominational, and some individual congregations

Mainline (moderate to liberal, not charismatic or born-again) African Methodist Episcopal, American Baptist, Christian Science, Church of Christ—Disciples of Christ, Church of Christ—Independent, Lutheran—ELCA, Presbyterian—USA, Unitarian Universalist, United Methodist

Roman Catholic (conservative, not charismatic or born-again)

REFERENCES

Alley, R. S. (1990). Television, religion, and fundamentalist distortions. In R. Abelman & S. M. Hoover (Eds.), *Religious television: Controversies and conclusions* (pp. 265-274). Norwood, NJ: Ablex.

Allport, G. W. (1954). *The nature of prejudice.* New York: Addison-Wesley.

Driedger, L., Currie, R., & Linden, R. (1983). Dualistic and holistic views of God: Consequences for social action. *Review of Religious Research, 24,* 225-245.

Fackler, M. (1990). Religious watchdog groups and prime-time programming. In J. P. Ferre' (Ed.), *Channels of belief: Religion and American commercial television* (pp. 99-116). Ames: Iowa State University Press.

Finnegan, J. R., Jr., & Viswanath, K. (1988). Community ties and use of cable TV and newspapers in a Midwest suburb. *Journalism Quarterly, 65,* 456-463, 473.

Hart, S. (1992). *What does the Lord require?* New York: Oxford University Press.

Heinz, D. (1983). The struggle to define America. In R. C. Liebman & R. Wuthnow (Eds.), *The new Christian right: Mobilization and legitimation* (pp. 133-149). New York: Aldine.

Hunter, J. D. (1991). *Culture wars: The struggle to define America.* New York: Basic Books.

Janowitz, M. (1952). *The community press in an urban setting.* Glencoe, IL: Free Press.

Lenski, G. (1963). *The religious factor: A sociologist's inquiry.* Garden City, NY: Anchor.

Liebman, R. C. (1983). Mobilizing the moral majority. In R. C. Liebman & R. Wuthnow (Eds.), *The new Christian right: Mobilization and legitimation* (pp. 50-74). New York: Aldine.

Merton, R. (1950). Patterns of influence: A study of interpersonal influences and of communications behavior in a local community. In P. Lazarsfeld & F. Stanton (Eds.), *Communications research 1948-49* (pp. 180-219). New York: Harper & Row.

Neuwirth, K., Salmon, C. T., & Neff, M. (1989). Community orientation and media use. *Journalism Quarterly, 66,* 31-39.

Park, R. P. (1929). Urbanization as measured by newspaper circulation. *American Journal of Sociology, 34,* 60-79.

Park, R. P. (1978). The natural history of the newspaper. In E. E. Dennis, A. H. Ismach, & D. M. Gillmor (Eds.), *Enduring issues in mass communication* (pp. 180-219). New York: Harper & Row.

Podesta, A. T., & Kurtzke, J. S. (1990). Conflict between the electronic church and state: The religious right's crusade against pluralism. In R. Abelman & S. M.

Hoover (Eds.), *Religious television: Controversies and conclusions* (pp. 207-226). Norwood, NJ: Ablex.

Roof, W. C., & McKinney, W. (1987). *American mainline religion: Its changing shape and future.* New Brunswick, NJ: Rutgers University Press.

Skillen, J. W. (1990). *The scattered voice: Christians at odds in the public square.* Grand Rapids, MI: Zondervan.

Smith, T. W. (1990). Classifying Protestant denominations. *Review of Religious Research, 31,* 225-245.

Stamm, K. R. (1985). *Newspaper use and community ties: Toward a dynamic theory.* Norwood, NJ: Ablex.

Stamm, K. R. (1988). Community ties and media use. *Critical Studies in Mass Communication, 8,* 357-361.

Stamm, K. R., & Fortini-Campbell, L. (1983). The relationship of community ties to newspaper subscribing and use. *Journalism Monographs, 84.*

Stamm, K. R., & Weis, R. (1986). The newspaper and community integration: A study of ties to a local church community. *Communication Research, 13,* 125-137.

Weaver, D. H., & Buddenbaum, J. M. (1980). Newspapers and television: A review of research on uses and effects. In G. C. Wilhoit & H. deBock (Eds.), *Mass communication review yearbook* (Vol. 1, pp. 371-390). Beverly Hills, CA: Sage.

10

The Role of Religion in Public Attitudes Toward Religion News

JUDITH M. BUDDENBAUM
STEWART M. HOOVER

Because newspapers have historically relegated religion news to a weekly church page filled with routine stories about local people and events (Mason, 1995; Nordin, 1975), they have often been criticized for covering primarily good news about established main-

AUTHORS' NOTE: Judith M. Buddenbaum thanks the Ball Brothers Foundation and the Center for Middletown Studies at Ball State University for grants supporting the research in Muncie, Indiana, and the Survey Research Center at Ball State University, which managed the Muncie survey. She also thanks Columbine CableVision and the *Coloradoan,* both of Fort Collins, Colorado; the Loveland, Colorado, *Reporter-Herald;* and the *Windsor Beacon* (Colorado) for commissioning the surveys referred to in this chapter. Students in her media research classes conducted the interviews as they learned media research procedures. Stewart M. Hoover thanks the Lilly Endowment for a grant supporting his research on religion news. He also thanks Religious News Service and Religion Newswriters Association for their interest and cooperation and Douglas Wagner for his help with data analysis. The national survey data were collected by the Gallup Organization.

135

line Protestant churches at the expense of attention to other religions and more meaningful information about trends and issues
(Buddenbaum, 1988, 1989; Dart & Allen, 1994; Hoover, Hanley, &
Radelfinger, 1989, 1993; Hoover, Venturelli, & Wagner, 1994;
Mattingly, 1983). Such coverage, however, may have served many
readers quite well. Root and Bolder (1966) found that readers generally liked the traditional church page. Preferred content consisted
of personality and feature stories, international and national church
news, and church notices and ads (Rarick, 1967).

Those findings are consistent with research stemming from Merton's
(1957) work that introduced the "localite-cosmopolite" orientations.
Roof and Hoge (1980), for example, found that a localite orientation,
as measured by agreement with the statement "Despite all the
newspaper and TV coverage, national and international happenings
rarely seem as interesting as events that occur in the local community in which one lives," is positively correlated with religious
activity. But because that measure is more strongly correlated with
conservative Protestantism than with other forms of Christianity
(Roof, 1972), "localite news" may be unattractive to many readers.

Root and Bolder (1966) found that only about one third of a
newspaper's subscribers read the church page regularly. Those who
did were typically female church members. Another study, based on
data collected a decade later, also found the typical readers to be
older women with low socioeconomic status who were active in
their church and generally conservative in their approach to life. But
actually, there were two audiences: the traditional one, whose news
interests were distinctly localite, and a more cosmopolitan one with
interests transcending the local community. Localites read religion
news along with stories about other kinds of local news; cosmopolites gravitated toward state, national, and international news, stories about issues, letters to the editor, and opinion columns
(Buddenbaum, 1982).

But by the time of that study, religion news was already changing,
fueled, perhaps, by visibility of the electronic church and growing
religio-political activity in the United States and abroad. Surveys
conducted in the 1980s show that reporters better educated in both
journalism and religion and more aware of diversity among their

readers began to staff the religion beat (Buddenbaum, 1984, 1987, 1988; Hynds, 1987).

Consistent with the findings from those surveys, content analysis confirms that stories have become longer, less local, and more issue oriented. They also have begun to appear more frequently outside the religion page (Mason, 1995). Change has not been uniform, however. Many papers, particularly in smaller communities, continue to emphasize local people- and event-oriented stories. In larger cities, some have abandoned traditional coverage, and even the religion page itself, in favor of in-depth, issue-oriented coverage in an effort to serve those with cosmopolite interests. Others try to serve both audiences by providing a mix of local features and hard news (Buddenbaum, 1984, 1987, 1988; Dart & Allen, 1994; Hoover et al., 1989, 1993; Hoover et al., 1994).

Each of those approaches has its critics. Much criticism focuses on sloppy journalism, but much also stems from disagreement, sometimes inspired by religious beliefs, about whether the traditional church page, the more recent trend toward hard news coverage, or some mixture best serves the public interest. In general, conservative Christians prefer localite news, often equating the hard news emphasis on issues and controversies with deliberate anti-Christian bias. Catholics, too, sometimes see deliberate bias, but both Catholics and more liberal Protestants more often complain about shallow coverage (Buddenbaum, 1990a, 1990b, in press; Hoover et al., 1989, 1993).

ABOUT OUR RESEARCH

Our focus in this chapter is on religious differences in public interest, readership, and satisfaction concerning religion news in general and in particular kinds of religion news. For this assessment, we draw on national and local surveys supplemented by in-depth interviews and content analysis.

Primary data come from face-to-face interviews with random samples of 1,100 respondents nationwide conducted in April 1988 and March-April 1989. These surveys allow us to generalize to the population as a whole, but analyzing the data forces us to treat as equivalent respondents living in different communities who may be responding to quite different religion news coverage.

Therefore, we also report findings based on a secondary analysis of a 1992 telephone survey of a random sample of 987 Muncie, Indiana, residents, and applied audience surveys conducted for local media in Fort Collins, Colorado, in 1988 and 1993, Loveland, Colorado, in 1990, and Windsor, Colorado, in 1995. These surveys allow us to examine responses in light of more intimate knowledge about the churches people attend and the religion news to which they are exposed through their local newspapers. This is particularly true of the Muncie data, which, like the national data, were collected as part of a large research project employing multiple methodologies.

AUDIENCES AND THEIR INTERESTS

Our survey data indicate that public interest in religion news is quite high, especially in comparison to interest in other kinds of specialty news on which newspapers lavish far more attention. In response to a question on the 1988 survey asking respondents to rate the importance of nine kinds of specialty news, religion ranked at the midpoint—significantly lower than education news that respondents rated as most important but well ahead of sports news that they rated least important.

Both readership and satisfaction with coverage, however, lagged behind the ratings for importance of religion news. With self-assessments of likelihood of reading as the test, education remained in first place but religion news slipped to sixth and sports moved up to seventh place. In reader satisfaction, however, sports moved into first place; education and religion fell to fifth and ninth place respectively (see Table 10.1).

Almost one fourth of all respondents gave religion news the highest rating for importance, but Evangelicals and those who attended church most regularly were even more likely than other Christians and those who less regularly attended church to give

Table 10.1 Mean Scores and Rank Orders for Nine Kinds of Specialty News[a]

Kind of News	Importance	Readership	Satisfaction
Arts	3.78 (7)	3.99 (8)	4.67 (6)
Business	4.85 (3)	5.82 (2)	5.29 (2)
Education	5.69 (1)	6.65 (1)	5.00 (4)
Entertainment	4.40 (6)	5.04 (4)	5.18 (3)
Food	4.54 (4)	4.81 (5)	4.99 (5)
Health	5.60 (2)	5.60 (3)	4.76 (6)
Personal Advice	3.72 (8)	3.88 (9)	4.39 (8)
Religion	4.50 (5)	4.56 (6)	4.32 (9)
Sports	3.46 (9)	4.22 (7)	5.74 (1)

a. All rankings are on a 7-point scale with 7 being the highest ranking for importance, likelihood of reading, and satisfaction with coverage in the newspaper read most often.

religion news the highest rating. Whereas 34% of the Evangelicals and 40% of those who most often attended church, regardless of their religious preference, gave it the highest rating, only 24% of the mainline Protestants and 22% of the Catholics attached similar importance to religion news. Among those who attended church no more than a few times a year, only 13% gave it the highest rating for importance. In general, women, older people, and those with less education rated religion news as significantly more important and were more satisfied with it than were men, younger people, and those with more education.

Consistent with the rankings of religion news against eight other specialties, for the sample as a whole and in all demographic and religious groups, a smaller proportion reported reading religion news whenever it was available. Even fewer gave it the top rating in response to a question asking how satisfied they were with religion news coverage. On that measure of satisfaction, 14% of all respondents, all Catholics, and all mainline Protestants, 21% of the Evangelicals, and 18% of those who attended church most often gave it the top rating. Women, older people, and those with less education were most satisfied with the coverage, but in those groups only about half as many respondents gave it the top rating for satisfaction as had given religion news the top rating on importance.

Although the finding that considering a subject important does not translate directly into readership may seem surprising at first, differences probably stem from an interaction between respondents' preference for a particular approach to news and the way they perceive journalists responding to their preference through actual news coverage.

A factor analysis of answers to questions in the 1989 survey asking respondents to rate the importance of 17 kinds of religion news stories identified localite and cosmopolite factors that together accounted for two thirds of the variance in importance. The localite factor included items such as stories about faith experience and local religious issues; cosmopolite interests included coverage of the role of religion in international and domestic politics, surveys, and religious issues and controversies (see also Hoover & Wagner, 1994).

Although those factors suggest two audiences for religion news, both the factor analysis and the demographic and religious characteristics correlated with each kind of news indicate there is much overlap in news interests. Seven items, including coverage of ethical and social issues that had the strongest loading on the localite factor and one of the strongest on the cosmopolite factor, were associated with both factors.

Being a female was significantly and positively correlated with ranking both localite and cosmopolite kinds of stories as very important, but cosmopolites were significantly more likely than localites to be more educated and affluent. These demographic differences may reflect a greater proportion of men in the cosmopolite group; they also point to lingering differences in socioeconomic status between conservative Protestants and other Christians. At the same time, the religious characteristics associated with the two factors suggest that more than socioeconomic status is at work.

The influence of beliefs on story preference can be detected in the finding that mainline Protestantism was less strongly associated with the localite factor and more strongly related to the cosmopolite factor than was conservative Protestantism. Although the correlations were quite weak and the difference insignificant, Catholicism was also more strongly related to the cosmopolite factor. Both the importance people attach to their religion and how often they attend

Table 10.2 Demographic and Religious Correlates of Importance of Localite and Cosmopolite Religion News

	Importance of	
Correlate	Localite Coverage	Cosmopolite Coverage
Gender	.14**	.06*
Education	−.17**	.20**
Income	−.15**	.13**
Salience of religion	.51**	.09**
Church attendance	.44**	.09**
Evangelical Protestant	.21**	−.02
Mainline Protestant	.05*	.02
Roman Catholic	.01	.04

*$p < .05$; **$p < .01$.

church were positively and significantly related to both factors; the stronger correlations between them and the localite factor are consistent with previous findings that the cosmopolite factor itself is split between religious people and those who have no religious affiliation (see Table 10.2).

A CLOSER LOOK AT NEWS CONTENT AND STORY PREFERENCE

Because newspapers cannot serve homogeneous audiences, mismatches between coverage and the interests of at least some people are inevitable. Therefore, we now turn to our local survey data to illustrate ways in which news coverage and audience characteristics may interact to influence interest, readership, and satisfaction.

Interest and Readership in Fort Collins

With a population of 100,000, Fort Collins, Colorado, is home to a major state university; its economic base rests on education and light and high-tech industry. Its residents are more highly educated and affluent but less religious than those in the other cities for which we have data. In the 1988 and 1993 surveys, more than half of all respondents reported no church activity; almost one fifth did not identify with any religion. Of those who did, mainline Protestants outnumbered both Catholics and conservative Protestants by more than two to one.

Reported interest in religion news was higher than in the national sample, but actual readership by all demographic and religious groups was lower than in other local communities for which data are available. Readership levels, however, were comparable to those found in other cities served by Gannett newspapers (Burgoon, Burgoon, & Wilkinson, 1981), which, like the Fort Collins one, had neither a religion page nor a journalist with the title of religion writer or editor.[1]

Although public interest in religion news was significantly and positively correlated with the need to make political decisions, in the Fort Collins paper, religion news consisted only of a weekly roundup of church announcements and an occasional feature story, usually picked up from the wire services or as a contribution from a freelance writer. Therefore, low readership most likely stems from the paucity of religion news compounded by a mismatch between available content and readers' interests.

Readership and Satisfaction in Loveland and Windsor

Located 15 miles south of Fort Collins, Loveland, Colorado, with a population of about 50,000, also has light and high-tech industry, but like the much smaller town of Windsor, Colorado, that is still largely a farming community, it remains closer to its agricultural roots. Residents of both towns were slightly less educated and affluent than Fort Collins residents but still well above the national average. They were also more religious than Fort Collins residents; only about 10% failed to identify with a religion or report any religious activity. As was true in Fort Collins, the largest number of Loveland residents were either Lutheran or Methodist. In Windsor, the dominant churches were Lutheran and United Church of Christ.

Both the daily newspaper in Loveland and the community weekly in Windsor provided community-oriented news that included a weekly religion page featuring stories about local churches, events, and people. In 1990, Loveland residents read religion news much more regularly than did people in Fort Collins and were generally satisfied with the amount of coverage in their paper.

Probably because Windsor residents subscribed to the weekly precisely for its local coverage, almost all subscribers surveyed in 1995 rated the church page as good or excellent. Satisfaction with the church page was also strongly and positively correlated with satisfaction with the paper itself. Satisfaction with religion coverage, however, was lowest among conservative Protestants and highest among Lutherans and members of the United Church of Christ, who presumably received more coverage than other groups simply because their churches were the dominant ones.

In Loveland, a similar lack of satisfaction on the part of conservative Protestants showed up in the relationship between readership of religion news and general satisfaction with the newspaper and with the community itself. To some extent, this probably also reflects greater coverage of mainline churches than of those attended by the conservative Protestant minority, but in Loveland, the relationship probably also stems from the very human desire to "kill the messenger." Incensed that the city had purchased a statue depicting motherhood in the form of a young woman breast-feeding her infant, members of two large conservative churches mounted a protest against public display of the statue, claiming it was obscene and promoted incest. In response to a series of survey questions designed to assess public perceptions of the quality of life in Loveland, members of those two churches gave unusually low evaluations to the city, the arts, the parks, and also to the newspaper, apparently for its role in promoting the art in the parks program and then covering the controversy surrounding the city's latest acquisition (see Buddenbaum, 1992).

Readership in Muncie

Like Fort Collins, Muncie, Indiana, is home to a large state university. But unlike the Colorado communities, it is a blue-collar town with many more low-income residents who have less than a high school education. Religious activity was equivalent to that in

Loveland and Windsor. Methodism was the dominant religion, but Pentecostals and members of other fundamentalist churches out-numbered Catholics. The proportion of the population belonging to one of the fundamentalist churches equaled the proportion of Methodists in the community.

Unlike the Colorado communities, Muncie had two newspapers. Although both devoted much more attention to state, national, and international political news and carried more syndicated political columns than the Colorado newspapers, both emphasized local news coverage and had very similar traditional church pages. Despite those differences, readership of the church page was similar to that found in Loveland; however, in Muncie, readership was higher among men, those with higher education, and those who were active in mainline Protestant churches. Although those are not the kinds of people one would expect to read localite coverage, the relationships are undoubtedly affected by low levels of newspaper subscribing among Fundamentalists (see Chapter 9, this volume).

In-depth interviews with members of one Roman Catholic and three mainline churches suggest that their members considered the religion coverage shallow and uninteresting. Some read specifically for Michael McManus's syndicated religion and ethics column in the morning paper; others scanned the religion page to find out what was going on in town, whereas others read it simply because it was there. In contrast, members of the two largest conservative churches in town considered all mass media, including the local papers, biased against religion and avoided them as much as possible. In the case of the local papers, that judgment was based at least partly on stories of the "nun struck by lightning while playing golf with rabbi" genre used as fillers, rather than on the religion pages that generally provided neutral to favorable coverage of local people and events.

Although in-depth interviews conducted in connection with the national study indicate that people generally understand how newspapers operate and do not expect a daily paper to provide religious news, reactions to religion news coverage were similar to those of Muncie residents. Members of an Assembly of God congregation tended to see the media as deliberately biased against religion; Catholics also sometimes saw bias against the institutional church, but like mainline Protestants, they generally favored in-depth, issue-oriented reporting.

CONCLUSION

From these findings, we conclude that interest in religion news is widespread, but readership and satisfaction are lower because they are more closely related to the way people perceive religion news is being covered and the way they believe it should be covered. What people want from religion news is, itself, related to demographic characteristics and to religion.

As previous research indicates, attention to religion news may be part of both a localite and a cosmopolite news orientation. The localite, or traditional, approach to religion news is common in small-town newspapers; a more hard-news or cosmopolitan approach exists at many larger papers. Likelihood of reading probably is related to whether or not respondents see their local newspaper meeting their own news interests. Satisfaction may be more strongly affected by respondents' awareness that other approaches to religion news exist.

People with above-average socioeconomic status, members of mainline Protestant churches, and those with no religion may read and even be reasonably satisfied with localite coverage, but they are more likely to prefer cosmopolite coverage; conservative Protestants and those with lower socioeconomic status will, in most cases, be happier with localite coverage. Serious mismatches between readers' preferences and the way religion news is covered can depress readership and satisfaction. Satisfying readers, however, is not entirely a matter of giving them what they want in the religion pages. As the reactions of conservative Protestants in Loveland and Muncie indicate, both scattered, short items that make up a tiny fraction of the religion news and coverage of salient issues, even when they are not reported as religion news, may offend conservative Protestants who prefer supportive, localite coverage.

NOTE

1. Three of the newspapers examined by Burgoon et al. (1981) were included in a study of the religion beat (Buddenbaum, 1988). Information on the status of religion reporting at those Gannett papers is based on replies from "the person who usually handles religion news" at those papers.

REFERENCES

Buddenbaum, J. M. (1982). News about religion: A readership study. *Newspaper Research Journal, 3*, 7-17.

Buddenbaum, J. M. (1984). *Religion in the news: Factors associated with selection of stories from an international religion news service by daily newspapers.* Unpublished doctoral dissertation, Indiana University.

Buddenbaum, J. M. (1987, August). *Religion journalists' perceptions of religion news and its audience.* Paper presented at the annual meeting of the Association for Education in Journalism and Mass Communication, San Antonio, TX.

Buddenbaum, J. M. (1988). The religion beat at daily newspapers. *Newspaper Research Journal, 9*, 57-70.

Buddenbaum, J. M. (1989). Developing religion news, not religious news. *Coaches' Corner, 4*, 1-2.

Buddenbaum, J. M. (1990a). Network news coverage of religion. In J. P. Ferre' (Ed.), *Channels of belief: Religion and American commercial television* (pp. 57-78). Ames: Iowa State University Press.

Buddenbaum, J. M. (1990b). Religion news coverage in commercial network newscasts. In R. Abelman & S. M. Hoover (Eds.), *Religious television: Controversies and conclusions* (pp. 249-264). Norwood, NJ: Ablex.

Buddenbaum, J. M. (1992, August). *Newspaper ties, community ties and the evaluation of a local community.* Paper presented at the annual meeting of the Association for Education in Journalism and Mass Communication, Montreal, Canada.

Buddenbaum, J. M. (in press). The mass media and religion. In M. A. Blanchard (Ed.), *Mass media history in the United States: An encyclopedia.* New York: Garland.

Burgoon, M., Burgoon, J. K., & Wilkinson, M. (1981). Dimensions and readership of newspaper content. *Newspaper Research Journal, 3*, 74-93.

Dart, J., & Allen, J. (1994). *Bridging the gap: Religion and the news media.* Nashville, TN: Freedom Forum.

Hoover, S. M., Hanley, B., & Radelfinger, M. (1989). *The RNS-Lilly study of religion reporting and readership in the daily press.* Philadelphia: Temple University and New York: Religious News Service.

Hoover, S. M., Hanley, B., & Radelfinger, M. (1993). Who reads religion news? *Nieman Reports, 47*(2), 42-47.

Hoover, S. M., Venturelli, S., & Wagner, D. (1994). *Religion in public discourse.* Boulder: University of Colorado, School of Journalism and Mass Communication.

Hoover, S. M., & Wagner, D. (1994, October). *Exploring religious and demographic correlates of media use.* Paper presented at the annual meeting of the Society for the Scientific Study of Religion, Albuquerque, NM.

Hynds, E. C. (1987). Large daily newspapers have improved coverage of religion. *Journalism Quarterly, 64,* 44-48.

Mason, D. (1995). *God in the news ghetto: A study of religion news from 1944 to 1989.* Unpublished doctoral dissertation, Ohio University.

Mattingly, T. (1983, January). Religion news: No room at the inn? *The Quill, 71,* 12-19.

Merton, R. K. (1957). *Social theory and social structure.* Glencoe, IL: Free Press.

Nordin, K. D. (1975). *Consensus religion: National newspaper coverage of religious life in America, 1849-1960.* Unpublished doctoral dissertation, University of Michigan.

Rarick, G. (1967). Readership of the church page. *ANPA Research Report, 2,* 34-35.

Roof, W. C. (1972). The local-cosmopolitan orientation and traditional religious commitment. *Sociological Analysis, 33,* 1-15.

Roof, W. C., & Hoge, D. R. (1980). Church involvement in America: Social factors affecting membership and participation. *Review of Religious Research, 21,* 405-426.

Root, R., & Bolder, H. D. (1966). The church page: Do readers like it? *ANPA Research Report, 2,* 42-43.

11

The Passionate Audience

Community Inscriptions of
The Last Temptation of Christ

THOMAS R. LINDLOF

This chapter considers one of those rare moments when interpretations of a media event become publicly and passionately competitive, when a transgressive text provokes individuals to articulate their assumptions about media and the locus of authority for recognizing a cultural "offense." Such a discourse swirled around the 1988 film, *The Last Temptation of Christ*, which offered an innovative treatment of the Jesus narrative. The question of whether the film should be shown had the prismatic effect of eliciting and separating the spectra of interpretive strategies that would otherwise remain diffuse and private.

The furor over *The Last Temptation of Christ* was one episode in the emerging "culture war," an intense, wide-ranging debate over the roles of personal choice and public policy in U.S. culture. This putative war represents a crisis in the national consensus of values, the most serious since at least the 1960s. The list of contributing factors is lengthy, but we can briefly acknowledge the rise of scientific rationality and moral relativism, the nation's growing multicultural demography, the profound changes in status and opportunities for women, and the impact of electronic media. Fundamentalism may owe its resurgence largely to the anxious reactions of many Americans to these and other advances of modernity, but it is not a retreat from the conflict that created it. Many of the traditionally orthodox compete for the resources and technological ability to voice their concerns in the wider cultural arena (Ammerman, 1991; Hunter, 1991).

In the issues central to the culture war, adherents to traditional orthodoxies see an encroaching secular, pluralist society that disrespects the sacred in public life and privileges the expressive and sovereign individual. Media corporations in particular are said to encourage this drift by their lack of sensitivity to traditional verities and their promotion of violence, cynicism, and hedonism (cf. Medved, 1992).

Therefore, the culture war continues to be waged primarily as conservative-led opposition to the expansion of rights such as abortion, protections for groups such as women and gays, and access to pornography and support for others such as school prayer.

But confining analysis to those issues would overlook the patterning of the communication that sustains, and arguably constructs, the terms of the debate. In essence, the culture war is a contest of incommensurable worldviews that are enacted ritualistically by the actors in distinctive vocabularies and rhetorical acts (e.g., Dubin, 1992; Hunter, 1991). It is the conduct of the dialogue itself through recurring symbols and interpretive strategies, as much as the substance of the issues involved, that defines culture war in a given instance.

A few studies have toured semiotic sites of the conservative Christians' mass-mediated world by means of critical exegesis (McGee, 1984) and audience analysis (Hoover, 1990), but they have looked within communities to discover their sense-making strategies with the result that we know little about the nature of contestation *between* them. This chapter explicates discourse between contestants concerning *The Last Temptation of Christ.* In it, I address two broad questions: (a) What coherent interpretive strategies can be discerned when the text in question is one that reconstructs a sacred narrative? (b) How do people define and defend their readings when they must compete with other, variant interpretations of the same event in public space? Through this analysis, we glimpse an instance of the culture war—here, a controversy over a mass-mediated retelling of the central Christian story—as expressed in the words of ordinary people rather than in the pronouncements of moral entrepreneurs.

ANALYTIC FRAMEWORK: RELATING AUDIENCE TO COMMUNITY

For any issue to engage people as public actors, it must be salient for them and move them to interrogate their own interests as "audience members" by asking what is at stake if they consent to, or resist, some problematic media content. To state those interests and to be persuasive in doing so, they must be able to forecast the validity of arguments as they might be interpreted by the community or by meaningful segments of it. It is the act of deliberately inserting oneself into a public dialogue, then, that brings forth a sense of community and all of its resonances for the speaker or author.

Despite their seeming proximity, the concepts of *community* and *audience* have had an uneasy coexistence. Community has its origins in ideas of what people hold *in common*, as in common goods, interests, customs, identity, and faith (Williams, 1983). Relations of mutual obligation, not self-interest, are the dominant chord. This sense of solidarity is often accompanied by a territorial aspect; a community "has spatial properties—borders, a center, outskirts. It also has a name and a set of symbols associated with it" (Griswold, 1994, p. 139). Its authenticity derives from both the immediacy of everyday relationships and the conjoined continuities of a place, a people, and a history.

Audience, by contrast, is an occasioned collectivity. In its modernist usage in mass communication, audience often refers to anonymous, heterogeneous, noninteracting individuals who receive messages from a central source (McQuail, 1994, pp. 38-39). In this scheme, media reception disembeds people's time and attention from pursuits as members of community-based groups. The audience becomes an artifact of the message, existing as a unit of reception (Ang, 1991). To the extent that this reception circuit is closed, invasive, and monosemic, its effects on community can only be debilitating. Of course, researchers now recognize and study the social character of media attendance and use and the varying meanings that persons assign to their media experiences. Yet the rise of the media audience is still seen as contrary to the interests of true communities, contributing to the erosion of the values and practices that sustain solidarity (cf. Harvey, 1989; Jensen, 1990). Although mass media may be no more a sole causal agent in this alleged decline than the interstate highway system, media influence is often thought to fragment and mystify people's understandings of themselves in subtly thorough ways.

Considering mass media experience and community building as separate and antagonistic depends on the premise that communities are stable, natural (as opposed to symbolically constructed), autonomous, and structurally tied to their physical settings. A different theoretical view, founded on pragmatist arguments, conceives communities as historically contingent formations whose identities emerge through distinctive linguistic practices (e.g., Rorty, 1989; Taylor, 1977). Herbst (1994), for example, contends that "community is not necessarily a physical place, or a geographic location, but a constellation of people and ideas, as well as the media individuals create to communicate with each other" (p. 182). Her historical studies of politically marginal communities point to the importance of communication infrastructures that permit the creation of common rituals, symbols, and contexts for conversation. Along the same lines, Morley (1992) argues that "analysis of . . . 'cultural identities' needs to be grounded in an analysis of the everyday practices and domestic rituals through which contemporary 'electronic communities' are conducted and reconstituted (at both micro- and macro-levels) on a daily basis" (p. 79). Communities take shape out of a meeting of activities, interests, and ethos that are signified by and to the membership through communicative action.

Similarly, qualitative studies of media use have documented that textual meanings are routinely negotiated and expressed in the intimate spheres of family, peers, and subcultures. These meanings vary, but when audience "readings" seem to cohere either within or across social groups, we can speak of an *interpretive community* (Jensen, 1991; Lindlof, 1988; Schroder, 1994). The concept accounts for the shared generative strategies (or codes) that are learned and practiced not only in media reception contexts but also in the major social networks an individual inhabits. Such strategies constitute reliable methods for generating meaning in encounters with media. As used by audience researchers, interpretive community is a conceptual device that drives empirical studies of how a genre (Lindlof, Coyle, & Grodin, in press) or a text (Schaefer & Avery, 1993) is decoded by its knowledgeable following or how readers signal ideological differences (Steiner, 1988). What seems key to the interpretive community is the idea of a *special discourse* made up of distinctive tropes, themes, and narratives, as well as schemata for the appropriate social occasions and rules for using them. The discourse grows out of people's experiences with the histories, pleasures, and problems of social collectivities in which media use is a core activity. Notions of audience and community merge in such a way as to lose the disadvantages of social isolation in the former and locational fixity in the latter.

THE STUDY: SUBJECT, SITE, AND DATA

On August 12, 1988, MCA-Universal and the theater chain Cineplex Odeon released a motion picture, *The Last Temptation of Christ*, directed by Martin Scorsese and originally adapted by screenwriter Paul Schrader from the novel by Nikos Kazantzakis (1960). Inspiring some of the most heated attack ever on a Hollywood film, the nine-city premiere was preceded by more than 2 months of denunciations of the film and its corporate sponsor, as well as protest events and campaigns aimed at stopping its release.[1] *The Last Temptation of Christ* was also a media cause célèbre in the summer of 1988, drawing attention from national news media and in statements from individuals ranging from Clint Eastwood, Jack Valenti, and the Rt. Reverend Paul Moore, Episcopal Bishop of New York, supporting its right to be shown, to Jerry Falwell, Mother Teresa, and Mario

Cuomo, who denounced it. From theatrical release through its un-publicized video release, the film was plagued by grassroots boycott efforts and threats of economic retaliation against distributors, many of them successful.

At the heart of the tempest were charges of the film's blasphemy, distortion of scriptural "facts," and blatant disrespect for the sensi-bilities of Christians. To be sure, *The Last Temptation of Christ* offered an inviting target for those who prefer a literalist approach to gospel texts. Kazantzakis's (1960) novel retold the familiar stories of Jesus in a 20th-century existentialist framework. The Jesus in *The Last Temptation of Christ* continually encounters ordinary temptations to sin as he struggles against fear and doubt to understand his messi-anic identity. The "last temptation" is Satan's offer to Jesus, enacted in an hallucinatory scenario, to come down from the cross and live out his days as a comfortable family man. Jesus rejects this offer and, true to biblical narrative, fulfills his mission of dying for the sins of humanity. Probably the most notorious of the film's scenes were the initial ones in which Jesus showed the greatest resistance and doubt about God's expectations and those involving Jesus (played by Willem Dafoe) and Mary Magdalene (Barbara Hershey), that is, first, when Dafoe's Jesus visits the Magdalene's brothel and later in the last-temptation sequence after they have married when she and Jesus are briefly shown making love. Some philosophically more daring elements—the psychological perspective taken on Jesus, his willing collaboration with Judas, and the deconstructionist impulse suggested by the encounter with the apostle Paul (see Babington & Evans, 1994; Lefebvre, 1990)—however, did not attract much ire or even discussion.

Unquestionably, an aspect of *The Last Temptation of Christ* furor that distinguishes it from most other media panics is that its oppo-nents typically argued against the film's content without having seen it, even after they had the opportunity to do so. Such was the case in Lexington, Kentucky, in July 1988.[2] Several individuals formed an ad hoc committee to mobilize locally against the film, mostly through petition drives centered in church congregations, after a July 11 radio broadcast by Focus on the Family's James Dobson advised audiences about the film and told how they could take action against it (Bailey, 1988a, 1988b). The intent was to per-

suade Loews Theaters, which owned all of Lexington's screens at
the time, that there was sufficient opposition to warrant not showing
it. About a month later, having submitted a reported 20,000 signa-
tures, the committee's leader was able to announce Loews would
not show *The Last Temptation of Christ* in Lexington.

The *Lexington Herald-Leader*, the city's only daily newspaper, ran
several articles both before and after Loews's decision, treating
different aspects of the controversy. On August 15, the newspaper
printed an announcement soliciting viewer opinions. Just 2 days
later, six letters addressing the film appeared, initiating a stream of
letters printed almost daily for the next 7 weeks. A computer search
produced a total of 164 letters in 1988 mentioning *The Last Temptation
of Christ*. This is a very large number of letters to appear on one
subject; however, it is not surprising given the newspaper's call for
letters, the charged atmosphere engendered by the national media,
and the fact that "hot" issues involving morality tend to elicit the
greatest volume of letters.

Following the idea that audience dynamics can be reconstructed
historically (Jensen, 1993), several attributes of letters to the editor
make them useful for analyzing communitywide rhetoric. Letters as
a communicative forum are accessible to all, prominently displayed,
and widely read—the only such arena available to the entire community. Writers may address virtually any subject as long as it is
judged to hold some current interest; their letters are published
quickly, resulting in a discourse that is chronological, correlatable to
benchmark events, and capable of being assessed for issue salience
in the community. By intending to speak to the community-at-large,
writers invoke their conceptions of whatever they believe to be vital
to its identity, ideals, morality, good functioning, or even amusement. Because those who are highly interested in the subject self-
select into the discourse, with no material incentive for their participation, the letters are also valuable as an unobtrusive qualitative
measure.

Yet letters present certain difficulties as data. They cannot be said
to represent the entire population's awareness of or evaluative
orientation toward an issue. Many letters, for example, are not published.[3] Some writers are regular contributors, acting out of idiosyn-
cratic motives; however, this bias is mitigated somewhat by the

policy of the *Lexington Herald-Leader* that limits writers to one contribution per month. Also, editing performed for aspects such as length and grammatical expression leaves unresolved the question of how closely the letter-as-published resembles the letter-as-sent.

These difficulties notwithstanding, letters to the editor represent a slow-motion unfolding of cognitions and feelings concerning a contested issue. Hypothetically, community members who read and interpret the daily wave of letters construct memories of the public's disposition that are obviously distinct individually but that also represent to some degree a collective reference. A subset of these readers then chooses to write, submit, and have on display their own contribution to this forum, subject to the newspaper's willingness to extend the "conversation." The few external constraints on this process enable writers to express themselves in a disarmingly direct manner; confidence in the letters' capacity to map the contours of community argumentation probably increases when the volume of letters is high, as with *The Last Temptation of Christ*. What results, then, is a record of self-crafted reader statements that is not only chronological and cumulative but also dynamic and dialogic.

ANALYSIS: HOW TO READ
THE LAST TEMPTATION OF CHRIST

Because the issue of whether the film would be, or should be, shown was the principal "peg" in local media stories and was arguably the controversy's determinant question, the 164 letters were evaluated for evidence of their support for or opposition to *The Last Temptation of Christ* being seen either locally or anywhere at all. In all, 42 letters explicitly favored the film not being exhibited, and 19 letters implicitly favored this position, resulting in 61 letters in a group I will call Con-LTC. On the side of wanting the film shown, 13 letters explicitly took this position, whereas another 48 letters implicitly supported it, yielding 61 letters in a group I will call Pro-LTC. The remaining 42 letters did not reveal any apparent position on showing the film.

What is striking about this pattern—other than the equal numbers of letters supporting and opposing (presumably not by design of the editorial page staff)—is the large number of Con-LTC writers explicitly favoring the film not being shown relative to the low number of explicitly Pro-LTC writers. As the next section illustrates, this result probably stems from a deep sense of affront among Con-LTC writers that was not found to the same degree among Pro-LTC writers. To some extent, it can be seen as a rhetorical extension of the petition action (in which many claimed to have participated), which asked signers to "Just Say No."

The mean lengths of letters, compared across subgroups, also displayed differences:

Explicit Con-LTC:	3.63 cm
Implicit Con-LTC:	5.32 cm
Explicit Pro-LTC:	5.65 cm
Implicit Pro-LTC:	6.17 cm
No position:	4.83 cm

Explicit Con-LTC writers expressed their stance economically, sometimes accompanied by a biblical passage or a reference to something repugnant in the film. They seldom developed extended arguments for their position. Combining explicit and implicit letters, the mean length of Con-LTC letters was 4.16 cm compared to 6.06 cm for Pro-LTC letters.

Reading the (Absent) Film: Against

The two most consistently appearing Con-LTC themes during the period of this study were those of *blasphemy* and *denigration of Jesus*. Blasphemy, Lawton (1993) writes, "stands for whatever a society most abhors and has the power to prosecute. It is a form of religious vituperation against those who have transgressed the timeless truths that a society cherishes" (p. 3). Contrasted with heresy, which is a violation of proper doctrine, blasphemy is a violation of proper speech or the proper way to symbolize. It is wrong because it has been *said wrong*. Declarations of blasphemy not only single out a text or utterance for blame, they identify for a community the things that should be regarded as impure and therefore not admitted.

The Con-LTC letters charging blasphemy were among the shortest, often bluntly naming the offense and stating the writer's wish that the film not be shown. Many, like this writer, gave a biblical warrant for considering the film to be blasphemous: "I think anything that shows Christ as a sinner is blasphemy. As any Christian knows, Christ was without sin. The Bible specifically states that to think it is to commit it." Others included supporters in the offense: "This film says, in essence, that Jesus did sin. . . . [But] Jesus' deity (Jesus is God) is . . . absolute. . . . This movie is directly attacking Christ and Christianity. Anybody who would support this film is blaspheming God."

Because firsthand encounters with *The Last Temptation of Christ* were not possible in Lexington except through brief footage on television newscasts, its blasphemous character had to be learned from other sources. In fact, many writers implicitly credited local pastoral leadership with the authority to make the correct diagnosis. For these writers, it was not necessary, or even right, for them to make their own personal evaluation. One wrote "I agree with the religious leaders who are opposing *The Last Temptation of Christ* that this film should not be shown here." Another expressed that idea by comparing the film to exposure to the AIDS virus before asking, "In like fashion, isn't it reasonable to heed advice given us by mental and moral experts?"

If blasphemy is the naming of moral pollution in biblical terms, some writers used a language of effluence to express the problem in more direct, vivid terms. Descriptions such as "trash," "sewage," "garbage," "filth," "slimy," "rot," and "dirt" conveyed the film as a waste product issuing from Hollywood. *The Last Temptation of Christ* was cast as an exploitative tool, putting it in league, as one writer put it, with "pornography, homosexuality, lesbianism, nudity (nudist camps), X-rated movies, burlesque shows, kiddy porn." Another stated that the film's callous use of Jesus Christ "placed [MCA-Universal] on the same level as the tabloids at the checkout counter, where a famous name is used to entice people to read their garbage." These terms of effluence had the effect of a blanket condemnation. Like blasphemy, they divided the world in binary fashion into the pure and impure. Blasphemy, then, was a common way for opponents to name the crime and indict its makers. For these writers, *The Last Temptation of Christ* represented a violation of the most basic kind for which there could be no ambiguity or debate. By its nature, blasphemy is an absolute judgment. It demands the absolute remedy of expulsion.

Others, however, saw the film as slander, "a smear on the impeccable name of Jesus Christ." Denigrations of the person of Jesus are related to blasphemy, but they were usually articulated with more specificity and formed a variety of interpretations. Many Con-LTC writers were disturbed that the film had illegitimately depicted Jesus as being engaged in sexual temptations or sexual activity. A writer claimed that "it's . . . very doubtful that Jesus was indulging in sexual fantasies while hanging on the cross. . . . His focus was totally other-centered." She then cited gospel passages to demonstrate that in the penultimate event of his life, Jesus was thinking entirely of his mission. Others used words such as "fornicator," "womanizer," "tramp," and "oversexed" to describe the sordid manner in which the film had described their Savior. Yet most Con-LTC references to a sexually tempted Jesus in *The Last Temptation of Christ* operated through the words "sin," "sinner," and "sinful" to cover nearly any human foible but most particularly to the carnal desires that the film allegedly showed Jesus having.

The notion that Jesus could be shown as doubting his divinity or being troubled by it also disturbed Con-LTC writers. Some interpreted this as Christ's mental instability or insanity, a characterization protest leaders often made in statements to the media. But the issue of Dafoe-as-Jesus's "weakness" or wavering resolve did not come up as often in letters as the media coverage would suggest. The question of how the film treated Christ's personality and his relation to God was more often embedded in the broader issue of historical accuracy. To Con-LTC writers, the way *The Last Temptation of Christ* took liberties with the founding texts of Christianity—by inventing scenes or revising events, characters, and relationships— was inexcusable or confused at best.

For most of these people, as with Fundamentalists generally (Ammerman, 1987), the Bible should be read literally as the word of God and nearly all events in the world and their own personal lives can be interpreted directly through its teachings and with unfailing insight. Typical of writers who considered the Bible to be the benchmark of historical accuracy was one who wrote, "The true historical evidence of Jesus as the son of God is found in the Bible—from beginning to end. The credibility of the Scriptures is higher than any other known book."

The Bible's authority might be taken for granted by Con-LTC writers, but it still needed to be pointed out to the *Lexington Herald-Leader* readers. Chapter and verse citations, scriptural quotes, and paraphrased teachings were used by several writers to inform readers' understandings of the film. For example, one wrote the following:

> [The film] is a typical example of blasphemy as definitively illustrated in the Holy Scriptures. When Satan is given credit for holiness from God or when God is blamed for something unholy that is from Satan, the act is blasphemous.

Thus, the writer calls the Bible's concept of blasphemy "definitive" and goes on to provide it in the technically correct terms. No mention is made of offending scenes in the film, but it is clear to this writer that its content is typically blasphemous. The Bible also gave this writer the authority to perceive *The Last Temptation of Christ* as a site of confrontation between God and Satan. Such references to the film as the workings of Satan or the devil or as a portent of the anti-Christ were common.

In some of the lengthier letters, the issue of accuracy centered on why the figure of Christ needed to be revised fictionally at all when a perfect version of his life already existed, one that held so much significance for so many. To refute the suggestion that filmgoers should recognize the last-temptation sequence as a fictional "dream" that could not threaten anyone's faith, some writers made up their own scenarios. Drawing a parallel to *The Wizard of Oz*, one writer, for example, asked readers whether they thought that Dorothy's experiences in Oz were any less real because they occurred while she was unconscious, after the Kansas tornado hit.

Others developed similar, but less elaborate, parallels between the offense of *The Last Temptation of Christ* to Christians and the hypothetical outrage by other constituencies (presumed to be more sought after by Hollywood than Christians, generically defined) that would follow if films were released that disparaged figures such as Martin Luther King, Mohammed, Gandhi, or "a leader of the feminist movement." The underlying logic of such complaints is expressed by this writer: "There is no place for a 'biography' which contains little or no factual information. . . . If that be the case, why not use a fictional name?"

Every fictional film is "inaccurate," of course, but no source is believed as profoundly by as many people as the Bible. Therefore, one of the predominant responses of the protest sympathizers to Pro-LTC writers was to remind them of the need to submit to God. Although one writer expressed sympathy for them, because they were "living in a darkness," more typically Con-LTC writers warned them about spiritual danger or instructed them in how to achieve a right interpretation: "Those who saw *The Last Temptation of Christ* are giving over to the flesh. Therefore, they cannot please Christ. One must learn to keep the flesh under subjection."

But by far the most frequent and forcefully stated response of the Con-LTC writers to the other side was to assert their right to take legal action against a wrongful moral offense and to challenge the supporters of the film to do the same. These answering letters only began to appear in mid-September after approximately 85 letters had been published, many of them Pro-LTC writers who criticized the petition drive and its outcome. There was a strong sense of satisfaction among the Con-LTC writers at having mobilized a communitywide consciousness, no matter how temporarily, to affect a decision by a media corporation. A representative letter states, "We're elated to see Christians . . . band together to put a stop to the showing of *The Last Temptation of Christ*. If those who have a different view want the movie shown, they should fight for it."

Some writers, though, showed an awareness of the marginal nature of the victory in the face of a commercial cultural tide that usually runs indomitably against their interests. One letter expressed frustration with "the self-righteous humanists who insist that the world be run their way," and another compared the other side to the losing opponents in an election: "The funniest letters are the ones that assign the censor label to the 20,000 persons who expressed their opinion to Loews' management. . . . The people who don't vote are the people who complain the most about the election results." One woman, however, warned against "the venom and hatred spewed by both sides of *The Last Temptation of Christ* controversy. We just have no toleration for others, much less love." At the time of her letter, the 137th of the eventual 164, it was apparent from the increasingly reactive character of the debate that the Con-LTC writers' earlier task of "witnessing" the offense of the film had been a much more vibrant, heroic, and cohesively performed rhetoric than this desultory endgame of answering to charges of censorship from persons who seemed not to understand at all why they acted as they did.

Reading the (Absent) Film: Supporting It

Whereas the Con-LTC writers freely discussed what they knew to be in the film, despite not having seen it, there was much less discussion of the film among the Pro-LTC writers, particularly during the first month in which letters appeared. Instead, Pro-LTC writers were preoccupied with issues having to do with the protest and the nonrelease of the film and their implications for freedom of speech, freedom of access to media content, the economic and political power of conservative Christians, and the community as a whole. Most tellingly, Pro-LTC writers stridently criticized the anti-*The Last Temptation of Christ* people for attacking a film they had not seen and about which they often had erroneous information. Thus, they tended not to defend the film so much as the community's right to see it.

What Pro-LTC writers did have to say about the film, though, was revealing in its contrast with the Con-LTC interpretations. One argument that was made in varying ways was that of *framing the film for what it is—just a movie.* The intent of this line of argument was to let the air out of the debate and to deflect it away from doctrinal fidelity and toward what the writers considered to be the real issues at stake. Two coauthors, seeing a threat to the Constitutional guarantee of free speech, addressed those supporting the economic pressure on Loews: "It's a movie. It's not life. It's not real. It has no value-threatening impact on religion. Movies are entertainment, plain and simple, and should always be viewed as such. No more, no less." Another hinted at an element of arbitrariness, or double standard, in the target of the protest: "Perhaps [the opponents] need to be reminded: It is just a movie, a form of entertainment. *The Exorcist* and *The Omen*, both movies with religious connotations, didn't receive the condemnation that this movie is receiving."

One woman—who expressed no position on the film being shown but nevertheless criticized the Fundamentalists' actions—called on readers to take seriously MCA-Universal's disclaimer about the film not being based on the Gospels at face value: "The film, a collection of surrealistic fantasies, has been consistently billed as exactly that— not an interpretation of the Gospel nor an attack on the traditional teachings of Judeo-Christianity." For this writer and for other Pro-LTCs, the Con-LTCs blind refusal of *The Last Temptation of Christ* was a clear sign that they could not stand intelligent, empathic engagement with their own religion. These Pro-LTC writers, therefore, insisted on accepting the film's fictional framing of Jesus as not only appropriate but as the only correct way for all people to approach it. First and foremost, *The Last Temptation of Christ* has a fictional job to do; any discussion of its artistic or theological merits comes only after accepting that point. Another group of writers also argued for reducing the importance of the controversy by comparing it to the more urgent problems in the community, such as the homeless and AIDS. For them, *any* movie is *only* a movie.

A second strand of interpretation among the Pro-LTC writers gave primacy to *the artist and issues of the film's artistic or representational competence.* One writer stated the case this way: "To attempt to ban *The Last Temptation of Christ* is an attempt to censor a film that should be allowed to rise or fall on its own intrinsic merits." Several writers argued for the special value of creativity, which should be provided a wide berth in society, particularly when exercised by a "serious" film director. (It is likely that this argument would not have been as prominent if *The Last Temptation of Christ* had not been directed by an auteur such as Scorsese or if its cinematography and production design had been more conventional.) For these following two writers, the protest to prevent the film's exhibition denies a part of humanity that is actually part of God's work:

People are wrong to deny an author and a director the sanctity of creativity. Christians especially must affirm human creativity as a sign of our origin in the creativity of God. . . . We must [also] ask: Are the intent and its manner of expression true and worthy of their subject, creators, and audience?

Art has . . . struggled with incarnation. . . . In Renaissance art, when Jesus' flesh was reaffirmed, he is portrayed without clothing and with his genitalia displayed. All of this to strengthen and . . . to remind the faithful that Christ understands because he became one of us.

According to these Pro-LTC writers, any move to stifle artists when they engage spiritual subjects diminishes everyone, especially those who are believers. Several others recalled the cruel history of war, hatred, persecution, and political repression that had been carried out in the name of Christianity. The enforcement of only one version of Christ and God, they implied, leads to such disasters. It is but a short distance from there to the view that the more interpretations of Jesus conceived and discussed by unfettered individuals the better. Such a view endorses the historical contingency in notions of "accuracy" and values the process of generating heterodox interpretations. One writer articulated this stance in relation to *The Last Temptation of Christ:*

There are a myriad of questions concerning the validity of the Bible. The majority . . . of us view the Gospels with varying degrees of belief; and we exercise our freedom to argue interpretations. Scorsese's film is a sincere and artistic endeavor based on his personal vision of faith. No one person, regardless of education or conviction, is more privy than the next to judge the accuracy of *The Last Temptation of Christ.*

Only one writer made a claim for a convergence between the historical authenticity of the gospel accounts and the Kazantzakis/Scorsese version. There was a broad current of opinion among the Pro-LTC writers, and many of the No Position writers, however, that no matter how dubious its theology, *The Last Temptation of Christ* was both a legitimate cultural product and a text that might generate a worthwhile reexamination of religious precepts for those willing to take the risk.

Four writers did report having encountered *The Last Temptation of Christ*—two as readers of the Kazantzakis (1960) novel (their letters published early, in mid-August) and the other two as viewers of the Scorsese production in another city (these published relatively late, in the third week of September). All four described their experiences with the elusive, torturously analyzed film, in letters having the quality of war dispatches to the domestic front. All four complimented the work's artistry and power. But more important, they reported reading or viewing a narrative that they believed was very compatible with the essential message of Christ. Each writer led the reader from a brief story of his or her experience with the text to a "lesson" the experience should hold for the protesters of the film. The first is from a reader of the Kazantzakis novel; the second saw the film.

> I find it ironic that it is the fundamentalists who are so upset that Christ may have been tempted to change his destiny. I would expect that they, of all people, would understand how men who are completely human could be tempted to forgo their perceived destiny in exchange for earthly pleasure.

> That scene [the last temptation] was wonderfully rich in theological meaning. But the protesters know nothing of that. Nor do they seem to know of the quotation from the novel's author that precedes the film, explaining that his fiction was an attempt . . . to come to terms with the divine and the human within himself. . . . It is true that if the protesters saw the film, they wouldn't find there the Jesus they have taught themselves to believe in; but they would find out a lot about themselves.

According to these excerpts, the protesters are wrong for not wanting to embrace "his humanness," a "wonderfully rich" scene, or a search to "find out a lot about themselves." But these lessons may be exactly what Con-LTCs would reject without hesitation. Unwavering belief, not struggle, and fidelity in truth, not temptation, are choices the Fundamentalist has already made. They are unlikely to revisit those choices, particularly on advice from someone who has seen *The Last Temptation of Christ*.

CONCLUSION

The Last Temptation of Christ provoked debate, even in its absence, not just because it bent some genre expectations rather rudely. Like Rushdie's (1988) *The Satanic Verses* and Andres Serrano's photograph *Piss Christ, The Last Temptation of Christ* upset some of the most fundamental social rules there are: the unwritten ones that regulate the image of a god and mark one group's truth from the brush of another's imagination.

For the opponents of *The Last Temptation of Christ*, the meaning of the film was in its effect, a dangerous intervention in a world alive with eternal and transcendent forces of love, judgment, and evil. For those who wrote against the film, there can be only one meaning for everything. This meaning is recognized and acted on in its relation to the codes given in their Scriptures and the community of believers who make those codes literal in their lives. To be faced with a text that goes against their codes is to dislocate the community and arouse its passion.

The film's supporters saw *The Last Temptation of Christ* as one possible version of truth. For them, everything has different codes and multiple meanings that travel historically and situationally through many communities of interest. No effect of a film can last for long, because its meaning mutates rapidly as the object is taken up in discourse. To be an audience member in this world is to be able to entertain choices of what is true. It is to always be discerning the conditions in which something can be true. To be faced with a loss of choices is to dislocate this community, arousing its passion. *The Last Temptation of Christ*, then, was a site of dislocation for both.

NOTES

1. A detailed version of the prerelease campaign against MCA-Universal, written from the perspective of two of its major participants, can be found in Poland (1988).

2. Located in the bluegrass region, Lexington is a city of about 220,000 with an economy based in light industry, auto manufacturing, regional distribution, and higher education. Its culture can be described as New-South conservative, albeit with progressive interests and diverse lifestyles. The county has traditionally voted more Republican than the rest of the state. The leading denomination is Southern Baptist

(26% of total adherents), followed by Catholic (18%), Methodist (12%), Church of Christ (11%), Black Baptist (9%), and Disciples of Christ (6%). During the last two decades, Lexington's evangelical Christian and fundamentalist congregations have grown most rapidly, primarily at the expense of mainline Protestant churches.

3. The paper does not publish letters if they (a) are written to a third party, (b) address another letter writer personally, (c) give one side of a private dispute, (d) quote extensively from other sources, (e) are merely thank-you letters, (f) are vehicles for self-promotion by an organization, (g) are in poor taste or potentially libelous, and (h) are likely to be unclear to many readers.

REFERENCES

Ammerman, N. T. (1987). *Bible believers: Fundamentalists in the modern world.* New Brunswick, NJ: Rutgers University Press.

Ammerman, N. T. (1991). North American Protestant Fundamentalism. In M. E. Marty & R. S. Appleby (Eds.), *Fundamentalisms observed* (pp. 1-65). Chicago: University of Chicago Press.

Ang, I. (1991). *Desperately seeking the audience.* London: Routledge.

Babington, B., & Evans, P. W. (1994). *Biblical epics: Sacred narratives in the cinema.* Manchester, UK: Manchester University Press.

Bailey, R. (1988a, July 23). Film about Jesus sparks local outrage. *Lexington Herald-Leader,* p. B2.

Bailey, R. (1988b, August 12). Protests block film: *Last Temptation of Christ* not coming to Lexington. *Lexington Herald-Leader,* p. A1.

Dubin, S. C. (1992). *Arresting images: Impolitic art and uncivil actions.* London: Routledge.

Griswold, W. (1994). *Cultures and societies in a changing world.* Thousand Oaks, CA: Pine Forge.

Harvey, D. (1989). *The condition of postmodernity.* Cambridge, MA: Blackwell.

Herbst, S. (1994). *Politics at the margin.* Cambridge, MA: Cambridge University Press.

Hoover, S. (1990). The meaning of religious television: The *700 Club* in the lives of its viewers. In Q. J. Schultze (Ed.), *American Evangelicals and the mass media: Perspectives on the relationship between American Evangelicals and the mass media* (pp. 231-249). Grand Rapids, MI: Academie.

Hunter, J. D. (1991). *Culture wars.* New York: Basic Books.

Jensen, J. (1990). *Redeeming modernity.* Newbury Park, CA: Sage.

Jensen, K. B. (1991). When is meaning? Communication theory, pragmatism, and mass media reception. In J. A. Anderson (Ed.), *Communication yearbook 14* (pp. 3-32). Newbury Park, CA: Sage.

Jensen, K. B. (1993). The past in the future: Problems and potentials of historical reception studies. *Journal of Communication, 43,* 20-28.

Kazantzakis, N. (1960). *The last temptation of Christ.* New York: Simon & Schuster.

Lawton, D. (1993). *Blasphemy.* Philadelphia: University of Pennsylvania Press.

Lefebvre, M. (1990). The Scriptures through postmodern strategies: Challenging history. *Canadian Journal of Political and Social Theory, 14,* 219-229.

Lindlof, T. R. (1988). Media audiences as interpretive communities. In J. A. Anderson (Ed.), *Communication yearbook 11* (pp. 81-107). Newbury Park, CA: Sage.

Lindlof, T. R., Coyle, K., & Grodin, D. (in press). Is there a text in this audience? Science fiction and interpretive schism. In C. Harris & A. Alexander (Eds.), *Theorizing fandom: Fans, subcultures, and identity*. Creskill, NJ: Hampton.

McGee, M. C. (1984). Secular humanism: A radical reading of "culture industry" productions. *Critical Studies in Mass Communication, 1,* 1-33.

McQuail, D. (1994). *Mass communication theory* (3rd ed.). Thousand Oaks, CA: Sage.

Medved, M. (1992). *Hollywood vs. America: Popular culture and the war on traditional values.* New York: HarperCollins.

Morley, D. (1992). Electronic communities and domestic rituals: Cultural consumption and the production of European cultural identities. In M. Skovmand & K. C. Schroder (Eds.), *Media cultures: Reappraising transnational media* (pp. 65-83). London: Routledge.

Poland, L. (1988). *The last temptation of Hollywood.* Highland, CA: Mastermedia.

Rorty, R. (1989). *Contingency, irony, and solidarity.* Cambridge, MA: Cambridge University Press.

Rushdie, S. (1988). *The satanic verses.* New York: Viking.

Schaefer, R. J., & Avery, R. K. (1993). Audience conceptualizations of *Late night with David Letterman. Journal of Broadcasting and Electronic Media, 37,* 253-274.

Schroder, K. C. (1994). Audience semiotics, interpretive communities and the "ethnographic turn" in media research. *Media, Culture, & Society, 16,* 337-347.

Steiner, L. (1988). Oppositional decoding as an act of resistance. *Critical Studies in Mass Communication, 5,* 1-15.

Taylor, C. (1977). Interpretation and the science of man. In F. R. Dallmayr & T. A. McCarthy (Eds.), *Understanding and social inquiry* (pp. 101-131). Notre Dame, IN: University of Notre Dame Press.

Williams, R. (1983). *Keywords* (rev. ed.). New York: Oxford University Press.

PART IV

Case Studies

The chapters in Part III provided evidence that religious beliefs have behavioral consequences. But in many cases, the very weakness of the evidence points toward what is, perhaps, the only firm conclusion from more than 50 years of communication research: Messages have effects, but they are not a magic bullet always producing uniform effects on everyone, everywhere.

A more complete understanding of the relationship between religion and mass media use requires a conceptual shift in thinking about religion and religiosity. Emphasis on the substantive nature of religion—religion as a set of church teachings—underemphasizes both its private and public aspects. As White (1970) points out, the model positing a direct link between beliefs and behavior is at heart a psychological one carrying with it the implicit assumption that people seek cognitive consistency between church teachings and their own understanding and behaviors. Although such a model focuses on individuals, it tends to ignore potentially important individual differences in cognitive ability and emotional needs. At the cognitive level, people vary in their ability to understand and apply church teachings. At the emotional level, people may join the same church seeking to fulfill quite different needs. They may also express their religiosity in a variety of ways.

In his pioneering research, Lenski (1961) discovered that indexes of religious involvement—communalism and associationalism—can be much better predictors of the influence of "the religion factor" than measures for beliefs such as "Christian orthodoxy" or religious affiliation. That finding points to the public dimension of religion. Religion may be a private affair, but religion of the type examined in this book is also a group phenomenon.

All groups, including religious ones, have their own normative structure and their own mechanisms for enforcing sanctions on group members who deviate from those norms. Those norms and sanctions are created and enforced by members as they interact with one another. As Marty (1976) points out, people who choose to join or remain members of a religion are often seeking both personal identity and a sense of purpose and commitment. In joining, people may tacitly place themselves under group authority, but in a society in which religious freedom is guaranteed, they are free to decide for themselves their level of commitment to the group.

They also are free to choose their group. It may be true that the existence of varying religious traditions represents a kind of tribalization within U.S. society (Marty, 1976), but tribes often are made up of clans, each with its own distinctive identity. If the tradition or denomination is taken as the religious equivalent of a tribe and congregations are considered clans, one can often find differences among those clans that belong to the same religious tribe that are as great or even greater than those between clans belonging to different tribes.

A more thorough understanding of individual differences and of group influences requires using methods other than surveys of large and diverse populations. Such surveys are an excellent methodology for producing large quantities of reliable, generalizable data. But the analysis of data from that kind of survey requires treating as equivalent both individuals and groups who are not truly equivalent. Therefore, the chapters in Part IV adopt a case study approach. That is, instead of making comparisons across religious traditions, each chapter provides a closer look at responses to the media by members of one particular religion.

In Chapter 12, Sam G. McFarland presents evidence from experimental research to demonstrate the utility of religious orientations in explaining within-group differences in media use. His finding—that among Fundamentalists those who scored high on measures of "religion-as-quest" were more willing than those with low quest orientations to read antifundamentalist articles as well as articles supporting their religious beliefs—provides one explanation for within-group differences in levels of use and in attention to content deemed unsuitable by church leaders.

Chapter 13 is an examination of differences in media use among women who are religiously devout. The divergence in institutional definitions and counsel versus individual interaction with mass media is explored. JoAnn Myer Valenti and Daniel A. Stout suggest that mass media not only allow for but provoke diversity and argue against communication to perceived cultural or segmented audience stereotypes. Effective communication, according to the authors, requires recognition of diversity even within groups identified by common gender, shared religious beliefs, and other traditionally measured demographics.

Next, Judith M. Buddenbaum's study of media use by members of a Quaker meeting presented in Chapter 14 illustrates how group norms may simultaneously encourage a quest orientation and provide protection for core group values. This is a sharp contrast to research cast within the secularization framework that portrays openness to multiple viewpoints as evidence of secularization.

Unlike the Quakers who actively encourage media use, Mennonites have learned to adapt to it. As Sharon Hartin Iorio explains in Chapter 15, Mennonites in northwest Oklahoma, like the Quakers in Middletown, have developed strategies for maintaining group identity both in the face of and through strategic use of mass media.

Cheryl Renée Gooch examines in Chapter 16 the views of black church leaders regarding the use of "gospel rap." This new form of religious music has captured the ears of young African Americans who are embracing the messages of rap for social identity. Gooch uncovers the complexity of issues leading some church leaders to embrace the musical form and others to reject it. Similar issues are addressed in Chapter 17, in which Daniel A. Stout, David W. Scott, and Dennis G. Martin describe two divergent "interpretive communities" among members of the Mormon Church. This research points out that religiosity is a complex phenomenon relative to mass media, as members of both groups set boundaries by drawing on multiple dimensions of their faith to decide whether or not to expose themselves to media messages criticized by their church.

REFERENCES

Lenski, G. (1961). *The religious factor.* Garden City, NY: Doubleday.
Marty, M. E. (1976). *A nation of behavers.* Chicago: University of Chicago Press.
White, R. H. (1970). Toward a theory of religious influence. In P. E. Hammond & B. Johnson (Eds.), *American mosaic: Social patterns of religion in the United States* (pp. 14-23). New York: Random House.

12

Keeping the Faith

The Roles of Selective Exposure and Avoidance in Maintaining Religious Beliefs

SAM G. McFARLAND

Psychologists of religion have given remarkably little attention to the psychological processes used by believers to maintain their faith. Because challenges to any faith are readily available—sometimes almost unavoidable—in the modern world, one may marvel that so many believers are unaffected. Somehow, many seem able to not attend to these challenges or to dismiss them easily. In either case, the near immunity of religious belief from doubt in our secularized, scientific, and pluralistic world is a psychological puzzle.

Two processes by which some believers apparently maintain their faith are (a) selectively attending to sources such as religious television, books, magazines, and music, which bolster their religious beliefs, and (b) selectively avoiding sources such as the secular mass media, which might challenge their faith. Although many theorists have regarded selective exposure and avoidance as two facets of a single process and have used a forced-choice paradigm in experimental studies, the two processes are logically distinct, and recent research indicates that they are influenced in part by different motivations.

Although a few studies reporting religious differences in levels of mass media use (Rigney & Hoffman, 1993) and in content preference (Buddenbaum, 1982; Hamilton & Rubin, 1992; Roberts, 1983) suggest conservative Protestants selectively avoid some sources and content while selecting others, most research has been conducted on how viewers' religious beliefs influence their selection of religious television programming.

Those studies indicate that Protestants with conservative religious and sociopolitical attitudes are more frequent viewers than others of religious television programs that advocate these attitudes (Gaddy & Pritchard, 1985; Tamney & Johnson, 1984). Religious television viewing is related to demographic characteristics that are correlated with religious faith—older age, female, and lower education (cf. Gaddy, 1984). Protestants watch Protestant shows (Buddenbaum, 1981), and older Catholics and those more involved in parish life are more likely to watch Catholic religious television (as opposed to Protestant programming or none) than are younger and less involved Catholics (Welch, Johnson, & Pilgrim, 1990).

The roles of selective exposure and avoidance in maintaining cherished beliefs were central to Leon Festinger's (1957, 1964) theory of cognitive dissonance. According to dissonance theory, all people have a strong need to maintain consistency among their beliefs, values, and behaviors. Inconsistencies generate an emotional distress called dissonance, which results in a drive to restore consistency. The more important beliefs and behaviors are to an individual, and the stronger commitment to them, the greater the dissonance created by inconsistent information and the stronger the drive to restore consistency. When the commitment to a set of beliefs is strong, public, and felt to be unchangeable, the likelihood increases that, rather than seeking information with an open mind, a believer will hunt for belief-supportive information because that information will decrease dissonance (selective exposure) and will try to avoid information that contradicts the beliefs because the information increases dissonance (selective avoidance). Because a person's religious faith is often the most treasured of beliefs, dissonance theory strongly suggests that selective exposure and avoidance will be used by believers to maintain their faith.

Early experimental research—all outside the domain of religion—supported the proposition that individuals often seek belief-supportive information (Brehm & Cohen, 1962) but not that they avoid dissonant information or that they generally prefer supportive over dissonant information when given a choice (Freedman & Sears, 1965). Due to these early failures, experimental research by psychologists on selective exposure and avoidance diminished greatly. Almost no effort was made to examine selective exposure and avoidance regarding religious beliefs.

The failure of the early research was due in large part to several methodological problems. First, most studies used issues that were probably not very important to participants: judgment of guilt in a mock trial, evaluation of the suitability for employment of an unknown fellow student, selecting one of two students as a partner in an experiment, and the like. Second, even when clearly important issues (such as cigarette smoking and cancer) were used, the early research failed to consider factors that might obscure selective exposure and avoidance.

Later research indicates that an individual is likely to seek belief-supportive information and to avoid nonsupportive information when the beliefs are freely chosen and felt to be unchangeable and when the individual is deeply committed to them. An individual may seek nonsupportive information, however, when the individual believes that information will be useful or can be easily refuted or when the individual feels obligated to be fair to both sides (Perloff, 1993). Also, selective exposure and avoidance appear linked to personality traits such as dogmatism (Clark & James, 1967; Innes, 1978; Kleck & Wheaton, 1967), repression on the repression-sensitization dimension (Olson & Zanna, 1979), and manifest anxiety (Frey, Stahlbert, & Fries, 1986).

Zillmann and Bryant (1985) have proposed that selective exposure and avoidance can be reduced to the simple hedonistic principle that "individuals are motivated to terminate noxious, aversive stimulation . . . and to perpetuate and increase the intensity of gratifying, pleasurable experiential states" (p. 158). To Zillmann and

Bryant, understimulation as well as overstimulation may be noxious. Following this logic, people may seek nonsupportive but easily refuted information because that information is experienced as gratifying rather than noxious. Furthermore, it may be that individual differences in selective avoidance associated with dogmatism, repression, and manifest anxiety are all due to individual differences in thresholds of noxiousness.

Such a reductionism is plausible, although its validity cannot be established at this time. The studies cited earlier simply indicate that religious believers use selective exposure and/or selective avoidance, but they do not distinguish between the processes. Some research, however, does reveal such a distinction.

In two studies, Abelman (1987, 1988) identified three kinds of viewers of religious TV via canonical analysis of viewing patterns and motives of high consumers of religious television. Ritualized viewers use religious TV for diversionary, entertainment-related reasons. Instrumental viewers, apparently motivated by strong religious beliefs, positively seek the religious talk shows and Bible study programs that reinforce or elaborate on their faith. Finally, reactionary viewers are motivated largely by their aversion to secular television. A reactionary viewer is "generally dissatisfied with commercial television programming and usually avoids such fare. Seeking the spiritual guidance and moral support not typically found in secular programming, these viewers purposefully select religious television as an alternative" (Abelman, 1987, p. 304).

Abelman's studies are noteworthy for their identification of types of viewers of religious television. In particular, the delineation of those who actively seek religious television from those who use religious television to avoid the unwanted influence of commercial programming parallels the distinction between selective exposure and selective avoidance suggested earlier.

Whereas Abelman's research is based on survey data, three experimental studies have examined selective exposure and avoidance of information relative to religious beliefs. Brock and Balloun (1967) asked college students to listen to six taped speeches, including one titled *Christianity Is Evil*. Students were told that the speeches were filled with static due to a poor recording device, but that they could temporarily eliminate the static by pressing and releasing a button on an electronic filter. When the button was pressed, the static discontinued for 3 seconds. The number of times the students pressed the button to hear the message clearly was the dependent variable. Because frequent churchgoers and those who prayed frequently consistently pressed the button much less often to hear *Christianity Is Evil* than those who infrequently attended church or prayed but did not differ in their button pressing for religiously neutral messages (e.g., smoking leads to lung cancer, no military draft for college graduates, etc.), the findings suggest frequent churchgoers and those who prayed often selectively avoided messages that opposed their religious beliefs. Their less religious counterparts did not appear to differentiate between the antireligious and religiously neutral messages.

Two experimental studies have examined the influence of different religious motivations or orientations on selective exposure and avoidance. Schoenrade (1987) asked 100 students from Christian backgrounds with at least a "moderate" interest in religion to choose one of two essays to read on life after death. The titles made it clear that one essay strongly supported belief in life after death (*A New Beginning: The Reason Death Does Not Hold Terror for Me*), whereas the other opposed that belief (*Belief in Afterlife Is a Denial of Death's Reality*). Comments, supposedly written by other students who had already read the essays, reinforced this distinction.

Overall, 70% of these religious students chose the proafterlife essay. The more strongly a student believed in life after death, the more likely he or she was to choose the essay supporting it, although the relationship was weak; scores on Batson and Ventis's (1982) "religion-as-ends" (an internal, intrinsic religious orientation toward Christian orthodoxy) measure correlated somewhat more strongly with preference for the proafterlife essay. Thus, it appears that having a religion-as-ends orientation either motivated these students to seek belief-supportive information, to avoid belief-discrepant information, or both. Schoenrade (1987), however, used a forced-choice paradigm. Therefore, one cannot tell whether the students' choices were based on selective exposure or avoidance.

More recently, Warren and I (McFarland & Warren, 1992) proposed that the intrinsic religious orientation, which is a central component of religion-as-ends and theoretically reflects a sincere

and selfless commitment to one's faith (Allport, 1966), should mo-
tivate individuals to want to read materials that support and elaborate on their faith. Because intrinsic religion does not directly reflect
the believer's open- or closed-mindedness and is not correlated with
dogmatism (Kahoe, 1974), it should not predict the avoidance of
belief-discrepant materials. Religion-as-quest, however, theoretically reflects three components of Allport's (1950) mature religion:
a willingness to ask existential questions without reducing their
complexity, a willingness to doubt, and an awareness that "the
mature religious orientation involves a continual search for more
light on religious questions" (Batson & Ventis, 1982, p. 149).

Although Schoenrade (1987) found no significant relationship
between religion-as-quest and essay preference, Warren and I hy-
pothesized that quest should be correlated with the desires to read
both information that supports one's faith and information that
contradicts one's beliefs because each of the components of quest
suggests that individuals high on religion-as-quest should display
"a willingness, if not an eagerness, to consider very broad evidence
and divergent points of view regarding one's own religious faith"
(McFarland & Warren, 1992, p. 165).

Testing our hypotheses required that we abandon the forced-
choice format used by Schoenrade (1987). From our perspective,
Schoenrade's finding that religion-as-quest was unrelated to essay
selection was likely due to the fact that those high on religion-as-
quest were motivated to read *both* articles rather than to select one
over the other.

For our study, adult religious Fundamentalists were asked to read
the titles and short abstracts of 24 articles as part of a field survey
"designed to select the kinds of articles which would interest Christian readers" (McFarland & Warren, 1992, p. 166), ostensibly for a
new journal to be titled *Christian Reflections*. The respondents rated
each article on a 7-point scale, from –3 ("definitely do not want to
read") to +3 ("definitely want to read"). Six of the articles supported
fundamentalist beliefs (on the biblical account of creation, the flood
of Noah, the accuracy of the Old Testament prophecies of Jesus, the
harmony of the four Gospels, divine guidance in the compiling of
the 66-book Bible, and the authority of the biblical moral commands
for the modern world); six other articles opposed these beliefs. The

12 remaining articles were on nonreligious issues of social interest, such as ecology and the war on drugs.

The sample, all Christian Fundamentalists, displayed a clear preference for the profundamentalist articles. The respondents averaged between +1 ("mildly want to read") and +2 ("want to read") for the fundamentalist articles but between 0 ("neutral") and −1 ("mildly do not want to read") for the antifundamentalist articles. As expected, the intrinsic religious orientation correlated significantly with the desire to read the profundamentalist articles ($r = .30$, $p < .001$) but was uncorrelated with wanting to read the antifundamentalist articles ($r = .02$, ns). The sample was divided at one standard deviation below the mean, the mean, and one standard deviation above the mean, creating four groups varying in intrinsicness. Consistently, the more intrinsic the group, the more they wanted to read the profundamentalist articles ($F (3, 101) = 3.96$, $p < .01$). The least intrinsic group averaged between "neutral" and "mildly want to read" these articles; the most intrinsic group averaged "want to read" them. These four groups did not differ in their desire to read the antifundamentalist articles, however.

Quest, measured by McFarland's (1989) revised scale, correlated with both the desires to read the profundamentalist articles ($r = .21$, $p < .05$) and the antifundamentalist ones ($r = .32$, $p < .001$). Batson and Schoenrade's (1992a, 1992b) revised quest scale yielded virtually identical results. When divided into four levels of quest (as with intrinsic religion, above), the greater a group's quest, the greater the group's desire to read the profundamentalist articles, and the more willing they were to read the antifundamentalist articles. Those lowest in quest averaged "mildly want to read" the profundamentalist articles but "do not want to read" for the antifundamentalist articles. In contrast, those highest in quest averaged "want to read" the profundamentalist articles and "neutral" for the antifundamentalist essays. From these data, it appears that high quest predicts a willingness, rather than an active desire, to read religious materials that contradict one's faith. Low quest, however, portends a clear desire to avoid these contradictory materials.

These few studies of selective exposure and avoidance regarding religious beliefs leave many unanswered questions. They do not show *why* religious individuals prefer belief-supportive over beliefcontradictive materials and choose not to listen clearly to anti-Christian messages or why the intrinsic and quest religious orientations influence selective exposure and avoidance as they do.

Do intrinsic religious believers seek belief-supportive arguments to strengthen their shaky faith, to gather material that might prove useful in discussions with others, to enlarge their own knowledge of their religion, or for still other reasons? Does the willingness of those high in quest to read belief-contradictory articles reflect a genuine openmindedness or perhaps simply a greater confidence that they can refute the information contained in these articles? And do these same relationships between the religious orientations and selective exposure and avoidance hold for nonfundamentalist believers as well?

The extrinsic, intrinsic, and (low) quest orientations seem very comparable to Abelman's (1987, 1988) ritualized, instrumental, and reactionary viewer types, but no study as yet has combined these categorizations. Nor have any studies used these orientations in an effort to explore religious differences in mass media use. The experimental exploration of selective exposure and avoidance regarding religious beliefs is just beginning. The topic clearly merits further investigation. The findings to date, however, suggest that the same psychological motivations that led some Fundamentalists to avoid belief-discrepant religious messages and others to express willingness to read both supportive and nonsupportive magazine articles may explain why some believers avoid the mass media, or at least certain media content, whereas other apparently equally devout Christians do not.

REFERENCES

Abelman, R. (1987). Religious television uses and gratifications. *Journal of Broadcasting and Electronic Media, 31,* 293-307.

Abelman, R. (1988). Motivations for viewing *The 700 Club. Journalism Quarterly, 65,* 112-118.

Allport, G. W. (1950). *The individual and his religion.* New York: Macmillan.

Allport, G. W. (1966). The religious context of prejudice. *Journal for the Scientific Study of Religion, 5,* 447-457.

Batson, C. D., & Schoenrade, P. A. (1992a). Measuring religion as quest: 1.) Validity concerns. *Journal for the Scientific Study of Religion, 30,* 416-429.

Batson, C. D., & Schoenrade, P. A. (1992b). Measuring religion as quest: 2.) Reliability concerns. *Journal for the Scientific Study of Religion, 30,* 430-447.

Batson, C. D., & Ventis, W. L. (1982). *The religious experience: A social-psychological analysis.* New York: Oxford University Press.

Brehm, J. W., & Cohen, A. R. (1962). *Explorations in cognitive dissonance.* New York: John Wiley.

Brock, T. C., & Balloun, J. L. (1967). Behavioral receptivity to dissonant information. *Journal of Personality and Social Psychology, 6,* 413-428.

Buddenbaum, J. M. (1981). Characteristics and media-related needs of the audience for religious TV. *Journalism Quarterly, 58,* 266-272.

Buddenbaum, J. M. (1982). News about religion: A readership study. *Newspaper Research Journal, 3,* 7-17.

Clark, P., & James, J. (1967). The effects of situation, attitude-intensity, and personality on information seeking. *Sociometry, 30,* 235-245.

Festinger, L. (1957). *A theory of cognitive dissonance.* Stanford, CA: Stanford University Press.

Festinger, L. (Ed.). (1964). *Conflict, decision, and dissonance.* Stanford, CA: Stanford University Press.

Freedman, J. L., & Sears, D. O. (1965). Selective exposure. In L. Berkowitz (Ed.), *Advances in experimental social psychology* (Vol. 2, pp. 57-97). New York: Academic Press.

Frey, D., Stahlbert, D., & Fries, A. (1986). Reactions of high and low anxiety subjects to positive and negative self-relevant feedback. *Journal of Personality, 54,* 694-703.

Gaddy, G. D. (1984). The power of religious media: Religious broadcast use and the role of religious organizations in public affairs. *Review of Religious Research, 25,* 289-301.

Gaddy, G. D., & Pritchard, D. (1985). When watching religious TV is like attending church. *Journal of Communication, 35,* 123-131.

Hamilton, N. F., & Rubin, A. M. (1992). The influence of religiosity on television viewing. *Journalism Quarterly, 69,* 667-678.

Innes, J. M. (1978). Selective exposure as a function of dogmatism and incentive. *Journal of Social Psychology, 106,* 261-265.

Kahoe, R. D. (1974). Personality and achievement correlates of intrinsic and extrinsic religious orientations. *Journal of Personality and Social Psychology, 29,* 812-818.

Kleck, R. E., & Wheaton, J. (1967). Dogmatism and responses to opinion-consistent and opinion-inconsistent information. *Journal of Personality and Social Psychology, 5,* 249-252.

McFarland, S. G. (1989). Religious orientations and the targets of discrimination. *Journal for the Scientific Study of Religion, 28,* 324-336.

McFarland, S. G., & Warren, J. C. (1992). Religious orientations and selective exposure among fundamentalist Christians. *Journal for the Scientific Study of Religion, 31,* 163-174.

Olson, J. M., & Zanna, M. P. (1979). A new look at selective exposure. *Journal of Experimental Social Psychology, 15,* 1-15.

Perloff, R. M. (1993). *The dynamics of persuasion.* Hillsdale, NJ: Lawrence Erlbaum.

Rigney, D., & Hoffman, T. J. (1993). Is American Catholicism anti-intellectual? *Journal for the Scientific Study of Religion, 32,* 211-222.

Roberts, C. L. (1983). Attitudes and media use of the moral majority. *Journal of Broadcasting, 27,* 403-410.

Schoenrade, P. (1987, October). *Belief in afterlife, religious orientation, and openness to belief challenge.* Paper presented at the annual convention of the Society for the Scientific Study of Religion, Louisville, KY.

Tamney, J. B., & Johnson, S. D. (1984). Religious television in Middletown. *Reviews of Religious Research, 25,* 303-313.

Welch, M. R., Johnson, C. L., & Pilgrim, D. (1990). Tuning in the Spirit: Exposure to types of religious TV programming among American Catholic parishioners. *Journal for the Scientific Study of Religion, 29,* 185-197.

Zillmann, D., & Bryant, J. (1985). Affect, mood, and emotion as determinants of selective exposure. In D. Zillmann & J. Bryant (Eds.), *Selective exposure to communication* (pp. 157-190). Hillsdale, NJ: Lawrence Erlbaum.

13

Diversity From Within

*An Analysis of the Impact of
Religious Culture on Media Use and
Effective Communication to Women*

JOANN MYER VALENTI
DANIEL A. STOUT

The role of media in the lives of members of mainstream religious denominations is a topic of growing interest among mass communication researchers. In the past decade, social scientists have investigated the phenomenon of televangelism (Peck, 1993; Schultze, 1990), analyzed religious television programming (Abelman & Hoover, 1990; Abelman & Neuendorf, 1985), and studied the relationship between news organizations and religious organizations in the United States (Buddenbaum, 1990; Dart & Allen, 1993). Much of this work, however, emphasizes the content dimension of mass communication processes relative to religious culture. Religion as a social phenomenon and the role the media play in various religious communities, however, cannot be easily assessed through descrip-

183

tions of media content alone. A social science examination begins from an audience perspective, recognizing the need for additional empirical investigations of how members of religious groups describe their own media-related behavior (Gaddy & Pritchard, 1985; Hamilton & Rubin, 1992; Roberts, 1983). This chapter addresses how members of a conservative subculture assess the role of the media when their religious institution articulates rules and guidelines for media use.

Drawing on ideas expressed in Peter Berger's work in the sociology of religion (Berger, 1967; Berger & Luckman, 1966), we explore the role of mass media at the level of the audience's religious life rather than at the institutional level of "public rhetoric" about media effects (see Berger, 1967, p. 134). By shifting the unit of analysis to audience members themselves, such study can more effectively address the question of how audience members make sense of mass media messages when organizations suggest a particular way of thinking about its effects on religious and cultural values.

To accomplish this objective, we examine media uses, attitudes, and behaviors of a sample of Mormon women. Mormon women are an appropriate audience for this research for two reasons. First, the Mormon Church advocates traditional roles for women and family (Campbell & Campbell, 1981; Gottlieb & Wiley, 1986; Wilcox, 1987) and has publicly stated that the media may undermine religious values. These official declarations about the media make the question of media use diversity among Mormons a compelling one. For example, appropriate television and movie viewing have been emphasized in the Mormon Church's biannual General Conference, which, in addition to holy Scripture, is considered to be an important guide for living (Ballard, 1989). In addition, Mormon women are instructed about the media in a special lesson titled "The Powerful Influence of the Media," which is contained in *Come Unto Me: Relief Society Personal Study Guide* and serves as the primary source of Sunday religious study for Mormon women (Church of Jesus Christ of Latter-day Saints, 1991), as well as through a number of articles in *Ensign*, the official monthly magazine of the church (see, e.g., "Making the Most of TV," 1990; Strong-Thacker, 1991).

A second reason why Mormon women may experience conflict associated with the media stems from an increasing diversity of lifestyles within a conservative religious culture. For example, Goodman and Heaton (1986) found that the number of Mormon women going into the workforce increased, despite encouragement by church leaders to stay in the home. As Hall (1990) suggests in *Women and Identity*, television and other media "communicate clearer messages of support" for contemporary women's values than ever before, and these values often conflict with traditional values supported by their denominational structures (p. 9).

JUSTIFICATION OF THE STUDY

How individuals define conflicts between traditional and modern values remains an important topic in sociological discourse. As Bassis, Gelles, and Levine (1984) point out, members of contemporary society in the United States are forced to choose between dual- and single-career marriages, single parenthood and traditional marriage, nontraditional religious commitments and traditional religious participation, and ethnic reidentification and assimilation, as well as a number of other value-related options (p. 536). These types of conflicts often accompany the rise of industrialization and urbanization (Bellah, Madsen, Sullivan, Swidler, & Tipton, 1985; Hall, 1990) or precede significant cultural change in a society (Zablocki & Kanter, 1976). During these periods, "traditional values" often preserved by religious institutions come into conflict with "modern values" fostered by pluralistic societies that uphold a wide range of cultural norms.

In recent years, a number of religious interest groups have placed the media at the center of such value conflicts. The Christian Leaders for Responsible Television (see Hamilton & Rubin, 1992) and the Christian Film and Television Commission (see Medved, 1992), for example, have sought to reduce television conflict thought to be inconsistent with mainstream "religious values." The primary argument posited by these groups is that mainstream Christian religious communities tend to define much of popular media as conflicting with traditional values and media decision makers should recognize this in selecting appropriate content for their audiences. Three popular books, *Hollywood vs. America: Popular Culture and the War on*

Traditional Values (Medved, 1992), *Children at Risk: The Battle for the Hearts and Minds of Our Kids* (Dobson & Bauer, 1990), and *Television and Religion: The Shaping of Faith, Values, and Culture* (Fore, 1987), describe a conflict of worldviews between the U.S. media industry and mainstream religious organizations. In the last book mentioned, Fore (1987) writes,

> In contrast to television's worldview that we are basically good, that happiness is the chief end of life and that happiness consists of obtaining material goods, the Christian worldview holds that human beings are susceptible to the sin of pride and will-to-power, that the chief end of life is to glorify God. (p. 70)

In *Children at Risk,* Dobson and Bauer (1990) use the term "incompatible worldviews" (p. 19) in a similar manner, and in *Hollywood vs. America,* Michael Medved (1992), a movie and television critic, asserts that "tens of millions of Americans now see the entertainment industry as an all-powerful enemy, an alien force that assaults our most cherished values and corrupts our children" (p. 3).

How accurate are these assessments of the way church members define the role of the media in their lives? What impact do such treatises have on fueling group stereotypes? Are communication practitioners being misled and, therefore, ineffective in reaching the full audience of those identified as church members? Popular books and public rhetoric about media effects on religious communities often make their predictions based on analysis or perceptions of content alone. Yet content-centered analysis is problematic in that it fails to describe the diversity of media interpretation that may exist within conservative cultures. Content analysis often implies a homogeneous conceptualization of audience attributed to organizational affiliations. This "passive" definition of audience is criticized by contemporary theorists working in the domains of uses and gratifications (Katz, Blumler, & Gurevitch, 1974), diffusion theory (Rogers & Adhikarya, 1979), critical studies (Slack & Allor, 1983), and social semiotics (Anderson & Meyer, 1988).

This study, therefore, is a departure from the often flat definitions of audience emergent in traditional, demographically based research. We address the question: Is there media diversity within conservative religious subcultures, and, if so, what effect might this have on how media are used? Our goal is to add to the understanding of audience individuality, what we are calling diversity within audiences, and to prevent communication ineffectiveness resulting from presumed homogeneity of media use within a group.

METHODOLOGY

Data collected in two separate research programs were merged to compare and combine information gathered from the population of Mormon women living in states located in the western and southwestern regions of the United States. Three study samples in which significant differences were found are presented separately and as a merged data set where appropriate. In instances in which questions lacked uniformity, for example, analysis is separated.

Merging data sets raises concerns over potential intervening factors resulting from differences in population sampling, methods, and question design. Ask a statistician, as we did, and you'll have no trouble discovering a whole host of real and perceived potential bias traps and invisible land mines. There are distinct advantages to social researchers, however, particularly with improvements in expanding sample size and using advances in computerization (Rosenthal, 1984; Schmidt & Hunter, 1983; Stiff, 1986). Because we are addressing these data for descriptive purposes and not attempting to establish quantitative measures for hypothesis testing, we acknowledge the limits and possible disturbances caused by merged data. We offer these findings as a starting point for the development of hypotheses to be tested and a contribution to the ongoing theoretical understanding of audiences and the effects of diversity on mass communication.

Study 1

The first study employed purposive stratified random sampling of Mormon women in three large western U.S. urban centers: Los Angeles, California; Houston, Texas; and Salt Lake City, Utah. Data collection began in January 1992. Of 702 questionnaires, 29% were mailed to Mormon women living in Houston, 34% to women in Salt Lake City, and 37% to women in Los Angeles. The mailing yielded a response rate of 61% (n = 428). When compared to the demographic data compiled by Goodman and Heaton (1986), the sample is more representative of Mormon women who are highly educated, affluent, and married than Mormon women in general. The sample is comparable, however, to the larger population in terms of family size and number employed outside the home.

The questionnaire contained six categories of survey questions: media behaviors, television program choice, attitudes about television, media use, demographics, and religiosity.

Studies 2 and 3

Women attending a daylong conference held in April 1993 in Salt Lake City, Utah, were surveyed as part of an ongoing health and risk communication research program. Those in attendance at the conference, called "Spaces and Silences: An Enhanced Women's Conference," were invited to complete a three-part questionnaire that measured media habits, risk-taking predispositions and behaviors, and general background information about themselves. Some 150 (n = 151) women participated in the study. This reflects an intercept response from close to half of those attending. Data gathered from the first and last sections in this survey are reported here.

Using this same questionnaire, data were also gathered during the same week at an annual 2-day conference held in Provo, Utah, sponsored jointly by the Relief Society of the Church of the Latter-day Saints and Brigham Young University (BYU). Women who attend the conference come from all over the state of Utah and the western region, including Idaho, Wyoming, Washington, Colorado, California, Montana, Nevada, and Oregon. As in the Salt Lake City study, a table was set up in an area near registration tables or in the general traffic path of conference attendees as they moved between sessions in the program. Two female graduate students and the principal researcher invited conference attendees to participate in a self-administered study. Survey instruments on a clipboard were offered to each willing respondent. Each woman spent from 10 to 15 minutes completing the questionnaire. No incentive or reward was offered in either Study 2 or 3; a cover release letter on BYU letterhead explained that the study was approved by the human subjects review board at the university. Nearly 400 (n = 387) women attending the Provo conference volunteered to assist in the study, reflecting an intercept participation rate of some 6% of the attendees.

FINDINGS

Although Mormon women share membership in a conservative religious community, their uses of mass media reflect diversity. We begin by reporting demographic similarities and then offer our findings on media use in this study sample.

General Description of Sample Population

Demographic measures included age, education, income, marital status, number of children at home, occupation, and religiosity. In the merged data set, more than 50% were between the ages of 32 and 49. In this sample, 29% were 50 or older, and the remaining 17% were under 31. (Note: Where percentages equal less than or slightly more than 100%, discrepancy is due to rounding off or missing values.)

The average level of education was high. More than 60% were college educated with another 20% holding graduate degrees. This seemingly overrepresentation of highly educated women is actually not unexpected in this population; Mormon women tend to finish college at higher rates than the general female population (Goodman & Heaton, 1986), attributable to the emphasis on education from church leadership. About 15% had only a high school degree and fewer than 1% did not have at least a high school diploma.

Overall household incomes indicated an affluent sample (49% reported incomes at $50,000 or more); however, this may, in part, be due to the number of southern California residents in one of the merged studies. Nearly 30% indicated a $30,000 to $50,000 annual range.

These women tended to be housewives; nearly 45% reported primary occupation as "housewife." Interestingly, some reported their occupation as both housewife and professional, possibly a unique nondilemma for women in this church in which validation for family and work inside the home is high. Some 44% listed full or part-time professional occupations outside the home. In this sample, fewer than 4% (3.9%) were retired and 6% reported their occupation as student.

Contribution to population statistics from Mormon families is near legend in folklore. In this sample, however, more than half (54%) had three or fewer children. Less than 9% had six or more children. Very few were single parents; 85% were married.

Because it was assumed in selecting Mormon women for study that church attendance would be high (81% reported regular church attendance), religiosity was also measured in terms of reported religious publications subscribed to or read. Slightly more than 70% subscribed to *Ensign*, the official monthly magazine of the Church of Jesus Christ of Latter-day Saints. The remaining 30% also reported reading other religious publications.

Media Use and Preferences
Among Sampled Mormon Women

About 39% of respondents were considered heavy users of television, defined as viewing 5 or more hours per day and 5 or more days per week. Another 40% were considered medium users, defined as watching television 2 to 4 hours per day and 2 to 4 days per week. Some 20% were low users, viewing TV less than an hour per day, one day or less per week.

In Study 2 and Study 3, respondents ($n = 523$) named their favorite television programs. Thirty-one percent listed news shows, and 33% identified sitcoms and drama. Only 2% listed religious programs.

In Study 1, respondents' admiration for female television characters reflecting both traditional and contemporary roles was measured (see Table 13.1). Claire Huxtable of the *Cosby Show* was named most often as the most admired (72%) and Elyse Keaton of *Family Ties* was admired by half (51%) of these Mormon women. Both characters are working mothers with children. On the other hand, some other contemporary television female roles in highly rated

Table 13.1 Rank Order of Percentages of Mormon Women Who Agree
With the Statement "I Admire This Female Television
Character" (*n* = 428)

	Agree	*No Opinion*	*Disagree*
Claire Huxtable	72.3	22.7	5.0
Aunt Bea Taylor	56.1	37.2	6.7
Elyse Keaton	50.8	42.6	6.7
Lucy Ricardo	49.0	29.4	21.6
Mary Richards	48.0	46.0	6.0
Harriet Nelson	46.5	47.7	5.7
Margaret Anderson	40.2	55.7	4.0
Murphy Brown	19.5	62.9	17.6
Roseanne Conner	10.0	17.3	72.7
Rebecca Howe	9.0	50.1	40.9
Peg Bundy	1.5	43.1	55.4

some other contemporary television female roles in highly rated
programs fared less favorably. Roseanne Conner was admired by
only 10% of these respondents, whereas Murphy Brown drew
slightly more fans (19.5%) than nonadmirers (17.6%). Rebecca Howe
(*Cheers*) and Peg Bundy (*Married With Children*) were the least admired television characters. We can only speculate about the relatively large number of respondents who checked "no opinion" in
responding to several characters on the list. Audience members may
have seen a particular character but did not recall the specific name
used in the show. Responses are less likely attributed to response
bias or the reluctance to disclose admiration for controversial characters; after all, 73% reported strong feelings about Roseanne
Conner. It is also important to note, for example, that the questionnaire was administered before then Vice President Dan Quayle
commented about the character Murphy Brown, elevating familiarity with this television personality.

Attitudes about television viewing were measured in the first
study by asking respondents whether they agreed with a series of
statements. Statements with which Mormon women reported less
than 75% agreement are listed in Table 13.2. Although nearly 42%
agreed that television is an important source of entertainment for

Table 13.2 Statements With Which Mormon Women Show Less
Than 75% Agreement in Their Attitudes About Television
(in percentages; n = 428)

	Agree	No Opinion	Disagree
TV is an important source of entertainment for me	41.9	10.5	47.5
Children are better off without TV	46.0	6.2	47.9
I watch TV to get away from the ordinary cares and problems of the day	38.5	9.0	52.5
TV keeps me company when alone	57.0	8.9	34.2
Television is a consistent part of my daily routine	36.5	7.1	56.4
I often feel guilty watching TV	27.4	14.2	58.5
Television viewing is something I look forward to each day	26.2	17.0	56.9

value to their lives. There was equal diversity of opinion in response to whether they felt children are better off without TV. Although 46% agreed that children are better off without television, nearly 48% seemed to find some benefit for children from television. Some 36% of those Mormon women who responded to this question reported that television is a consistent part of their daily routine.

As with television viewing, newspaper usage was generally high. Slightly more than 70% of these respondents read newspapers fairly regularly. High newspaper usage, defined as reading a newspaper 5 or more days per week, was reported by 39.1% of the respondents in the merged data set; medium or moderate use, defined as reading a newspaper 2 to 4 days per week, was reported by 34% of this population. Only 26.7% said they did not read a newspaper or read a newspaper only once a week.

Although some magazine preferences were measured in all three studies, only use of religious magazines could be merged adequately as reported earlier in the discussion of religiosity. Radio-listening habits and overall magazine-reading habits were measured in Study 2 and Study 3 (n = 523). More than half of the surveyed women reported medium or high reading habits for magazines (n = 477), and 39.5% (n = 448) reported listening to the radio nearly every day.

DISCUSSION AND CONCLUSIONS

Despite strong institutional encouragement to curtail media use (see Church of Jesus Christ of Latter-day Saints, 1991; Strong-Thacker, 1991), women in the studied conservative religious culture showed diverse patterns in their television-viewing, newspaper- and magazine-reading, and radio-listening habits. Respondents' attitudes toward media reflect a diversity of opinion even though the sampled population shared a compellingly similar demographic profile. These findings suggest that conservative cultures may provide fertile ground for mass communication audience researchers. Members of organized conservative groups demonstrate a diversity of responses as they confront institutionalized definitions of the role of media from a conflict perspective.

What this suggests for mass communication scholars and mass media professionals is that membership in a conservative religious community is not always an accurate predictor of media behavior. Media not only may allow for diversity but may even provoke it, a slight variation on Turow (1989). This is surely a contrary media descriptor from those who define media by their content and judge the media guilty of stereotyping. Indeed, when evaluated from the audience as primary, media appear in this study to encourage individual diversity within a strong conservative culture admonishing members to be wary of the power and dangers of mediated messages. The institution may be clinging to a model that worries about media telling us what to think about, but some in the flock apparently know where they belong and know how to think and decipher for themselves what not to think about. Religiosity within this sampled group of women is consistently high; their media use is diverse.

As research in cognitive response suggests, in this highly educated population of women, need for cognition and opportunities to process information may be too strong to override (Cacioppo, Petty, & Morris, 1983; Chaiken & Stangor, 1987; Petty, Ostrom, & Brock, 1981). These findings may also support Eagly's (1978) explanation (for gender differences in influenceability) that there is a tendency for women to be oriented to interpersonal goals in group settings. Future research with this population and within religious or other conservative cultures should seek to recognize gender differences in the way people are experiencing the world and using media for knowledge discovery (Deming, 1989; Gallagher, 1989).

Practical lessons to be gained from such insight are more easily applied in hindsight. Perhaps if former Vice President Dan Quayle had considered the range of diversity within conservative religious cultures, he would not have so completely misread his assumed constituency when he attacked the storyline and character of television's Murphy Brown. Quayle's content-centered assumption did not allow for those who shared his religious family doctrine but remained fans of Ms. Brown. Nearly 20% of the women in this study report admiration for Murphy Brown.

Quayle, or more likely his advisers, and media critics such as Michael Medved (1992) have ignored the audience by focusing on content. Future research should focus on how media-provoked diversity manifests itself in behavioral outcomes. What we are suggesting is that rather than considering religion to be a causal factor in many attitudes and behaviors, insight may be gained from a lens shift to diversity within audiences, even those who are clustered into organized conservative cultures. Our concern is that market-driven segmentation and audience-targeting shortcuts have misled mass communication to audience negligence. Some may be guilty of audience stereotyping and overgeneralization, just as the literature has so often deplored in media content, and in the broad swipe, we fail to communicate effectively.

Nothing in this initial analysis reveals startling new paradigm shifts, nor do the findings contribute much in the way of ferment fodder. Stereotyping audience members may not lead the field astray, but as Katz (1987) suggested in reference to the model of limited effects, such misinterpretation (of audience, in this instance) may easily exhaust its welcome in an era of globalization and sensitivity to diversity issues. Our initial summary is a gentle reminder: Do not assume that religious audiences are inattentive to a diversity of media offerings.

Our analysis suggests a need for further conceptualizations of audience, unblinded to market segmentation or demographic-driven assumptions. There is diversity within.

REFERENCES

Abelman, R., & Hoover, S. M. (Eds.). (1990). *Religious television: Controversies and conclusions.* Norwood, NJ: Ablex.

Abelman, R., & Neuendorf, K. (1985). How religious is religious television programming? *Journal of Communication, 35,* 98-110.

Anderson, J. A., & Meyer, T. P. (1988). *Mediated communication: A social action perspective.* Newbury Park, CA: Sage.

Ballard, M. R. (1989, May). The effects of television. *Ensign,* pp. 78-81.

Bassis, M. S., Gelles, R. J., & Levine, A. (1984). *Sociology.* New York: Random House.

Bellah, R. N., Madsen, R., Sullivan, W. M., Swidler, A., & Tipton, S. M. (1985). *Habits of the heart: Individualism and commitment in American life.* New York: Harper & Row.

Berger, P. L. (1967). *The sacred canopy: Elements of a sociological theory of religion.* Garden City, NY: Doubleday.

Berger, P. L., & Luckman, T. (1966). *The social construction of reality: A treatise in the sociology of knowledge.* New York: Doubleday.

Buddenbaum, J. M. (1990). Network news coverage of religion. In J. P. Ferre' (Ed.), *Channels of belief: Religion and American commercial television* (pp. 57-78). Ames: University of Iowa Press.

Cacioppo, J. T., Petty, R., & Morris, K. J. (1983). Effects of need for cognition on message evaluation, recall, and persuasion. *Journal of Personality and Social Psychology, 45,* 805-818.

Campbell, B. L., & Campbell, E. E. (1981). The Mormon family. In C. H. Mindel & R. W. Habenstein (Eds.), *Ethnic families in America: Patterns and variations* (pp. 386-416). New York: Elsevier.

Chaiken, S., & Stangor, C. (1987). Attitudes and attitude change. *Annual Review of Psychology, 83,* 575-630.

Church of Jesus Christ of Latter-day Saints. (1991). The powerful influence of the media. In *Come unto me: Relief society personal study guide 3* (pp. 194-199). Salt Lake City, UT: Author.

Dart, J., & Allen, J. (1993). *Bridging the gap: Religion and the news media.* Nashville, TN: Freedom Forum.

Deming, C. J. (1989). Must gender paradigms shift for themselves? In B. Dervin, L. Grossberg, B. J. O'Keefe, & E. Wartella (Eds.), *Rethinking communication* (Vol. 1, pp. 162-165). Newbury Park, CA: Sage.

Dobson, J. C., & Bauer, G. L. (1990). *Children at risk: The battle for the hearts and minds of our kids.* Dallas, TX: Word.

Eagly, A. H. (1978). Sex differences in influenceability. *Psychological Bulletin, 85,* 86-116.

Fore, W. F. (1987). *Television and religion: The shaping of faith, values, and culture.* Minneapolis, MN: Augsburg.

Gaddy, G. D., & Pritchard, D. (1985). When watching religious TV is like attending church. *Journal of Communication, 35,* 123-131.

Gallagher, M. (1989). A feminist paradigm for communication research. In B. Dervin, L. Grossberg, B. J. O'Keefe, & E. Wartella (Eds.), *Rethinking communication* (Vol. 2, pp. 75-87). Newbury Park, CA: Sage.

Goodman, K. L., & Heaton, T. B. (1986). LDS church members in the U.S. and Canada. *AMCAP Journal, 12*(1), 88-107.

Gottlieb, R., & Wiley, P. (1986). *America's saints: The rise of Mormon power.* San Diego, CA: Harcourt Brace Jovanovich.

Hall, C. M. (1990). *Women and identity: Value choices in a changing world.* New York: Hemisphere.

Hamilton, N. F., & Rubin, A. M. (1992). The influence of religiosity on television viewing. *Journalism Quarterly, 69,* 667-678.

Katz, E. (1987). Communications research since Lazarsfeld. *Public Opinion Quarterly, 51,* S25-S45.

Katz, E., Blumler, J., & Gurevitch, M. (1974). Utilization of mass communication by the individual. In E. Katz, J. Blumler, & M. Gurevitch (Eds.), *The uses of mass communications: Current perspectives on gratifications research* (pp. 19-32). Beverly Hills, CA: Sage.

Making the most of TV. (1990, October). *Ensign,* pp. 70-71.

Medved, M. (1992). *Hollywood vs. America: Popular culture and the war on traditional values.* New York: HarperCollins.

Peck, J. (1993). *The gods of televangelism.* Creskill, NJ: Hampton.

Petty, R., Ostrom, T., & Brock, T. (Eds.). (1981). *Cognitive responses in persuasion.* Hillsdale, NJ: Lawrence Erlbaum.

Roberts, C. L. (1983). Attitudes and media use of the moral majority. *Journal of Broadcasting, 27,* 403-410.

Rogers, E. M., & Adhikarya, R. (1979). Diffusion of innovations: An up-to-date review and commentary. In D. Nimmo (Ed.), *Communication yearbook 3* (pp. 67-82). New Brunswick, NJ: Transaction Books.

Rosenthal, R. (1984). *Meta-analytic procedures for social research.* Beverly Hills, CA: Sage.

Schmidt, F. L., & Hunter, J. E. (1983). *Meta-analysis: Cumulating research across studies.* Beverly Hills, CA: Sage.

Schultze, Q. J. (Ed.). (1990). *American Evangelicals and the mass media: Perspectives on the relationship between American Evangelicals and the mass media.* Grand Rapids, MI: Academie.

Slack, J., & Allor, M. (1983). The political and epistemological constituents of critical communication research. *Journal of Communication, 33,* 208-219.

Stiff, J. B. (1986). Cognitive processing of persuasive message cues: A meta-analytic review of the effects of supporting information on attitudes. *Communication Monographs, 53,* 75-89.

Strong-Thacker, K. (1991, July). TV free: Giving up the daytime habit. *Ensign,* pp. 29-31.

Turow, J. (1989). Television and institutional power: The case of medicine. In B. Dervin, L. Grossberg, B. J. O'Keefe, & E. Wartella (Eds.), *Rethinking communication* (Vol. 2, pp. 454-473). Newbury Park, CA: Sage.

Wilcox, L. P. (1987). Mormon motherhood: Official images. In M. Ursenbach-Beecher & L. Fielding-Anderson (Eds.), *Sisters in spirit: Mormon women in historical perspective* (pp. 208-226). Urbana: University of Illinois Press.

Zablocki, B. D., & Kanter, R. (1976). The differentiation of lifestyles. *Annual Review of Sociology, 2,* 269-298.

14

Use of Mass Media for Political Information in a Middletown Quaker Meeting

JUDITH M. BUDDENBAUM

I n his examination of the yellow press, Park (1927) notes that there are two schools of thought concerning news. One school, represented at the turn of the century by journalists from established newspapers, believed that "if God let things happen that were not in accordance with the conceptions of the fitness of things," it was their duty to protect public morals by suppressing news about "things that they knew ought not to have happened." The other, represented by the increasingly popular Hearst and Pulitzer newspapers, thought it their right and their duty to report "anything that God would let happen" (p. 7).

AUTHOR'S NOTE: The author thanks the Center for Middletown Studies at Ball State University and the Ball Brothers Foundation, both of Muncie, Indiana, for providing funding for this study. She also thanks the Quakers of Middletown for welcoming her into their meeting and their homes.

Today the opinion that news about unseemly things "God would let happen" should be suppressed or reported to reflect particular religious beliefs about "the fitness of things" comes most often from conservative Protestants who reject the idea that making truly moral decisions depends on reason and free choice (Alley, 1990). When news emphasizes conflict, sex, and violence or reports on alternative religions or lifestyles, their belief that such coverage leads only to the destruction of moral values makes these Christians quick to claim the mass media are at best areligious, at worst antireligion (Buddenbaum, 1990a, 1990b).

Certainly independent research indicates that the press has criticized the New Christian Right (Buddenbaum, 1990a, 1990b; Fields, 1984). At the same time, both journalists (Entman & Paletz, 1980) and scholars (Hunter, 1991) have accepted the Christian Right's framing so that the conflict appears to be between religious people committed to timeless standards of decency and secular humanists for whom "anything goes."

This framing can create the impression that all Christians want news filtered through a conservative Christian interpretation of the Bible. Lost is the possibility that the debate may not be between religion and secularity. Instead, it may stem from different views of the Bible, different concepts of spirituality, and different styles of moral reasoning (Wuthnow, 1989). In an effort to show that strong religious beliefs, not just secularism, can lead to an appreciation of and support for a marketplace of ideas, this chapter describes Quaker beliefs and their implications for how members of the Religious Society of Friends should relate to the media. It then examines support for and use of the mass media for political information in one local meeting before concluding with a discussion of the consequences for the church and its members.

Quakers were chosen for this study because their beliefs are such that they score very low on Christian orthodoxy scales. They would, therefore, be treated as secular in many analyses even though their "unorthodox" beliefs are an integral part of their religion.

Because the Quaker religion is noncredal, there are no standard theological texts or doctrines that all Quakers must accept to be members in good standing. Most, however, consider Quaker writings, and especially those of their founder George Fox, to be instructive. Therefore, the religious beliefs and their implications presented in this chapter are those found in classic Quaker writings (Barbour & Roberts, 1973; Fox, 1925, 1972, 1991; Laughlin, 1969; Lippincott, 1959).

The analysis of how those beliefs are communicated to Quakers, the extent to which they inform Quakers' use of the media, and the consequences for individuals and for the meeting come from participant observation in a Quaker meeting in Middletown, in-depth interviews with 10 congregation leaders, and questionnaires filled out by the leaders and by a random sample of congregation members. Like many Quaker meetings (Brinton, 1969; Trueblood, 1969), the Middletown meeting is small. Therefore, the 23 Quakers who completed the survey represent about one third of the households in the congregation. Data were gathered during the 3 months preceding the 1992 presidential election as part of a larger study that included observation in five other Middletown congregations and a survey of 987 Middletown residents.

QUAKER BELIEFS
AND THEIR IMPLICATIONS

Failing to find the spiritual truth and peace he sought in the established churches of his day, George Fox came to believe that God can and does speak directly to each person according to that person's condition. According to Fox, the "true Light, which lighteth every man that cometh into the world" described in John 1:9 is an Inner Light or Inner Voice within each person. Everyone can know God directly by being still, listening to that voice, and then using God-given reason to test initial understanding to see if it is in accord with God's timeless truth.

Although such an empowering doctrine was immensely appealing to people confused by and tired of constant sparring among powerful religio-political factions, it posed a serious threat to both church and state. Fox taught that tax support for churches is wrong. But more important, the fact that God speaks to everyone implied a radical equality of all persons. Believing that there is an inherent dignity and worth in each person, Quakers made no distinction among peoples based on sex, race, or social class. They refused to go to war. Instead, they insisted on listening to other people and taking them seriously, for even enemies have an Inner Voice and may be speaking God's truth.

Because Quakers insisted on "speaking truth to power" whenever they felt led to do so by their Inner Light, Fox was imprisoned eight times between 1649 and 1673 on charges of heresy or sedition. Between 1650 and 1689, thousands of other Quakers were arrested and convicted on various charges; several hundred died in prisons.

In the course of those trials, Fox and other Quakers became quite adept at using verses from the Bible to defend themselves against charges of heresy. They also defended themselves through arguments for freedom of speech that were in many ways similar to those of Fox's contemporary, John Milton, but in other ways went far beyond Milton (1969).

Edward Burrough (1973), one of the early Quaker leaders, wrote,

> And we believe that to oppose false opinions and unsound doctrines and principles, seeking to convince them that oppose themselves, by exhortation or sharp reproof, by word or writing, ought not to be counted a breach of the peace; or to strive about the things of the Kingdom of God, by men of contrary minds or judgments, this ought not to be punishable by the magistrates and their laws. For we believe, the outward laws and powers of the earth are only to preserve men's persons and estates, and not to preserve men in opinions. (pp. 302-303)

The reference to "men of contrary minds or judgments" suggests that Quakers, unlike Milton, would have extended the freedom they sought for themselves to other religions. On trial for his preachings, William Penn framed his arguments for tolerance as protections for the jurors; later, he incorporated tolerance for dissent into laws governing the Pennsylvania colony (Penn, 1726/1971; see also Barbour & Roberts, 1973, pp. 441-450; Morris, 1993).

As Powe (1991) notes, a willingness to protect all viewpoints "rests on a belief in objective truth and in the predominance of rational thought, and an almost religious faith that truth will prevail" (p. 239). But for the Quakers, there is nothing "almost" about any of that. Their views about freedom of expression are an integral part of their religious belief.

Because of their experiences with persecution, early Quakers such as Burrough and Penn recognized what John Stuart Mill (1859/1947) later described as the "tyranny of the majority." Thus, they probably saw that their greatest protection would come by extending freedom of expression to everyone. For Burrough (1973), the right flowed logically from the belief that God speaks directly to everyone and that those who would follow God must speak as led by the Inner Light. Because God's commands are above and beyond those of the state, the government has no right to enact laws that would interfere with God's commands. Similarly, Penn's extension of freedom of expression to everyone stemmed from the Quaker beliefs that God's truth is recognizable by people following their Inner Light and using their God-given reason and that all people are equal in God's eyes and must be treated with dignity and respect.

These early Quakers believed that anyone, even a person whose opinions appeared to be wrong, may be speaking God's truth, but they never assumed that everyone would listen to their Inner Light or understand perfectly what God might be saying to them. Although they were quite aware that falsehoods would circulate in the marketplace of ideas, they did not consider erroneous views a threat to those who would follow God. In a 1652 letter to his followers, Fox (1991) wrote, "Fear not the powers of darkness" (p. 218). In his journal he declared, "If you love it [the Inner Light] and come to it . . . it will bring you off from all the world's teachers and ways . . . and will preserve you from the evils of the world, and all the deceivers in it" (Fox, 1991, p. 99).

In accord with classic libertarian philosophy, he placed the responsibility for finding and heeding truth on the hearer, not the speaker. But with freedom comes responsibility. Although the Quaker religion is highly experiential and individualistic, the Quaker approach to spiritual guidance is a disciplined one bounded by the Bible, Quaker writings, and the sense of the meeting. The goal is a consensus that reflects God's will. Therefore, instead of silencing divergent viewpoints, Quakers insist on listening and understanding so that, like God, they may speak to each person according to that person's condition (Case, 1969; Keiser & Keiser, 1993-1994; Lippard, 1988; Trueblood, 1969).

ENCOURAGEMENTS
TO MASS MEDIA USE

This emphasis on listening to and understanding others suggests a surveillance function for the mass media that, in fact, figures quite prominently in more modern Quaker writings. According to Jessamyn West (1959), the author of the classic Quaker novel *Friendly Persuasion*, writers and journalists

> should be the eyes of the public, [seeing] as much as possible and [reporting] as fully and as meaningfully as [their] talents permit. Otherwise society is wasteful. . . . When the artist is made to scamp his proper work by the pressure of the community, it is as if the community willingly lopped off a finger or bound up one eye. (pp. 169, 174)

Consistent with the essentially libertarian philosophy of the early Quakers, many modern Quakers see greater danger in silenced voices than in exposure to diverse viewpoints. Case (1969), for example, argued that protecting truth and freedom cannot be accomplished by silencing dissent. Seeing protection only in free communication, he complained about the tendency of the mass media to suppress news or color it to avoid displeasing advertisers. He saw greater danger, however, in a public that wants "someone to do their thinking and problem-solving for them" (p. 144).

But Quakers are not immune to that desire, as West (1959) points out,

> One of the most unhappy facts that the beginning writer encounters: the fact that within his own family, his own church, his own community are those who urge that he put on paper, not the truth as he sees it, but the fiction they desire to see; the fiction that most completely bolsters their own psychic ease and moral self-esteem. (p. 169)

Thus, both Quaker beliefs and writings support freedom of expression. They also encourage attending to messages that may be unsettling or that contradict one's beliefs. But even as West suggested that censoring writings according to what people want to see or hear would be "wasteful," she acknowledged pressures in that direction from members of her own church.

Within the Religious Society of Friends, emphasis is on unity in the Spirit rather than doctrinal conformity. Therefore, some meetings undoubtedly encourage their members to avoid sources that might conflict with the basic Quaker message. That was not true, however, in the Middletown meeting itself.

Each of the nine newsletters mailed to members during 1992 included at least one item recommending listening to and learning from nonchurch sources. A January article, for example, suggested members might want to subscribe to or read the church's copy of *News/Views* published by the Atlanta Friends Meeting for its variety of perspectives on important issues culled from mass media sources; a March item suggested cable television, and an April article recommended using the public library.

Only once were members told they should attend to a particular source. In her October 11 announcements, the pastor expressed the hope that as many people as possible would use their VCRs to record the vice presidential debates so they could hear what the candidates had to say and also attend a "Politics With Integrity" program that was scheduled for the same time at the church.

Only once was media use discouraged. In a January newsletter article adapted from a publication by the Green Alliance, the last item in a list of 61 "thoughts on the art of living" suggested decreasing TV watching. But even on that occasion, the context made it clear that only passive, noncritical viewing was being discouraged. The complete wording was "Decrease TV watching and increase creative learning." Twelve items in the list began with the words "learn," "discover," "research," or "listen" ("Some Thoughts," 1992, p. 2).

Through newsletter articles and announcements in church, members were repeatedly encouraged to use the mass media. But free inquiry was always presented in a way that gave it purpose. And at the same time, members were encouraged to learn about and from God and from each other. Just as each newsletter contained at least one item recommending use of the mass media, each also contained at least one announcement about Christian education classes, discussion groups, or Quaker readings. This dual emphasis was best explained in a summer newsletter article that described the distinctive function of the local meeting as providing a place for worship and reflection and "an environment which promotes freedom of inquiry and concern for others" ("Friends Memorial Meeting," 1992, p. 2).

MEDIA USE

Consistent with the encouragement to media use that they received, data from the questionnaires indicate that Quakers were significantly more likely than members of conservative Christian churches to use the mass media regularly for political information. Although there were few differences in responses to the specific survey questions about media use between Quakers and Lutherans or United Methodists, both the in-depth interviews and answers to other survey questions suggested some important differences.

More than three fourths of the Quaker leaders and members said they used newspapers and television some or a lot for political information; more than half of each group said the same for radio and magazines. Responses from Lutherans and United Methodists with similar socioeconomic status indicated similar amounts of use for each of those media, but the Quakers were somewhat more likely to use multiple sources within each medium.

Instead of naming a favorite television channel for state and local news, Quakers tended to monitor several channels. Furthermore, although subscribing to both local newspapers and reading the capital city newspaper at least occasionally were common among all liberal Protestants, Quaker leaders were the most likely to read at least one elite newspaper regularly. Two subscribed to the *Christian Science Monitor.* Another Quaker leader was the only one of six college professors in the study to make a regular practice of going to the university library to read elite newspapers.

As those findings suggest, the Quakers preferred print media because they perceived them as providing the most substantive coverage. In fact, a pile of reading material was a common sight on desks, tables, or the floor beside a favorite chair in Quaker homes. Although many of the members and one leader read either *Time* or *Newsweek* regularly, most also read professional journals, trade magazines, or publications from special interest organizations that could be counted on for in-depth attention to particular issues.

Although the Quakers also used network and local television newscasts and radio for political information, they preferred cable television because the programs more often provided substantive coverage and multiple viewpoints. Programs most often mentioned as favorites for political information were the *McNeil-Lehrer News Hour,* documentaries, and C-SPAN I and II. For radio news, they relied on National Public Radio rather than commercial AM or FM stations.

Despite being such heavy users of the mass media for political information, Quakers did not consider the media particularly trustworthy. As was true in the other churches and in the population as a whole, most Quaker leaders and members judged radio, magazines, and newspapers only somewhat trustworthy as sources of political information. Most members said the same of television news, but 6 out of 10 leaders called television news very untrustworthy. Although those evaluations were not much different than ones obtained from leaders and members in the other churches or from the general survey of Middletown residents, Quaker leaders most often tempered their judgments.

In an explanation very similar to Case's (1969) contention that the marketplace of ideas is being limited by commercial pressures, one Quaker leader complained that reporters were "afraid to tell half of what they see and know to be true" but quickly added that he understood how hard it is when "you're getting criticism from the public, your editor refuses to stand up to advertisers, and your job is constantly on the line." The major problem, as these leaders saw it, was with inadequate, shallow, and repetitive news.

Because most used so many media, they readily detected differences in news coverage but attributed those differences to the human condition rather than to deliberate attempts to slant or distort the news. As one leader explained,

I'm certain they're biased. You can't have a reporter . . . somebody
seeing and writing things . . . without being biased even though they
try not to be. . . . No matter how unbiased you try to be, you'll get your
own bias in there. Something that you agree with or that you think is
important—you'll bring it out just a little more.

Although these Quakers saw bias in the news, many considered
it natural and valuable. They deliberately chose sources for their
diversity of opinions. When asked where they got information on
political issues that most concerned them, one couple quickly
named more than a dozen sources ranging from *Mother Jones* and
The Progressive to William F. Buckley. Leaders who read *Christian
Science Monitor* valued it partly for its in-depth coverage but also for
its distinctive Christian science perspective that, they noted, was not
always confined to the editorial page or the religious columns.
Similarly, they liked the *McNeil-Lehrer News Hour*, *Face the Nation*,
and *Issues and Answers* and were watching the presidential debates
because they could be counted on to provide diverse viewpoints.

Unlike many people who believe it is the media's duty to provide
"the truth," these Quakers took full responsibility for finding truth.
As one woman explained,

When I go to vote, I shouldn't be going just to go through the motions.
When I mark off a certain box, I should have known as much as I can
about whatever it is that I'm voting on—which actually is quite
difficult. . . . You just want to try to be exposed to as much information
as you can be and then you just have to sift through it.

To decide for whom to vote, one man said he first made a list of
important issues and issue positions and then used both newspapers and candidate scorecards from several different organizations
to check off the strengths and weaknesses of each candidate.

CONSEQUENCES AND CONCLUSIONS

Interview and survey data from leaders and members in six
churches and from the general population indicate that Quakers
were among the heaviest users of the mass media for political

information, but there were characteristics of that use that marked it as consistent with the teachings of their religion and the messages they received through the local meeting.

Taught to value freedom of inquiry and to use a variety of sources to learn about and understand the world and its peoples but also to draw their own conclusions on the basis of reason and the urgings of their Inner Light, the Quakers gravitated to media that provided the most substantive information. They also favored sources that provided diverse viewpoints.

As a result, Quakers were among the most knowledgeable on political issues and candidates. Both leaders and members were able to identify the issues they considered most important, give their positions on those issues, and explain why they had taken those positions. They could also describe differences in candidates' positions.

Quakers were also more able to connect their political positions to their religious beliefs than other liberal Protestants. They were almost as likely as conservative Christians to say they had taken political positions because of their religious beliefs and almost as adept in quoting the Bible to support their opinions. They were more likely, however, to voluntarily point out why others might prefer a different position.

Because the ways these Quakers used the media are consistent with Quaker teachings, it is tempting to say that religion explains attitudes toward and use of mass media. Information collected at one point in time from a handful of people from one meeting, even when compared to other subjects from other churches and to the general population, however, cannot support that kind of generalization. In fact, even the findings from this investigation suggest that religion is, at best, only part of the explanation.

Half of the Quaker leaders were born into the faith. In most cases, they had attended the same meeting all their lives. The other half, however, joined as adults. There were no differences between the two groups of Quakers in their attitudes toward or use of the media. From their explanations of how they came to be convinced Quakers, however, it was clear that the converts were first attracted to the faith because it provided a religious justification for the desire to learn, ask questions, and make up their own minds. Therefore, at most, we can conclude that if a religion encourages members to learn from many different sources and to consider diverse opinions before making up their minds, most members will act accordingly. Those who are not comfortable with that kind of freedom will most likely find another church.

At the same time, the findings from this study provide little support for those who contend that exposure to alternate viewpoints leads to a breakdown of religious values. Differences in religious and political beliefs among these Quakers were quite small. Although some considered themselves religious liberals and others described their beliefs as conservative, all stressed the importance of the Inner Light. All disagreed or strongly disagreed with a literal interpretation of the Bible, but they agreed it is true and valuable. In fact, most used the same Bible verses and very similar language to explain what they believed about God and about the Bible and to justify their political positions.

Despite the fact that some considered themselves political conservatives and some liberals and some were Republican and some were Democrats, political differences were more often over methods than goals. As members of a traditionally pacifist church, all opposed war. All leaders and almost half of the members considered a reallocation of the military budget to programs that would promote peace and justice one of the most important issues in the presidential election campaign. Where they differed was on the programs that should receive first priority in that reallocation.

That both leaders and members held very similar religious and political opinions despite that they were encouraged to learn from a variety of sources, to use their reason, and to follow their Inner Light wherever it might lead can partially be attributed to the fact that church membership is voluntary. Those with truly deviant opinions most likely will switch to a more compatible congregation. The fact that political opinions within the Quaker congregation were less diverse than in the Lutheran and United Methodist ones, however, can best be attributed to Quaker practices.

Encouraged to voice their concerns in worship and business meetings but also to listen and learn, they gradually came to understand each other and draw each other to similar conclusions. Whereas that may occur in all groups, here it was probably strengthened by the Quaker practice of making decisions by consensus.

REFERENCES

Alley, R. S. (1990). Television, religion, and fundamentalist distortions. In R. Abelman & S. M. Hoover (Eds.), *Religious television: Controversies and conclusions* (pp. 265-273). Norwood, NJ: Ablex.

Barbour, H., & Roberts, A. O. (Eds.). (1973). *Early Quaker writings: 1650-1700*. Grand Rapids, MI: Eerdmans.

Brinton, H. (1969). The theory of worship. In S. B. Laughlin (Ed.), *Beyond dilemmas* (pp. 75-103). Port Washington, NY: Kennikat.

Buddenbaum, J. M. (1990a). Network news coverage of religion. In J. P. Ferre' (Ed.), *Channels of belief: Religion and American commercial television* (pp. 57-78). Ames: Iowa State University Press.

Buddenbaum, J. M. (1990b). Religion news coverage in commercial network newscasts. In R. Abelman & S. M. Hoover (Eds.), *Religious television: Controversies and conclusions* (pp. 249-264). Norwood, NJ: Ablex.

Burrough, E. (1973). Declaration to all the world of our faith. In H. Barbour & A. O. Roberts (Eds.), *Early Quaker writings: 1650-1700* (pp. 298-303). Grand Rapids, MI: Eerdmans.

Case, C. M. (1969). Friends and social thinking. In S. B. Laughlin (Ed.), *Beyond dilemmas* (pp. 125-151). Port Washington, NY: Kennikat.

Entman, R. M., & Paletz, D. L. (1980). Media and the conservative myth. *Journal of Communication, 30*, 154-165.

Fields, E. E. (1984). *Preachers, press, and politics: The media career of a conservative social movement*. Unpublished doctoral dissertation, University of Oregon, Eugene.

Fox, G. (1925). *Short journal and itinerary journals* (N. Penney, Ed.). Cambridge, MA: Cambridge University Press.

Fox, G. (1972). *Narrative papers of George Fox* (H. J. Cadbury, Ed.). Richmond, IN: Friends United Press.

Fox, G. (1991). *George Fox and the children of light* (J. Fryer, Ed.). London: Kyle Cathie.

Friends Memorial Meeting—Its reason for being. (1992, Summer). *Newsletter* (Friends Memorial Meeting, church newsletter, Muncie, Indiana).

Hunter, J. D. (1991). *Culture wars: The struggle to define America*. New York: Basic Books.

Keiser, E. B., & Keiser, R. M. (1993-1994). Quaker principles in the crucible of practice. *Cross Currents, 43*, 476-484.

Laughlin, S. B. (Ed.). (1969). *Beyond dilemmas*. Port Washington, NY: Kennikat.

Lippard, P. V. (1988). The rhetoric of silence: The Society of Friends' unprogrammed meeting for worship. *Communication Quarterly, 36*, 145-156.

Lippincott, H. M. (Ed.). (1959). *Through a Quaker archway*. New York: Sagamore.

Mill, J. S. (1947). *On liberty*. Oxford, UK: Blackwell. (Originally published in 1859)

Milton, J. (1969). Aeropagitica. In J. Patrick (Ed.), *The prose of John Milton* (pp. 326-345). New York: New York University Press.

Morris, K. R. (1993). Theological sources of William Penn's concept of religious toleration. *Journal of Church and State, 35*, 83-111.

Park, R. E. (1927). The yellow press. *Sociology and Social Research, 12*, 3-11.

Penn, W. (1971). *The select works of William Penn*. New York: Kraus Reprint Co. (Original work published 1726)

Powe, L. A., Jr. (1991). *The fourth estate and the constitution: Freedom of the press in America.* Berkeley: University of California Press.

Some thoughts on the art of living. (1992, January). *Newsletter* (Friends Memorial Meeting, church newsletter, Muncie, Indiana).

Trueblood, D. E. (1969). The Quaker method of reaching decisions. In S. B. Laughlin (Ed.), *Beyond dilemmas* (pp. 104-124). Port Washington, NY: Kennikat.

West, J. (1959). Readers and writers. In H. M. Lippincott (Ed.), *Through a Quaker archway* (pp. 166-176). New York: Sagamore.

Wuthnow, R. (1989). *The struggle for America's soul: Evangelicals, liberals, and secularism.* Grand Rapids, MI: Eerdmans.

15

How Mennonites Use
Media in Everyday Life

Preserving Identity in a Changing World

SHARON HARTIN IORIO

The use of media as an element of social organization is a central concern in the study of mass communication. At issue are the long-term consequences of emerging media technologies and group development. In recent years, there has been a growing recognition that mass communication use involves interactive and interpretative processes (Schramm, 1983; Tuchman, 1988). New research strategies employing qualitative methods at the individual level have reconceptualized the audience role (Liebes, 1988; Lindlof, 1987; McQuail & Gurevitch, 1974). Yet not much progress has been made in understanding the links between media use and group life in a theoretically informed and grounded fashion. It is the aim of this research to move forward along this line. By locating the research within the theories of group boundary maintenance developed by

Frederick Barth (1969), this study will employ historical qualitative methods to address the relevancy of media to group identity maintenance. To do this, the history of the group is discussed and current use of mass media in daily life is explored. The group studied is a small[1] religious/ethnic minority who is visible and distinctive as part of the total population mix in northwest Oklahoma where the research was conducted. Although the importance of content in communication should not be ignored, the emphasis of this research is not on specific beliefs or opinions, neither those held by the group under study nor those generated by the media.

THEORETICAL OVERVIEW

A major obstacle in studying Mennonites as a subculture is the difficulty in defining the group. Mennonite identification covers a broad spectrum of religious doctrine. Moreover, several ethnic subgroups can be found among Mennonites as a whole. Followers of the faith have been divided into several denominations that have been organized to form a continuum (Barclay, 1967; Fretz, 1977), ranging from those who reject technological advances and live in communal, closed congregations, to those who ascribe to strict dress and behavior codes but associate marginally with the outside world through public education and employment, to those who integrate with the larger society and define their association as Mennonites through religious belief and practice. Among the latter are General Conference Mennonites and Mennonite Brethren. It is the more acculturated Mennonites who identify with the more liberal denominations who are most populous in northwest Oklahoma and compose the focus of this research.[2]

The characteristics of these groups were presented in a pioneering work on Anabaptists by Kauffman and Harder (1975). The only published study (Umble, 1990) to date that addresses Mennonites' relationship to mass communication is based on the data Kauffman and Harder collected. Surveys, however, are not designed to elicit information about group development and underlying values, beliefs, and norms of conduct. Neither are they adequate sources of data on the processes that underlie attitude formation.

Sawatsky (1978) attempted to rectify such conceptual and methodological deficiencies and found that denominationalism had resulted in progressive assimilation of Mennonites in U.S. society. His research suggested a linear mobility. Boldt and Roberts (1979) criticized the Sawatsky study and offered an alternative explanation of Mennonite assimilation. Regardless of differences in findings, both Sawatsky and Boldt and Roberts have assumed assimilation as positive, unidimensional, and linear, although the essence of Mennonite identity is not integration but separation. Furthermore, Mennonites have in some ways tended to survive better as Mennonites when society treated them with hostility than when they were accepted by society.

In contrast, Heatwole's (1974) research considered Mennonites as a part of pluralistic society. Separation of the group from society, he found, preserves the religious sect through attaching transcendental meaning to the distinctive values and culture of the religious group. This type of counteracting relationship between Mennonites and U.S. society at large has been pointed out in a variety of articles (Newman, 1973; Redekop, 1974; Redekop & Hostetler, 1977). Yet in looking at the qualities that distinguish Mennonite groups, pluralist interpretations of Mennonites often overlook significant movement toward integration. Such studies also fail to look at interpretation of religious/ethnic groups from the viewpoint of their members.

An alternative to assimilation and pluralist approaches that recognizes the interactive processes of ethnicity has been incorporated in studies of Mennonites (Boldt, 1979; Driedger, 1975; Kauffman, 1977; Rose, 1988) that build on a theoretical perspective developed by Barth (1969). Barth considered the dynamic nature of ethnic boundaries to be the critical aspect of minority groups. His theory is action oriented, allowing for expanding or contracting boundaries within groups. It is distinguished in its theme that ethnic groups are often built on interaction with other social systems. From Barth's perspective, it is not necessary for groups to depend on the absence of interaction to maintain identity. Interaction can actually support differences between groups. Boundaries persist despite a flow of personnel and information across them, and boundaries may also shift. Acculturation and assimilation are important considerations but represent only two of many types of boundary shifts. Studies of

Mennonites emerging from this theoretical perspective have noted the importance of individuals' identification (Driedger, 1977), system linkages (Kauffman, 1977), institutional completeness (Boldt, 1979), and modern migration to urban areas (Rose, 1988).

Barth's (1969) theory that recognizes the linkage of processes among the micro, group, and mass levels provides an opportunity for analyzing mass and individual communication as tools in group maintenance. Furthermore, recent developments in mass media research have fostered reintroduction of the "sociologies of everyday life" to media studies and awakened interest in broadening the definition of what constitutes the audience for mass media (McQuail, 1985; Schramm, 1983; Tuchman, 1988). This has led to several qualitative research projects focused on the audience as a participant in mass communication (Liebes, 1988; Lindlof, 1987; Lull, 1980). Nevertheless, no mass media research examining the part media play in religious/ethnic group development could be located. A line of inquiry, therefore, was established to study the connection of group identity to mediated communication.

Almost all of the sociological research about Mennonites as an ethnic group has sought to interpret lifestyle change. The basic research question was "Are Mennonites losing their identity?" The answer has been yes, no, and, at times, both. The question that this research addresses is not "Are Mennonites losing their identity?" But rather it is, "How have and how are Mennonites constructing their identity?" a topic not addressed by any previous research.

METHOD

Although an interactive orientation shaped my research perspective, I began the project with no a priori theories of how culture and communication worked in Mennonite life. When I undertook the study, I did not intend to embrace the social world of Mennonites through my research, nor did I want to become an "ethnic" specialist or create an ethnography. I instead focused analysis on one aspect of Mennonite life—mediated communication. I selected Mennonites as subjects because they formed a distinct and identifiable group and because I had lived in northwest Oklahoma, near these people, for more than 15 years. But more important than convenience, the Mennonites were an ideal group for the study because of their peculiar relationship to mass communication. Their strict rules of conduct, which at one time forbade the use of mass media by church members, have been relaxed gradually over the years. Mass communication now is part of the everyday life of these Mennonites.

My research was based principally on in-depth personal interviews held with persons of Mennonite heritage. To verify and augment the data gathered in the interviews, I entered into participant observation of the group. In addition, I researched primary and secondary sources to check the reliability and validity of the data I had gathered and to provide background for a summary of Mennonite culture, social organization, and development.

I interviewed more than 40 subjects selected purposively. Participation was voluntary, and subjects were assured anonymity. My long-time residence in the area preceded my role as participant member, so I decided to present myself straightforwardly as a researcher. My established marginality may have limited somewhat my ability to "get inside" the group. Nevertheless, when word of my project circulated, the number of willing participants snowballed.

To ensure the reliability and validity of the data, the subjects were selected to represent a wide range of individuals of Mennonite heritage. Some were active members of Mennonite congregations. Some were currently members of other Protestant denominations. Some lived in urban areas. Some lived on farms or in small towns. For purposes of verification by comparison, I interviewed several members in each of two Mennonite congregations of different denominations located in the same city. The majority of the interview participants were above-average in socioeconomic status and education. This is reflective of the majority of Mennonites in the area. All interviewed were adults.

I wanted to talk with those who had experienced change in the Mennonite way of life. Therefore, I concentrated on people who were from 55 to 75 years of age, but I interviewed many older and some younger, about half of them men and half women.

I also used unobtrusive primary and secondary sources of information as a second basis for my research. Among these sources were materials provided me by congregations from their local publications and from their denominational publications. I also used unpublished manuscripts provided by individuals I interviewed and published works from the personal libraries of the participants. I used newspaper articles and census data. Whenever possible, I checked the accounts given me against published fact. On the whole, I found the Mennonites' descriptions of their group's past to be accurate. The primary and secondary sources were used extensively in providing the record of the group's development in northwest Oklahoma. During and after the information-gathering process, I employed the technique of "constant comparison" (Glaser & Strauss, 1967) to organize and analyze the data.

MENNONITES, ASSIMILATION, AND MEDIA

Political, economic, and technological developments of the 20th century were followed by some Mennonite efforts to adapt and assimilate. They were among the first to make use of power-driven machinery and other laborsaving farm devices in the 1920s and 1930s. Listening to the new radio sets and attending picture shows, however, were different matters. Radio did become more acceptable as the years passed, partly because it was a source of news and information, particularly weather reports that were of vital interest to Mennonite farmers.

When World War II approached, church leadership worked against prevailing public opinion and overt discrimination to generate a selective service provision for conscientious objectors (Smith, 1950). Nevertheless, many Mennonite men entered the military service during World War II ("Pacifist View," 1942). With the passing of time, militarism came to be tolerated, if not accepted, by the majority of the group. Today the peace mission of most churches in northwest Oklahoma is focused on humanitarian aid. Nonresistance is a belief nurtured by the church but also an activity open to personal choice. This adaptation of the boundaries that identify Mennonitism to the outside world allowed the group to be tolerated by the larger society and still preserve its beliefs and values.

During the years after World War II, Mennonite life changed dramatically (Epp, 1977). Mechanization, increased production, and specialized, government-subsidized farming worked to dislodge the diversified, family farm operations that had been the major occupation and the foundation of the closed organization that bound Mennonites together as a religious/ethnic group. Largely through urbanization, professionalization of work, and affluence, the Mennonites steadily assimilated into mainstream society. Interest in political, economic, and social issues has become a part of the Mennonites' daily world. The group no longer attempts to shun society; instead, Mennonites actively participate in the larger social world embracing many forms of mediated communication. Old taboos against attending movies or using electronic media have been dropped.

At the same time the Mennonites have embraced the outside world, there has been an unprecedented amount of institution building, evangelism, and program activity (Hostetler, 1987; Wiesel, 1977). Local Mennonite churches use newsletters and other media. At the denominational level, publishing houses print books, magazines, and other materials. During the post-World War II years, there was a reorganization of the Mennonite ethic. The influence of mainstream Protestantism has continued to contribute to church life, as has the influence of Fundamentalism (Haury, 1981). The willingness to make use of material produced by a variety of Protestant religious denominations, Fundamentalists, or nondenominational groups is reflective of Barth's (1969) view that groups can persevere even when boundaries are permeable. The media creations of Protestant denominationalism and other allied groups generate support for a Christian ethic that does not conflict with Mennonite doctrine and is directly applicable to Mennonites' everyday life.

Some old world traditions lived on. Some unique forms of church life have evolved. A variety of public events and celebrations such as the auctions (Cox, 1988), the meat canning project, and disaster relief projects cut across denominational ties of Mennonites. These activities contribute substantially to a new sense of vitality and direction for the group. Mennonites today live within the larger social milieu. What sets them apart is not their behavior in the world but their way of looking at the world.

During the 20th century, the Mennonites of northwest Oklahoma have moved from poverty to prosperity, from nonconformity to integration, from closed congregations to evangelical mission, and from nonresistant pacifism to proactive peace initiatives and, for some, even military service. In the early 1990s, as many as 2,000 affiliate themselves with six General Conference and two Mennonite Brethren churches located in towns and small cities across northwestern Oklahoma. Their members minister to the needs of their local congregations and actively extend fellowship to the public at large.

Contemporary Mennonite society is vigorous. The group has been transformed from the outside and, perhaps more important, has transformed itself from the inside. The discussion to follow reveals how media are used in everyday life to construct the identity and boundaries of the group. Two types of mediated communication use emerged from the interviews conducted: Mennonites as active consumers of media and producers of media.

Mennonites as Consumers of Media

The group of Mennonites studied in this research is immersed in a media-oriented, technologically centered society. Without exception, all those interviewed for this research said they used media in a variety of forms daily. It would be uncommon today to find a Mennonite household without radio, television, stereo, magazines, books, and newspapers. Videocassette recorders, compact disk players, computers, and the like were found in fewer but still a sizable number of Mennonite homes. Many said they started their day being awakened by a clock radio. Many said they read a newspaper daily, and a clear majority indicated that at some time during the day they read the Bible or used some other form of published religious devotional material. Few of the Mennonites interviewed considered themselves to be heavy television users. On the other hand, few said they restricted the use of media in any way in their homes, although many at some time had restricted their children's television use.

Most commented on the poor quality of television programming and pointed to violence and sex as disagreeable, but few could recall a specific instance when they had turned off a program because it was offensive. Most regarded a lot of what is in the media as valueless, and a few thought television was actually harmful in some instances, but those who did said they did not know exactly *how* media harmed people.

One woman indicated that media, their quality, and their forms, were simply part of the "environment." This rationale for indiscriminate media use seems to fit within the Mennonites' broader frame of reference that has accepted lifestyles that conform to those of mainstream society. Mennonites believe they must now live within the world. The acculturative influence of all this media use was illustrated by one man:

> We had our three granddaughters with us last week. Well, I have a VCR. "Grandpa! We want to watch the movie." The first movie we saw—cute, interesting movie, trick photography in that thing like you wouldn't believe. The language was not that bad. Next movie we got, in terms of lifestyles, was very, very far fetched from any Christian values. I had three grandkids that in less than 24 hours saw that movie three times. And, of course, to them the fun thing was the baby. Well, they just howled. They didn't realize that baby was born out of wedlock. I mean that kind of issue was not in the kids' heads, but you know, for me, that's not where I'm at.

Instead of attempting to restrict the acculturating influences in media that may or may not be affecting them, Mennonites actively select and use certain types of media that reinforce their own value system, for example, the daily devotional. Daily Bible reading is still a widespread practice among Mennonites. The daily devotional and shared Bible reading serve as examples of symbolic expression of media use. Devotions generally are held either at breakfast, at the evening dinner hour, or before retiring at night. The devotions also are most usually observed in a ritualistic manner with Bible reading, the study of a lesson from printed material, and prayer, each addressed in a prescribed manner and particular order.

Bible reading often is augmented by other Christian readings that are historical or instructive in nature. Printed material published by the Mennonite denominations, *The Christian Leader* and *The Mennonite*, and other periodicals, are circulated widely. In addition, many books, pamphlets, and take-home Sunday school workbooks for children and adults put out by the Mennonite denominations also are found in Mennonite homes. Religious books and music printed by Protestant publishing houses or by fundamentalist groups are widely used, as well as videotaped religious subject matter.

Periodicals and other kinds of printed and video material that relate to the special interests of individuals are used by Mennonites. For example, literature from peace organizations and from antiabortion groups is circulated to members of the group. Special interest information geared to hobbies, sports, or business and professional people also can be found in Mennonite homes. Not only is material produced by other religious groups found in the homes of Mennonites, it is used in church services as well. Videotapes on church history and mission efforts of the Mennonite denominations are distributed widely and shown regularly to individual congregations.

Mennonites also engage in television watching and videotape and movie viewing as groups. The gathering of a congregation or smaller units within the church to share in media use has ritualistic and symbolic significance. It is a late 20th-century representation that reflects the group's bonding in the mid-16th century. Films on church history—the re-creation of the deaths of the early martyrs— are a means to instill in viewers the lessons of group identification as well as church doctrine. The review of the migrations of the group in search of religious freedom reinforces a historical association with Mennonite ethnicity. It serves as a badge of identification that is a positive, albeit self-imposed and entirely conceptual, label of marginality. Not all group viewing is restricted to lessons in ethnic history and church doctrine, however. A good deal of videotape watching is devoted to topics related to everyday life. The subjects of media content range from lessons on how to build a good marriage to effective estate planning. The consumption of media embodies ritualistic and symbolic expressions and reflects how people and ideas may flow across boundaries with the boundaries remaining intact.

The overriding perception is that the media, in their various forms, are acculturating. Much in the media is distasteful to Mennonites and, many think, probably harmful. But to attempt to disassociate one's self or one's family from media would be futile. On the other hand, the media also are perceived as an enjoyable pastime that offers some kinds of information. The acts of media consumption are a part of the process of active community organization. For a Mennonite, making a life that is "in the world, but not of the world" is a tightrope walked by a shared group experience assisted by creative media consumerism.

In summary, Mennonites, as a group, do not appear to restrict the flow of mass media into their homes in any regulated way. Although they often criticize it, they seem to involve themselves with many forms of media content and types of media technology. Individual members of the group actively seek out media that reinforce the denominational beliefs and values of the group and the religious values of constituent religious groups and material that appeals to other special interests that they might have. Outside their homes, in their churches, Mennonites avail themselves of materials, especially visual media, produced by fundamentalist or mainline Protestant organizations, and their own denominations make available movies and other kinds of printed and visual materials for use in local churches. Mennonites actively manipulate media by choosing media products that articulate and reinforce the group's identity.

Mennonites as Producers of Media

Mennonites create as well as consume media. As farmers in earlier years, they were among the first to adopt new agricultural technologies. Similarly, they readily adopt new media technologies. Mennonites use print and visual media, particularly visual media, to produce an experience of community. This activity goes beyond the formulation of content or the construction of materials. It involves, among other things, the selection of media form and subject, editing, and dissemination of the final product. For example, video cameras provide the group an opportunity to make movies. One congregation put together a script about their church, taped several different activities of their members, edited their work, and produced it all as a video recording that was broadcast on public access cable television. Another congregation regularly videotapes its Sunday morning church services for replay at a local nursing home in which several elderly members of the congregation are confined. Almost all Mennonite churches produce a weekly newsletter that contains information about congregational programs and events and is mailed to members' homes.

One minister of a congregation in an urban area uses a darkroom he set up at the church to produce a series of slides that he uses to accompany his weekly sermons. He said,

> I had never been into photography before and I took a class on it. I desperately wanted to communicate. I love the Bible and am thoroughly convinced that it's God's word to us, as old as it is. The principles are still the truth. I desperately wanted to communicate it. And I just realized the traditional sermon of a half-hour monologue wasn't doing it. I felt that having some kind of visual effect would help. That's basically my motivation and I really ought to think about other ways, you know.

Ministers or church lay leaders usually are involved in the media creation processes, often organizing the work of others. Although only a small portion of the membership is usually involved directly in producing mediated communication, the entire congregation generally participates in using what the few have produced. Furthermore, the congregations seem to identify with the work of the "media specialists" among their group and share in the ownership of the finished product. There is a certain amount of congregational pride associated with the projects, particularly the more creative applications of visual media. The activity provides a network of social ties that links the congregation to their common identity, intensifies positive group interaction, and is an important resource for perpetuating the formal structure of the group. Media production helps to undergird the normative organization of the congregation. Working with media, creating it, and using it is not only an individual experience. It is, at times, a shared experience.

The production of media is a multifaceted operation and is unique. Every congregation is involved on its own. It should be noted, however, that except for the weekly newsletters, the extensive production of media at the local level is limited and not undertaken by the majority of congregations, but active media use is growing both among individual members and congregations.

In addition to the media created by individuals and local churches, mediated communication also is created at the group level. The annual Mennonite relief sale is an auction of handmade quilts, hand-crafted clocks and toys, new and used farm equipment, and other items; it is an example of how media is used within the larger primary group. The relief sale project is an opportunity to raise money for Mennonite peace programs and an additional opportunity for the group to reify its ethnic heritage. It is highly publicized. Through brochures, announcements, and news releases sent to local, area, and statewide publications, an organized effort of volunteers uses public channels of communication to attract attention for the sale.

At a higher level of organization, the General Conference of Mennonite Brethren Churches and the Mennonite Church General Conference each maintain a publishing house to circulate material for church and home consumption. The denominational headquarters of the Mennonite organizations also produce and distribute films, videotape, and slides that emphasize church history and doctrine. One Mennonite woman living in northwest Oklahoma has published a book of religious stories for children through her denomination's press. She is an exception. The amount of media produced by individual Mennonites for their local congregations or denominations is not large, especially when compared to the amount of commercial media consumed by Mennonites.

The Mennonite production of media is obviously an expressive act and built within the shifting boundaries of the subculture. The media of today provide Mennonites opportunity for communication, extension of the group, and bonding, although in a much more expansive way than in years past. The rapid introduction of low-cost media production apparatus in the form of video camera recorders and video cassette recorders, desktop publishing, computer networking, and the like has revolutionized interactive communication among Mennonites. Not relegated to the position of passive receivers, Mennonites now have within their means the tools of production. These new tools of creativity allow individuals and small groups to play an initiative role in mediated communication. With financial barriers to the technology eroding, Mennonites can engage imagery through different media, visual as well as print, and, if not compete with commercial efforts, at least transcend its all-out pervasiveness. The current ease and affordability of communication technology have empowered individuals and local congregations with new tools of expression.

The main purpose of the media Mennonites produce is to extend the group's identity. The creation of media is an expression of the group that reinforces it. In the following instances, taking a video of church services to the rest home strengthens group ties. Producing a television film about church life heightens the group's identification with the general public. Writing children's books and photographing slides to accompany sermons have instructive value. The group puts out literature and imagery, and, although they may not have access to the media, they do access the media technologies and that in itself is a means to a transcendental end. The hoped-for effect is both temporal and a heavenly reward.

MEDIA AND BOUNDARY MAINTENANCE

Mennonites have undergone tremendous change in the almost 100 years they have spent in Oklahoma, from a closed community to an open one, from plain dress and restrictive codes of behavior to assimilation and acculturation into mainstream society, from nonresistance as religious doctrine to pacifism as personal choice, and from isolation to integration. The events and issues surrounding World War I forced change in the group's use of the German language, in the group's response to war, and in group culture overall. Conformity and accommodation permitted survival in a complex and rapidly changing society.

As the Mennonites of northwest Oklahoma consume and produce media, the current dominant trend toward assimilation, acculturation, and acceptance of the larger social world is undergirded by a strong effort to reify the group's religion/ethnicity. Although much of their media use is nonselective, Mennonite people do actively target some types of media for consumption, and they create their own media. They use a variety of religious and secular printed materials. Mennonites produce media in many forms, including church newsletters, advertisements for their activities, videotapes, and illustrated sermons. In recent years, the ease and affordability of the new communication technologies have empowered individuals and local congregations and allowed Mennonites to play an initiative role in mediated communication. By picking and choosing from content and technologies, individual Mennonites can be viewed as putting together the boundaries of their group and supporting their religion/ethnicity.

Although there is no attempt to generalize the findings of this study, the results do suggest that the popular view of media as a force that encourages homogeneity is not an entirely accurate conceptualization. The influence of media in the acculturation of minorities and ethnic groups certainly cannot be denied. Nevertheless, the uses of mass communication are hardly unidirectional. At the same time mediated communication acculturates, it cultivates religion/ethnicity, as this study of Mennonites of northwest Oklahoma shows. Furthermore, the study verifies that media technology, as well as its content, can be processed as an object of communication.

If, indeed, the concept of a global village (McLuhan, 1964) built by technology is true, it is also possible that life in the techno-village may be carried on in clans: clans whose bonds are welded by mediated as well as other forms of communication. For the Mennonites observed in this study, mediated communication is an important means through which individuals in the group express self-identification to the group, sustain beliefs and values, shore up frames of reference, and maintain group boundaries. In an era of instant and pervasive communication that touches the most remote and resistant of enclaves, Mennonite identity endures amidst great social change.

NOTES

1. According to the U.S. Bureau of the Census, Mennonites in 1985 numbered approximately 100,000 nationwide. Because of their small numbers, no accurate count of their membership in Oklahoma at preset could be determined. The number of Mennonites in northwest Oklahoma may range anywhere from 1,000 to 2,500.

2. Although the focus of this research is on the Mennonites who have acculturated and assimilated into U.S. society, those interested in modern Mennonites who remain separated from society may find a discussion of these groups in Barclay (1967), Defrange (1988), Eaton (1952), Hostetler (1980), and Redekop and Hostetler (1977). Only one such group, Holderman Mennonites, supports two church groups with an approximate total membership of 250 in northwest Oklahoma currently.

REFERENCES

Barclay, H. B. (1967). The plain people of Oregon. *Review of Religious Research, 8,* 140-165.

Barth, F. (1969). *Ethnic groups and boundaries.* Boston: Little, Brown.

Boldt, E. P. (1979). The plain people: Notes on their continuity and change. *Canadian Ethnic Studies, 11,* 17-28.

Boldt, E. P., & Roberts, L. W. (1979). Mennonite continuity and change: A comment on Rodney J. Sawatsky. *Canadian Journal of Sociology, 4*(2), 151-154.

Cox, A. (1988, November 28). Fairview: Mennonite sale nets $85,000. *Enid Daily News and Eagle,* pp. 1-3.

Defrange, A. (1988, June). A separate peace. *Oklahoma Today,* pp. 12-19.

Driedger, L. (1975). Canadian Mennonite urbanism: Ethnic villages or metropolitan remnant? *Mennonite Quarterly Review, 47,* 225-244.

Driedger, L. (1977). The Anabaptist identification ladder: Plain urbane continuity in diversity. *Mennonite Quarterly Review, 51,* 378-381.

Eaton, J. W. (1952). Controlled acculturation: A survival technique of the Hutterites. *American Sociological Review, 17,* 331-340.

Epp, F. H. (1977). *Mennonite peoplehood: A plea for new initiatives.* Waterloo, Ontario: Conrad.

Fretz, J. W. (1977). The plain and not-so-plain Mennonites in Waterloo County, Ontario. *Mennonite Quarterly Review, 51,* 377-385.

Glaser, T., & Strauss, A. (1967). *The discovery of grounded theory: Strategies for qualitative research.* Hawthorne, NY: Aldine.

Haury, D. A. (1981). *Prairie people: A history of the Western District Conference.* Newton, KS: Faith & Life Press.

Heatwole, C. A. (1974). Religion in the creation and preservation of sectarian culture areas: A Mennonite example (Doctoral dissertation, Michigan State University, 1974). *Dissertation Abstracts International, 35,* 6031A.

Hostetler, B. S. (1987). *American Mennonites and Protestant movements.* Scottdale, PA: Herald.

Hostetler, J. A. (1980). *Amish society.* Baltimore: Johns Hopkins University Press.

Kauffman, J. H. (1977). Boundary maintenance and cultural assimilation of contemporary Mennonites. *Mennonite Quarterly Review, 51,* 227-240.

Kauffman, J. H., & Harder, L. (1975). *Anabaptists four centuries later: A profile of five Mennonite and Brethren in Christ denominations.* Scottdale, PA: Herald.

Liebes, T. (1988). Cultural differences in the retelling of television fiction. *Critical Studies in Mass Communication, 5,* 277-292.

Lindlof, T. R. (1987). Ideology and pragmatics of media access in prison. In T. R. Lindlof (Ed.), *Natural audiences* (pp. 88-103). Norwood, NJ: Ablex.

Lull, J. (1980). The social uses of television. *Human Communication Research, 6*(3), 197-209.

McLuhan, M. (1964). *Understanding media.* New York: Signet.

McQuail, D. (1985). Sociology of mass communication. In R. H. Turner & J. F. Short, Jr. (Eds.), *Annual review of sociology* (pp. 93-111). Palo Alto, CA: Annual Reviews.

McQuail, D., & Gurevitch, M. (1974). Explaining audience behavior: Three approaches considered. In J. G. Blumler & E. Katz (Eds.), *The uses of mass communication: Current perspectives on gratifications research* (pp. 287-302). Beverly Hills, CA: Sage.

Newman, W. M. (1973). *American pluralism: A study of minority group and social theory.* New York: Harper & Row.

Pacifist view hard for young men to accept: War creates problems and heartaches for Mennonite clergymen and families. (1942, February 16). *Daily Oklahoman,* p. 1.

Redekop, C. (1974). A new look at sect development. *Journal for the Scientific Study of Religion, 13,* 345-352.

Redekop, C., & Hostetler, J. A. (1977). The plain people: An interpretation. *Mennonite Quarterly Review, 51,* 266-277.

Rose, M. (1988). Migration and ethnic persistence: A study of a rural Mennonite church. *Mennonite Quarterly Review, 62,* 167-176.

Sawatsky, R. J. (1978). Domesticated sectarianism: Mennonites in the U.S. and Canada in comparative perspective. *Canadian Journal of Sociology, 3*(2), 233-244.

Schramm, W. (1983). The unique perspective of communication. *Journal of Communication, 33,* 6-17.

Smith, H. C. (1950). *The story of the Mennonites.* Newton, KS: Mennonite Publication Office.

Tuchman, G. (1988). Mass media institutions. In N. J. Smelser (Ed.), *The handbook of sociology* (p. 601-626). Newbury Park, CA: Sage.

Umble, D. Z. (1990). Mennonites and television: Applications of cultivation analysis to a religious subculture. In N. Signorielli & M. Morgan (Eds.), *Cultivation analysis: New directions in media effects research* (pp. 141-156). Newbury Park, CA: Sage.

Wiesel, B. B. (1977). From separatism to evangelism: A case study of social and cultural change among the Franconia Conference Mennonites, 1945-1970. *Review of Religious Research, 18,* 254-263.

16

Rappin' for the Lord

The Uses of Gospel Rap and Contemporary Music in Black Religious Communities

CHERYL RENÉE GOOCH

RAP HAS FOUND GOD

He calls himself Mr. Solo, and he is a gangster, that is, a gangster of the gospel. After seeing many of his peers go either to prison or to their graves, Solo decided to turn his life around and use his rapping talent to worship God.

His group, "Gospel Gangstas," addresses through its songs popular subjects of rap music—sex and violence—but with a moral twist. Using hard-hitting, hip-hop lingo, they admonish their fans to overcome sexual desires with the help of Jesus in singing, "I had an A in fornication, but an F on my test, oh yes . . . I needed 2 be delivered. . . . Cause livin' in sin is like 5-2-10 in the pen. So I gave my life 2 Christ and got born again" (Solo, 1994b).[1]

Regarding violence, particularly between Black males and police, Solo, a former gang member, says gospel rap is intended to be redemptive, not retaliatory:

We just want to let brothers out there know we acknowledge police brutality and police harassment because we live in it . . . but we have answers to the problem. It's not in killing the police, it's not in violent retaliation. . . . It's in knowledge, it's in staying in school . . . getting yourself out of those situations . . . accepting Christ and asking God to direct your path. (Solo, 1994a)[2]

Blending religion and rhymes, groups within this burgeoning genre have captured the ears of young African Americans who are embracing the messages of rap and other popular music for social identity.

Although much has been written about rap music and its relationship to the Black[3] community, scholarly treatment of the emergence of gospel rap as a socially relevant, viable form of spiritual expression is rare. As more churches endeavor to address a fuller range of concerns in the Black community, especially in urban areas where youth increasingly are alienated, some church leaders may be amenable to incorporating alternative forms of music in their outreach programs. This chapter examines the views of some Black church and religious leaders regarding the use of gospel rap (and other contemporary sacred music) as a complement to praise, worship, or ministry, and the social and religious contexts that help shape some of these views.

OH HAPPY DAY: THE RELIGIOUS AND SOCIAL FUNCTIONS OF CONTEMPORARY BLACK GOSPEL MUSIC

From the early days of slavery to today, the church has played a vital role in the African American community, functioning both as a social and spiritual forum. Most Black Christians are affiliated with major, historically Black Baptist and Methodist denominations and Holiness-Pentecostal sects, although increasing numbers have joined the Roman Catholic Church and other predominately white religious sects, including the Jehovah's Witnesses and Seventh-day Adventists.[4]

The praise and worship styles observed in majority Black churches reflect the broad range of experiences of their communities

(McClain, 1990; Phelps, 1990). National Public Radio's 1994 *Wade in the Water* series traces the origins and development of Black sacred music from traditional to contemporary genres, while demonstrating how the varied song traditions have shaped the Black community along both spiritual and social lines. The creator and producer of the series sees Black gospel music as "a twentieth-century phenomenon, born of a people moving from rural communities to the urban centers of this country" (Reagon, 1992, p. 4) and, like numerous scholars, as an embodiment of the religious, cultural, and social dimensions of Black life in the United States (Cone, 1980; Dupree & Dupree, 1993; Spencer, 1990; Walker, 1979).

The 1969 recording *Oh Happy Day*, with its modern music tempo and number one slot on both pop and gospel charts, helped usher in the contemporary Black gospel music era. Since then, gospel has moved toward the mainstream with an updated religious sound that is especially appealing to urban contemporary music listeners, prompting some critics to question whether the message of gospel music is getting compromised. Singer Edwin Hawkins, however, the driving force behind *Oh Happy Day*, contends that the use of secular music does not dilute the message of the gospel. " 'It's not the style that makes gospel,' " he contends. " 'It's the message' " (Brown, 1988, p. 66).

Indeed, the messages of gospel music, both traditional and contemporary, have embodied a full range of concerns of the Black community. Examining the relationship between Black sacred music and social change, for example, Walker (1979) traces the continuum of the oral tradition of Black sacred music that commenced with the creation of the spiritual and all of its musical "cousins." He notes that today's gospel umbrella embraces both "the spiritual idiom and contemporary social comment," resulting in a "form of urban spiritual, a song of faith which rallies the hope and aspiration of the faithful in the face of devastating social conditions" (p. 127). Similarly, theologian James Cone (1980) says the fusion of spirituals and blues helps create "cultural structures for black expression. . . . Its purposes and aims [are] . . . directly related to the consciousness of the black community" (p. 5).

Of particular relevance to this discussion of contemporary gospel is Newman's (1988) analysis of the "soul synthesis," that is, how gospel, street-corner rhythm and blues (R&B) and big band jazz came together to form soul. For purposes here, the lyrical content and function of gospel and street corner R&B are most important. Both gospel and street-corner R&B, Newman notes, fostered a sense of community while contributing "to a growing sense of freedom and accomplishment" among Blacks (p. 163).

Similarly, the most contemporary form of rap, which became popular in the 1970s, provided the traditionally disenfranchised a voice with which to praise or protest prevalent social conditions. Now gospel rap, a derivative of socially relevant rap, is being used by groups such as "DC Talk" "to minister the gospel" (Dougherty & Carpenter, 1994, p. 85). The "DC" stands for Decent Christian and reflects the group's adherence to traditional Christian teachings such as salvation through Christ, importance of family, and the pitfalls of abortion (Rabey, 1991).

Still another group, "Transformation Crusade," uses the so-called devil's music to discourage violence among urban teenagers. One of the members, Andre Sims, a former gang member, says, "Basically we're trying to stop the violence of urban teen America. We recognized the fact that we needed to go back and reach folks who are doing the same things we were doing before we knew the Lord" (Jones, 1991, p. 46).

This continual "wedging together of sacred and secular music styles," as noted by an ethnomusicologist, "calls into question the artificial boundaries that historically have separated religious and secular styles, their performers, and their audiences" (Maultsby, 1992a, p. 32). This assertion evokes a point about contemporary gospel that even its critics must address: the strength that listeners derive from the message of the music. "Regular rap talks about sex and earthly things," explains a teenager who recently attended a gospel rap show near Chicago. But gospel rap music, he says, "teaches you about the Lord and that there is a higher place to look to" (Marriot, 1994, p. 64). A notable radio host also observes that "the music today is not confined to the church. It's moved beyond the church walls and . . . people are leaning towards it . . . because this is the day and time for it. Crime and killings have taken their toll on people" (Boehlert, 1994, p. 34).

In a candid discussion of the relationship between theology and music, leading Baptist minister and author Wendell Mapson (1984) notes, "It is necessary to continue to affirm the power and appeal of music in the Black church. In the Black church the two major attractions are still good preaching and good singing, although perhaps not always in that order" (p. 20).

The fact that music type is often a major drawing card for congregations, especially those with active youth outreach ministries, has been further documented. Exploring the growing numbers of Black youths flocking to traditional and evangelical churches, Poinsett (1990) observes that various youth subcultures may require new forms of evangelism. In an ever-changing social, political, and moral climate, the Black church has recognized the need to adjust and respond to new challenges facing the community, namely the family and youth. The results of a recent *Ebony* magazine survey reinforces this point. Most of the leaders of traditional denominations surveyed say they urge their congregations to address rising problems, including drugs, teenage pregnancy, and gangs, and almost all cited youth as the main target of their outreach ministries ("Changing Church Confronts," 1993). Jones (1992) further observes that "the churches that are growing by leaps and bounds are characterized by vibrant worship, . . . warm evangelical preaching . . . and aggressive social ministries" (p. 195).

Yet during a time when some African American congregations are experiencing a creeping decline in membership, partly due to unchanged leadership styles and programs (Jones, 1992), some leaders have not readily embraced gospel rap and other contemporary Christian music forms, the styles of music that have the ears of the nation's music-listening youth. For this study, representative Black church organizations were asked to provide formal statements or policies regarding the use of rap that had been issued. In most cases, the national headquarters indicated that such policies are left up to individual churches. According to the spokesperson for the Congress of National Black Churches, a coalition of seven major African American denominations (the three major Baptist conventions, the three major Methodist churches, and the Church of God in Christ) that has pursued broad priorities, including the media, evangelism, and human services, no particular statement on the use of gospel rap has been issued (Diane Hugger, personal communication, September 1994). Moreover, with regard to newer, more expressive gospel music styles, the views of some mainstream church leaders reveal that they are generally nonconversant about music styles that deviate from the traditional forms of sacred music and less than eager to incorporate even positive Christian rap in their music repertoires.

These views, in part, are a result of the stigma attached to secular rap as well as evangelistic styles of music historically associated with certain religious sects deemed to be out of the traditional Christian mainstream. Therefore, to better understand views about the use of gospel rap and other contemporary music in church services, it is important to consider some of the social and theological contexts in which church leaders decide what types of music to encourage their congregations to use.

MAKING A JOYFUL NOISE: THE MINISTRY OF MUSIC IN BLACK CHURCHES

The upbeat tone of Psalm 100:1-5 (KJV), "Make a joyful noise unto the Lord, all ye lands," encourages worshipers to praise God cheerfully and is recited in most African American churches and congregations before the choir performs any special presentation (*The Original African Heritage Study Bible*, 1993, p. 904). Another Scripture frequently quoted by celebration churches (including charismatic mainstream churches) to support expressive worship forms is Psalm 150, which admonishes believers to praise God openly, enthusiastically, and, when possible, with instruments. It reads, in part,

3. Praise him with the sound of the trumpet: praise him with the psaltery and harp.
4. Praise him with the timbrel and dance: praise him with stringed instruments and organs.
5. Praise him upon the loud cymbals: praise him upon the high sounding cymbals.
6. Let everything that hath breath praise the Lord. Praise ye the Lord!

Actually, numerous Scriptures condone the use of music, musicians, and musical instruments for various praise, worship, and ministerial purposes.[5]

Music has long been an integral part of worship services in Black churches, and some clergy have even proposed general guidelines for the qualitative use of music in the church (Harris, 1991; Mapson, 1984). Still, there are divergent perspectives about what styles are most appropriate and the conditions under which such styles should be incorporated into services and ministries; these views tend to be informed by denominational and other inextricably related sociocultural factors.

The Seventh-day Adventist church (SDA), which includes a significant number of Black congregations, defines "debased" music as "any melody partaking of the nature of jazz, rock or related hybrid forms" (*Seventh-day Adventists Believe*, 1988). To the more socially conscious, the definition presented here reflects a traditionally conservative, Eurocentric view that denigrates some of the expressive music that pervades most contemporary Black worship settings. For example, contemporary gospel music, as discussed earlier, is rooted in a fusion of jazz and blues. It also

> tends to be . . . upbeat . . . and highly emotional, with highly ornamented recitatives and imaginative instrumentation. . . . Choirs use a large range of instrumental accompaniment: electric organ, piano, horns, drums. . . . Choirs stage performances with music carefully chosen to elicit an audience response at the desired time. (*Abingdon Dictionary of Living Religions*, 1981, p. 108)

The SDA view, which is also held across many Christian denominations, typifies attitudes of some of the most ardent critics of contemporary gospel who generally regard the jazz/blues fusion and such expressive accompaniment (vocal and instrumental) as licentious.

Although less vitriolic of expressive gospel music styles, leaders of mainstream Black churches are still apt to employ more traditional forms of gospel music in their programs. In a survey of more than 2,000 Black churches nationwide, Lincoln and Mamiya (1990) found that

there are still some prominent segments within elite . . . Baptist and
Methodist churches and among some traditionalists who customarily
express annoyance with, or outright rejection of gospel music, both in
terms of its often problematic theology and because of its alleged
secularity. (p. 376)

Although the vast majority of pastors surveyed approved of use
of some form of gospel (usually traditional spirituals), the greatest
ambivalence was shown toward other types of Black music that
characterize contemporary gospel (Lincoln & Mamiya, 1990, p. 379).
Also, urban clergy expressed more willingness to experiment with
other types of Black music than did the rural clergy.

The observation of the traditional "outright rejection of gospel
music, both in terms of its often problematic theology and because
of its alleged secularity" (Lincoln & Mamiya, 1990, p. 379), warrants
further consideration in that it reflects some deep-seated class and
sociocultural differences in the Black community that often are
manifested in Black church settings. "In its developing stages," says
Maultsby (1992b), "gospel music emerged only in the Black folk
church" (p. 21). Associated with Holiness, Pentecostal, and Sancti-
fied sects, "the doctrines of the Black folk church encourage free
expression, which unveiled itself in spontaneous testimonies, prayers, and music" (Maultsby, 1992b, p. 21), while also nurturing a
"new style of singing, with its driving rhythms and percussive
instrumental accompaniment" (Reagon, 1992, p. 5).

A leader of one of the major Holiness-Pentecostal groups, the
Church of God in Christ (COGIC), which condones the use of
evangelistic music, including gospel rap, is keenly aware of the
ethnocentric bias that permeates the views of some leaders of traditionally mainstream churches. He notes,

In the "sophisticated" Black churches . . . there were several theories
ascribed to the deletion of Black religious music in worship service.
Among these is the idea that the Black music was held in ridicule, and
the persons performing it were after grotesque effects and laughter,
causing the Blacks themselves to become ashamed of their own
songs. . . . The dialect used in these songs was simply laughed at. . . .
This ridicule and persecution created the stereotyped image of the
Blacks as being stupid, ignorant and clownish. (McCoy, n.d., p. 5)

Of the various denominations contacted for this study, the COGIC provided the most clearly delineated and extensive statement of its musical philosophy: an official handbook. The ministry of music, the handbook states, uses songs "which will exalt God and render due benevolence to his great and marvelous name" (McCoy, n.d., p. 21). For the COGIC then, music is but a natural expression of church theology. "The Pentecostals have been the most innovative in terms of gospel development," because, according to Maultsby (Portia Maultsby, personal communication, September 1994), "unlike some other denominations, their doctrines do not restrict religious expression."

I also found that leaders of some traditional congregations who espouse more progressive views about the use of music in social ministry are more receptive to contemporary forms of gospel music.[6] In such cases, leaders indicated their sensitivity to the importance of making religious experiences relevant to the cultures of the communities they serve.

Like the COGIC, Black Catholics have endeavored to develop guidelines for the use of culturally relevant music that coincide with church doctrine. Recognizing the need to have music reflective of their heritage and faith, a group of Black Catholic bishops helped develop what is called the *African American Catholic Hymnal*. They noted, "We believe that liturgy of the Catholic Church can be an even more intense expression of the spiritual vitality of those who are of African origin, just as it has been for other ethnic and cultural groups" (*Lead Me, Guide Me: The African American Catholic Hymnal*, 1987).[7] Other charismatic leaders of the Catholic faith have provided guidelines for the creative integration of Black cultural characteristics into praise and worship services, namely, that the services be participatory, Spirit-filled, and celebratory (Bowman, 1987; Murray, 1987).

LIGHT TO THE GENTILES:
RAP AND ITS BIBLICAL CONNECTIONS

Acts 26:23 provides one clear biblical foundation for gospel rap. For some of those attempting to heed the apostle Paul's advice to Christians to witness to people outside the church in languages they understand, rap has provided a viable venue. The coordinator of music for the Crenshaw Christian Center, a well-known charismatic ministry based in Los Angeles, says that rap used in his church is "the spoken Word put to music . . . that opens the door for young people . . . and even the adults to relate to Christ" (Marcial Holmes, personal communication, May 8, 1995).

Echoing the contention that secular rap can be transformed to convey biblically inspired messages is Rodney Draggon, a Tacoma, Washington-based minister who specializes in youth ministry and drug prevention. Known as "The Message Man," Draggon says he uses rap because it is a language young people understand. "Rap was always accepted among inner-city youths," he explains, "because it deals with real situations and comes from the heart . . . and it's a way to reach them" (Rodney Draggon, personal communication, August 31, 1994). In his song, "Christian Rap," Draggon (1992a) addresses street life and drugs in a manner that encourages young people to see Jesus as a viable alternative. He sings,

> *So if young people, you want to have a fling,*
> *Give your life to Jesus, that's doing the right thing.*
> *You don't need drugs or taking any dope.*
> *Jesus is love and he'll bring you hope.*[8]

Listening to Draggon's rap, one is reminded of the straightforwardness of traditional Black preaching and gospel music, both of which involve interpreting biblical texts within the context of the struggles of day-to-day life (Franklin, 1982; Spencer, 1990), techniques that almost always render audiences captivated and responsive (Dupree & Dupree, 1993; McClain, 1990). Combining his preaching and singing talents in his song "Rapping Through the Bible," Draggon (1992b) tries to instill in his young listeners an interest in and respect for biblical truths as a basis for daily living with lyrics such as the following:

> *Now when you come to Jesus, he sticks like static cling.*
> *And in your heart, you really will sing.*
> *So brothers and sisters if you should fall,*
> *Get right back up and on his name you call.*[9]

Although the lyrics of gospel rap may coincide with biblical principles, the style of gospel rap strikes a less than resonant chord among some church leaders who for various social and theological reasons already discussed are more amenable to traditional sacred music forms. But although some churches have closed their doors to gospel rap, gospel rap is gaining momentum and support in secular settings. One of the major distributors of the music, Matthew Abraham (personal communication, May 6, 1995), president of CMN Distributors, says he gets calls telling about hundreds of "gang members and prisoners who are giving their lives to the Lord" after listening to positive, edifying rap. "That so-called lost generation, generation X, is lost," he says, "because no one is out there talking to them in a language they understand." Also, publishers of two of the leading gospel rap magazine publications, *Score* and *Heaven's Hip Hop*, predict that the growing popularity of positive rap music will prompt more churches to begin using this type of music to minister to youth populations.

Most churches and ministries that make use of positive rap are characterized by their more expressive worship forms reflective of the cultures of their communities. Leaders of such groups have an acute understanding of the appeal and effectiveness of communicating through a medium young people understand.

SEARCHING TO AND FRO: FINDING A PLACE FOR HEAVENLY HIP-HOP

The beginning of the rap "Christian Rap (Draggon, 1992a) goes:

> *I went seeking, I was searching to and fro.*
> *I'm trying to find peace of mind in this world below.*
> *You know, I needed Jesus to help me find my way.*
> *You know, I didn't know where to go, I was all alone.*
> *I heard Jesus say, "My child, why not come home?"*[10]

These lyrics hold dual meaning for Draggon, who, just a few years ago, struggled to find a church that would accept his rap music ministry. A Black, Seventh-day Adventist minister, Draggon recalls being rebuffed by some church leaders in his predominately Black church conference. Now in a predominately white conference, he says, he and his music have gained more acceptance and support. This scenario encapsulates a concern of some in traditional Black religious settings who are beginning to use this new form of rap to spread moral messages among young listeners: "Is there a place for heavenly hip-hop in the Black church?"

According to the pastor of the Macedonia Miracle Kingdom and Worship Center in Montgomery, Alabama, there is. Like his counterparts across the country, he sees rap as a viable part of praise and worship and outreach and evangelism and as a way to attract and maintain the youth membership of his charismatic congregation. Leo Lewis (personal communication, September 21, 1994) explains,

> Youth are drawn by this expression. As long as gospel rap exalts the name of Jesus and motivates others to follow Him, we see nothing wrong with it. Our battle comes when Satan attempts to pollute and pervert this form of expression.[11]

FISHING FOR SOULS

In Mark 1:17 (KJV), Jesus told his disciples, "Come ye after me, and I will make you fishers of men." Although the specific type of bait to be used was not specified, the spoken word has been handed down to Christian believers in the form of the Bible. Similarly, sacred music is regarded as the spoken and written word put to music.

Like earlier forms of evangelistic "Jesus" music associated with nonmainstream religious sects, gospel rap has not been readily embraced by fans of more traditional sacred music forms. It has communicated, however, often where no other language has, to groups for whom rap is a natural and familiar language.

Whereas generally characterized by its proclivity for preserving old traditions, the Black church has provided the impetus for social change from voting rights to human rights. Concomitantly, the church has accommodated both continuity and change in religious music styles. Given the burgeoning interest in and effectiveness of gospel rap both within and outside of the church, more churches are likely to consider using it to minister to youth populations. Although the styles and beats of religious music may vary, the message remains the same. As one minister said of the increasing success of gospel rap in outreach ministries: "It's the hope, the word of God."

NOTES

1. Gospel Gangstas lyrics courtesy of Frontline Music Group. "Testimony" written by Solo. Copyright © 1994 Broken Songs/Holy Terra Music (ASCAP). Recorded by Gospel Gangstas on *Gang Affiliated*. Label: Frontline Records. All rights reserved. Reprinted by permission.

2. Gospel Gangstas lyrics courtesy of Frontline Music Group. "Interrogation 2" written by Solo. Copyright © 1994 Broken Songs/Holy Terra Music (ASCAP). Recorded by Gospel Gangstas on *Gang Affiliated*. Label: Frontline Records. All rights reserved. Reprinted by permission.

3. This capitalized form is the author's preference for designating and referring to persons of African descent. The terms *Black* and *African American* are used interchangeably to acknowledge and encompass the terms most widely used by persons of African descent to define their cultural heritage and racial orientation.

4. Most mainstream congregations are affiliated with one of the historically Black denominations: the National Baptist Convention of America, U.S.A.; the National Baptist Convention; the Progressive National Baptist Convention; the African Methodist Episcopal Church; the African Methodist Episcopal Zion Church; and the Christian Methodist Episcopal Church. After the mainstream churches, Holiness-Pentecostal groups, such as the Church of God in Christ, constitute the largest religious category among Black Christians.

5. For a detailed list of such Scriptures, see Day (1992, pp. 300-303).

6. This coincides with the observations made by Jones (1992), Lincoln and Mamiya (1990), Poinsett (1990), and the *Ebony* study ("Changing Church," 1993).

7. This view is substantiated in the *Catechism of the Catholic Church* (1994), which states that "the harmony of signs (songs, music, words, and actions) is all the more expressive and fruitful when expressed in the cultural richness of the People of God who celebrate" (p. 299).

8. Reprinted from the song "Christian Rap on *The Name of Jesus* cassette with permission of Rodney Draggon.

9. Reprinted from the song "Rapping Through the Bible on *The Name of Jesus* cassette with permission of Rodney Draggon.

10. Reprinted from the song "Christian Rap on *The Name of Jesus* cassette with permission of Rodney Draggon.

11. The rap to which Leo Lewis refers is performed by "Sons of Thunder," a church-sponsored group that travels extensively and ministers the gospel.

REFERENCES

Abingdon dictionary of living religions. (1981). Nashville, TN: Abingdon.

Boehlert, E. (1994, August 13). Gospel's big boom inspires radio to add stations and increase airtime. *Billboard*, p. 34.

Bowman, T. (1987). The gift of African American sacred song. In *Lead me, guide me: The African American Catholic hymnal* (pp. 3-7). Chicago: G.I.A. Publications.

Brown, R. (1988, May). The glory of gospel: Will the message be lost in the contemporary sound? *Ebony*, p. 66.

Catechism of the Catholic Church. (1994). Liguori, MO: Liguori Publications.

Changing church confronts the changing Black family. (1993, August). *Ebony*, pp. 94-96, 98, 100.

Cone, J. H. (1980). *The spirituals and the blues.* Westport, CT: Greenwood.

Day, A. C. (1992). *Roget's thesaurus of the Bible.* San Francisco: Harper & Row.

Dougherty, S., & Carpenter, B. (1994, January). Rap finds God. *People Weekly*, p. 85.

Draggon, R. (1992a). Christian rap. On *The name of Jesus* [cassette].

Draggon, R. (1992b). Rapping through the Bible. On *The name of Jesus* [cassette].

Dupree, S., & Dupree, H. C. (1993). *African American good news (gospel) music.* Washington, DC: Middle Atlantic Regional Press.

Franklin, M. J. (1982). *The relationship of Black preaching to Black gospel music.* Unpublished doctoral dissertation, Drew University.

Harris, J. H. (1991). *Pastoral theology: A Black-church perspective.* Minneapolis, MN: Augsburg.

Jones, J. T. (1991, October). Transformation crusade: Rapping for the Lord. *Essence*, p. 46.

Jones, L. N. (1992, November). The new Black church: Activism and growth of the new denominations change the institution. *Ebony*, pp. 192, 194-195.

Lead me, guide me: The African American Catholic hymnal. (1987). Chicago: G.I.A. Publications.

Lincoln, C. E., & Mamiya, L. (1990). *The Black church in the African American experience.* Durham, NC: Duke University Press.

Mapson, J. W. (1984). *The ministry of music in the Black church.* Valley Forge, PA: Judson.

Marriot, M. (1994, November). Rhymes of redemption. *Newsweek*, p. 64.

Maultsby, P. (1992a). The impact of gospel music on the secular music industry. In B. J. Reagon (Ed.), *We'll understand it better by and by* (pp. 19-33). Washington, DC: Smithsonian.

Maultsby, P. (1992b). The use and performance of hymnody, spirituals, and gospels in the Black church. *Hymnology Annual: An International Forum on the Hymn and Worship, 2*, 12-26.

McClain, W. B. (1990). American Black worship: A mirror of tragedy and a vision of hope. In R. Maas & G. O'Donnell (Eds.), *Spiritual traditions for the contemporary church* (pp. 352-361). Nashville, TN: Abingdon.

McCoy, E. B. (Ed.). (n.d.). *C.O.G.I.C. official music handbook.* Memphis, TN: Church of God in Christ.

Murray, J. G. (1987). The liturgy of the Roman rite and African American worship. In *Lead me, guide me: The African American Catholic hymnal* (pp. 8-12). Chicago: G.I.A. Publications.

Newman, M. (1988). *Entrepreneurs of profit and pride: From Black appeal to radio soul.* New York: Praeger.

Phelps, J. (1990). Black spirituality. In R. Maas & G. O'Donnell (Eds.), *Spiritual traditions for the contemporary church* (pp. 332-351). Nashville, TN: Abingdon.

Poinsett, A. (1990, August). God and the rap generation. *Ebony,* pp. 64, 66-68.

Rabey, S. (1991, June). Rhymin' and rappin' 4d king. *Christianity Today,* pp. 13-14.

Reagon, B. J. (1992). Pioneering African American gospel music composers. In B. J. Reagon (Ed.), *We'll understand it better by and by* (pp. 3-18). Washington, DC: Smithsonian.

Seventh-day Adventists believe. (1988). Washington, DC: Ministerial Association General Conference of Seventh-day Adventists.

Solo. (1994a). Interrogation 2 [Recorded by Gospel Gangstas]. On *Gang affiliated* [cassette]. Garden Grove, CA: Frontline Records.

Solo. (1994b). Testimony [Recorded by Gospel Gangstas]. On *Gang affiliated* [cassette]. Garden Grove, CA: Frontline Records.

Spencer, J. M. (1990). *Protest and praise: Sacred music of Black religion.* Minneapolis: Fortress.

Walker, W. T. (1979). *"Somebody's calling my name": Black sacred music and social change.* Valley Forge, PA: Judson.

17

Mormons, Mass Media, and the Interpretive Audience

DANIEL A. STOUT
DAVID W. SCOTT
DENNIS G. MARTIN

In recent years, leaders of the Church of Jesus Christ of Latter-day Saints (Mormon) have become increasingly concerned about the effects of mass media on religious values (see Chapter 7, this volume). Describing contemporary television programs and movies, M. Russell Ballard (1989) of the church's Quorum of Twelve Apostles stated that "far too much programming is not wholesome and uplifting but is violent, degrading, and destructive to moral values" (p. 78).

Guidelines for appropriate television viewing can be found in church magazines ("Making the Most of TV," 1990; Schaefermeyer, 1991; Tucker, 1988), and Mormons are admonished to avoid R-rated movies (Benson, 1986; Peterson, 1993). On the other hand, church members are encouraged to use the media in ways that uplift and benefit the family. For example, it is recommended that they "have good magazines about the house, . . . read a good family newspaper, . . . go to the theater, . . . and use that most remarkable of all tools of communication, television, to enrich their lives" (Hinckley, 1975, p. 39).

Given that Mormon church leaders emphasize careful selectivity in media use, it is likely that audience members experience a number of dilemmas and conflicts in choosing television programs and movies. How do Mormons define and resolve such conflicts given their religious commitments? How do they describe their experiences with mass media in the context of everyday life?

These questions are important given that many of the assumptions, conjectures, and conclusions about the effects of media are based on descriptions of media content alone. Content analysis, however, has little capacity to expand knowledge about the ways media-related conflicts are defined and resolved within the broader context of social and cultural experience (Anderson & Meyer, 1988; Fiske, 1987; Lindlof, 1988; Morley, 1988). In other words, predictions about the effects of media based exclusively on what is on television or presented in movies are limited in that they ignore the personal, social, and cultural dimensions of message reception.

One way to address these limitations is to draw on recent work in the area of interpretive community, which recognizes that individuals may vary in their descriptions of media-related experience despite exposure to the same institutional definitions of media effects. According to Fish (1980), there are inevitable sublevel "strategies of interpretation" that emerge in the individual's network of social relations. This chapter is an effort to learn more about such strategies.

Recent work in the area of social semiotics, interpretive community, and critical mass communication research has examined the issue of how audiences discursively make sense of texts within environments of social practice. Some have termed this sublevel unit of analysis *interpretive community* (Fish, 1980; Lindlof, 1988; Radway, 1984). Here, the term interpretive community is used to address some of the questions raised by Lindlof, Coyle, and Grodin (in press), namely, how audiences define their boundaries when dealing with variant interpretations of popular culture. They argue that recent research often fails to account for "divergently correct ways of categorizing the textual object."

With this in mind, we begin to describe the nature and scope of interpretational strategies used by members of a conservative religious institution. Of particular interest is the range of diversity in the ways Mormons talk about media and what makes this diversity possible. At a theoretical level, this chapter searches for a broader understanding of the complex nature of religiosity as it applies to the interpretation of mediated texts. Fundamental issues of what "religious audiences" are and how they function drive the objectives of this research.

METHOD

Findings from two samples of members of the Mormon Church are reported here. The first project reports data from a 1994 study of students at Brigham Young University (BYU), a major Mormon educational institution. The second study, conducted in 1992, analyzes Mormon women's views on television viewing in three major cities in the western United States (i.e., Los Angeles, Houston, and Salt Lake City). The examination of two data sets provides cross-validation to the findings about how Mormons, both younger and older, talk about the media. Survey data were analyzed first. Next, open-ended written statements were categorized by an independent panel to identify dominant themes in the responses using a sorting technique similar to Browning (1978).

Although comparisons of dominant themes are made between the two samples, we do not in any way attempt to merge or synthesize the two data sets. The purpose here is to explore the variation in styles of talking about the media and how two samples of Mormons define and resolve conflicts associated with particular television programs and movies.

Brigham Young University Students and Movies

Full-time BYU students were sampled using survey questionnaires administered to customers at a local video rental store located near the BYU campus. An earlier random intercept survey of 210 BYU students indicated that 40% of the students sampled listed this particular store as one of two places where they rented movies most often.

A total of 326 individuals were intercepted inside the video store and asked to complete the questionnaire. As an incentive, respondents were offered a $1.00-off coupon to apply to their video rental if they participated. Patrons were not told anything about the purpose of the research. Those completing questionnaires were assured of complete anonymity.

The survey instrument was designed to gather information about students' video rental behavior as well as their attitudes about acceptable movie choices. In addition, several open-ended questions asked how religious values had an effect on movie selection. One important question asked respondents to share impressions of a current popular film with an R rating, *Schindler's List*.

Customers were intercepted on a Friday starting late in the afternoon until the store closed. Of the 326 original questionnaires, a total of 238 were subjected to analysis after eliminating non-BYU students. Women students composed 52% of the sample and male students 48%. All five traditional classes of students were represented in the sample, that is, freshmen (14%), sophomores (20%), juniors (29%), seniors (31%), and graduate students (6%).

Mormon Women and Television

This study selected names randomly from five congregational lists or "wards" in each of the three metro areas using stratified random sampling. The sample of 428 is more representative of Mormon women who are highly educated, affluent, and married than Mormon women in general. It is comparable to the larger population, however, in terms of family size and number employed outside the home. Higher levels of education and income are likely attributed to respondents from Los Angeles where household earnings tend to be higher.

RESULTS

A cluster analysis was performed on each data set. In the BYU student sample, all attitudinal questions were used in the cluster procedure. In the Mormon women study, the principal component factor analysis employed VARIMAX rotation (SASS) and identified seven items for a cluster analysis. Items were selected for the cluster analysis if they had a loading of .5 on a factor with an eigenvalue greater than 1.0.

Polarized Interpretive Audiences

Diverse interpretive audiences emerge from both studies. The Mormon women study yielded three sublevel audiences, but only two were identified in the BYU study. Of particular note were two audiences from each study that varied greatly in their style of "talking" about television and movies. Although a third cluster was identified in the study of Mormon women (see Stout, 1994), this chapter's primary goal is to describe similarly divergent interpretive strategies discovered in two separate samples. Of particular value here is the polarization of audiences within each sample, that is, two audiences from each study that were polarized in how they described their media-related experiences. Moreover, each study contained a conservative audience that was highly selective in media choice, as well as one that was more independent, choosing more broadly from available television programs and movies.

We named the first interpretive audience common to both samples *Traditionals*, who placed strong emphasis on what is considered "immoral" content in selecting movies and television programs and whose style of talking about the media reflected strong institutional influence, whereas the second audience was named *Independents*, who often described their media-related experiences in individual, goal-oriented terms and assessed their value more from a personal, private point of view rather than an institutional perspective. These interpretive audiences are not mutually exclusive, and we recognize that audience members may possess skills and abilities that allow them to apply a number of interpretive strategies not necessarily confined to these broad categories. In other words, although these clusters do not fully capture the complex processes at work when religious audiences view television and movies, they do provide an initial description of different critical strategies among highly religious audiences. In the BYU study, Independents were the largest cluster ($n = 114$), and Traditionals had 81 members. In the Mormon women study, Traditionals composed the largest cluster ($n = 197$), and Independents were smaller in size ($n = 95$).

Traditionals: Brigham Young University Study

Almost 70% of Traditionals in the BYU study were women. An analysis of 72 written statements from these students identified three themes in the ways Traditionals described the role of movie viewing in their everyday lives: First, *ratings:* Traditionals frequently mentioned the rating system in evaluating the quality of movies. Second, they often referred to *negative effects* of the media as described by church leaders. That is, there is a belief reflected in the statements of these students that movies may have corrosive effects on an individual's religious faith. The third and final category is *censorship*, where students expressed the need for more editing of controversial films so they can be viewed by religious audiences.

Ratings were a dominant theme (39 statements, 54%) among the students sampled. Several responded simply, "I do not watch R-rated movies." One student explained why the movie *Schindler's List* is not an appropriate movie:

> I will not see an R-rated film, as fond as I am of watching movies, and as much as I enjoy talented artists. A true artist is one who can create in the mind of the viewer certain important images in a limited amount of time, and in a tasteful way. By their nature, movies sacrifice realism to symbolism. *Schindler's List* is trying to create an event realistically instead of artistically. I won't see it because of the rating this realism brings.

Not all referred to ratings, however, in describing their feelings about inappropriate movies. Several (15 statements, 19%) cited church leaders in describing the harmful effects of movies. Examples are found in statements such as, "I am Mormon" or "I am LDS" when explaining the basis for their movie choices. Some said, "The general authorities have counseled us not to" or "We have been counseled by church leaders not to watch these things."

Students in this cluster were also unique in their desire to watch edited versions of R-rated films (11 responses, 14%). Some controversial films will be viewed if they are edited versions such as those shown during airline travel or in the Varsity Theater (an on-campus theater at BYU that edits movie scenes deemed to be inappropriate). Some students, for example, said they would not see the movie *Schindler's List* unless certain scenes were edited.

Traditionals: Mormon Women Study

Among Mormon women, Traditionals tended to be younger ($\chi^2 =$ 22.746; $df = 8$; $p < .01$) and were more likely to be married ($\chi^2 = 18.002$; $df = 4$; $p < .01$) and have more children ($\chi^2 = 16.352$; $df = 4$; $p < .01$). Traditionals were also more likely to marry in a Mormon temple ($\chi^2 = 133.995$; $df = 8$; $p < .01$), which is a good indicator of religiosity as individuals who marry in the temple must demonstrate high levels of institutional commitment.

An analysis of 91 written statements identified three dominant themes in the ways Traditionals in the Mormon women study described their television viewing. The first category of responses was labeled *distraction* (36 statements, 40%), which communicates a feeling that television always takes the place of something more important, especially church duties and responsibilities. Several of these comments revealed an intense concern about the value of time and how it is misused in watching television. For example, one respondent commented,

I consider TV on the whole, to be a terrible waste of human time and resources. I feel that anyone who watches it regularly is not contributing adequately to their home, community, or personal lives. There is almost always something more important to be doing than watching TV. The best years of our lives as a family were the 2 years that we did not have a TV in our home. In my opinion, the only reasons to keep the TV are to watch 1. family videos (home movies), 2. to entertain the children with a decent movie when we go out for the evening, 3. the news, 4. General Conference, 5. the viewing of church films for family home evening and 6. the occasional wonderful evening when we rented a great movie, popped popcorn and laid on the floor together as a family watching it. If it were not for these things I would not hesitate for even 5 seconds before throwing the TV in the garbage. I am not generally a radical in life, but I admit I am a radical in my disgust for TV!!!

Some Traditionals ascribed an addictive power to television that robs the viewer of precious time: "There probably isn't a way to tell how many people are addicted to TV in this survey, but it would be interesting to know. One woman I know couldn't get anything done (housework, etc. shower even) because of TV."

The second theme characterizing Traditionals' talk about television had to do with negative effects of television content (34 statements, 37%). The majority of these statements condemned television for what was considered to be excessive portrayals of sex and violence that were assumed to have a negative effect on the audience. When talking about television, terms such as *garbage, pornographic,* and *corruption* were often used to describe the potentially negative effects of the medium on one's spirituality. One respondent asserted, "I do not clutter my mind with the pornography of movies or TV so I can have divine inspiration to what is truly happening." Several respondents linked undesirable behaviors directly to television, including sexual promiscuity, bad language, and disobedient children.

Another category of responses was labeled *control* (14 statements, 15%), which described efforts to ensure that rules regarding television viewing were enforced. Some of these statements described arguments between husbands and wives, whereas others talked about efforts to monitor their children's viewing. "We have a lock which gives us control over the TV" commented one respondent, whereas others spoke of "screening" programs before allowing children to watch.

Independents: Brigham Young University Students

About 56% of Independents were men. Independents generally described their movie behavior in more personal, intimate language. In contrast with Traditionals, they were characterized by a more tolerant attitude about popular culture in general. They did talk about values, often conservative values, but they were less rigid about the way they decided whether or not to see a film. They were more likely to decide on a movie based on the advice of others instead of relying solely on institutional guidelines. In fact, the word rating was used rarely by this audience; it appears that ratings were not their primary way of evaluating or talking about a movie. When they did talk about the rating system, they tended to approach the conflict between institutional rules and individual values from a more critical, interpretive viewpoint.

Independents also tended to be less dogmatic than the Traditionals; that is, they were much slower to judge the value of a video or film based on ratings alone. Hence, Independents were more inclined to see R-rated films, especially if they judged them to have political, historic, or artistic merit. In marked contrast with Traditionals, when Independents talked about movies, very few mentioned the word censorship, and none suggested the need for editing R-rated films to make them acceptable for viewing.

A total of 85 statements from the BYU Independents cluster was analyzed. As noted earlier, to assess students' response to an historically significant film with an R rating, a question about *Schindler's List* was included. Three dominant themes emerged among the sampled students in the BYU study:

1. A stronger reliance on the opinions of peers for tips on which movies were worth seeing (13 statements, 15%)
2. Assessment of movie content over ratings (40 statements, 47%)
3. A reflective approach in which respondents tended to evaluate films based on more personal, private interests rather than relying on institutional guidelines (21 statements, 25%)

The first category of statements suggests that when faced with a decision about renting a particular movie, Independents were more likely to rely on the advice of others to determine if the film was appropriate, even if rated R. Rather than focusing on the standards and advice of church leaders (only 6 of 85 Independents mentioned or alluded to the Mormon Church), they asked their spouses or peers whether the movie was worth seeing based on its artistic merits. One student summarized this point when she said,

Sometimes [church] values affect my decision. But if I've heard it's good . . . I don't care what it is rated. I want to see *Schindler's List* because it's the best picture—but my husband says it looks too depressing. I want to see . . . what the big fuss is about, why it's the best picture, but my husband says it looks too depressing. . . . [When deciding on a movie], if the preview looks good, I'll definitely see it. I love watching all types of movies.

In the second category of responses, Independents talked about content that they found offensive. In discussing content, sex was mentioned most frequently, followed by violence, and then language. Independents were most opposed to watching films in which sex and violence dominated the story. It appeared, however, that they will endure a moderate amount of offensive content if it is deemed necessary for "realism" or artistic merit.

Forty statements suggested that content, not ratings, is the most important factor when Independents decided on a movie. A 22-year-old student talked about film content like this:

Sometimes movies really push my limits. Excessive and distasteful nudity, violence, and sex are turn-offs. I had to see *Schindler's List* because it exposed me to a very disappointing time in the world's history. I do not regret seeing it, but I don't think I could see it again.

Another Independent referred to objectionable content in *Schindler's List* in a value-oriented, critical way:

I don't really look at the ratings, but I research the content and the subject matter of the movie before I see it. The values portrayed in the movie are very important to me. . . . *Schindler's List* is absolutely one of the greatest works of art I've ever seen. Although I have heard complaints of nudity and violence, there is nothing in the film that was added to attract a crowd to those things. It is not pornographic and I believe all the scenes were created to get a message across.

Independents did avoid many R-rated films. In contrast with Traditionals, however, they were much more likely to examine a movie based on its specific merits rather than its rating alone. For example, when content added realism, they were more likely to justify nudity or violence, for instance, the student quoted previously who wrote, "I don't really look at the ratings, but I research the content and the subject matter."

In the final category, statements revealed a reflective approach in describing films. Just as Independents were inclined to take a neutral position regarding the attitudinal questions, they were also less parochial in their approach to interpreting value-laden issues and the media. Unlike the Traditionals who generally responded with a straightforward yes or no, Independents tended to be more reflective in making movie choices. Twenty-one qualified their responses to the attitudinal questions on religious or personal values. Rather than just saying yes, Independents were more likely to use expressions such as "I prefer," "I try," "Sometimes," and "To a degree." One young woman wrote,

> I like entertaining and stimulating movies and prefer them to be clean. However, our world isn't clean and some things need to be present to make a movie realistic. . . . I think *Schindler's List* should be seen by all who can handle the topic and the manner of dealing with the graphic subject matter. In this case, the rating should not factor in so much when deciding on the movie—it's a historical re-creation.

Notice how her attitude about realism and artistic merit contrasts with that of the earlier quote from the student who felt an artistic representation never needs graphic material. Her response differed substantially from the majority of Traditionals. Traditionals followed institutional directives rather closely, and hence they did not talk about preferring or trying to follow church leaders. Generally, they avoided R-rated films and thus eliminated the need to be reflective about what they considered forbidden material.

Independents: The Mormon Women Study

Compared with Traditionals, Independents were older, had fewer children, and were somewhat less likely to marry in the Mormon temple. Although Traditionals were primarily concerned with the undesirable effects of the media, Independents tended to define the activity more as an expressive outlet that serves a number of functions in everyday life. Unlike Traditionals, this audience described television as a "personal" and "private" experience and was much less critical of television content. Typical metaphors used by Independents in describing television included "teacher," "informer," "escape," and "link to the outside world."

A total of 44 statements from this cluster was subjected to analysis, and three dominant categories emerged: *situational uses* (17 statements, 40%), a series of comments with which Mormon women explained how television assisted them in dealing with particular problems and situations in their lives; *assessments of content* (14 statements, 33%), a pattern of statements evaluating various types of television programs; and *choice* (6 statements, 14%), which were requests for a more significant role in program choices in the home.

Whereas Traditionals spoke in terms of potential effects of television and described the conflicts it caused in their lives, Independents had a different style of television talk. The medium was described in more personal terms and was often related to some event or situation they were experiencing at that moment. One respondent, for example, placed her television viewing in the context of a struggle she was having in balancing career and family:

> Basically, I enjoy anything [on TV] that shows women in the working world, even if she is a parent, that she is not having a wonderful time baking cookies all the time. That she is struggling, trying to find out who she is, if she is trying to stay home and why.

Some respondents stated that television helped them in dealing with the challenges and pressures of homemaking. For example, one said that television took her "mind off a huge mountain of laundry and dishes." Another explained that she watched television because the "eyes are too tired" to read. A mother of three children seemed to imply that television was necessary in coping with the challenges of child rearing: "I would go crazy if we didn't have a TV in our home because my kids would be after me constantly to do things with them."

Like Traditionals, Independents also criticized television for its excessive violence and sexually explicit content. Independents, however, often praised many of the programs condemned by Traditionals. An interesting comment in this regard came from an active churchgoer in her 30s who praised the cartoon comedy program *The Simpsons:*

> Sometimes we watch TV shows together such as *The Simpsons* and discuss the social messages. If there is something inappropriate that unexpectedly comes on, I use that as a teaching opportunity to explain why we don't believe that way or do those things. I think it's important to teach children to do their own self-monitoring of what they watch. Parents won't always be around to turn off the TV as they get older and watch outside the home.

Comments such as this were revealing in that they reflected a reliance on the personal as well as the institutional dimension of religiosity in resolving conflicts associated with television viewing. The above comment, while stating that elements of the program might be inappropriate, also recognizes personal interpretations of a program that may justify viewing it if the family feels that a show stimulates discussion, is educational, or teaches self-monitoring.

Additional comments about talk shows seemed to suggest that despite institutional criticisms of these shows, some viewers felt they had a positive impact on personal religious values:

> I like talk shows because it gives me an opportunity to see how others live [with] the choices they've made and how those choices affected their lives. More often than not, I reaffirm my own beliefs and choices in life as being wise. I feel grateful for the influence of the church when I see others that don't have it and how unfortunate their lives have turned out.

These statements indicated that although the women sampled may have been active members of the Mormon Church, not all criticized the medium in the same way as the institution. That is, a distinction between Traditionals and Independents suggested by the written statements is an ability to divergently interpret the nature of television's effect despite common religious beliefs and behaviors.

SUMMARY AND DISCUSSION

Striking differences in the ways Traditionals and Independents talked about media is a compelling finding given that both audiences had strong religious commitments. It was apparent that respondents drew on multiple dimensions of their religiosity in making decisions about the media. Personal religiosity may have been just as salient as institutional guidelines in making decisions about media use. A movie such as *Schindler's List,* for example, was considered inappropriate by most of those referencing institutional standards. In contrast, it was praised by a more independent group who cited personal religious beliefs and feelings in describing how they were inspired by the film's strong moral message.

The question of what distinguishes those with an independent style of talking about television from those with a more traditional approach remains a challenging question. From the sample of Mormon women, it appears that age may be an important variable to consider in future research. Women over 35 seem more likely to maintain enough distance from institutional expectations about media use to satisfy personal needs regarding television and movie choice. This could, in part, be related to experience in raising teenagers as well as the luxury of having had several years to observe the role of media in the home. With the BYU students, reliance on friends for advice about media choice suggests another issue for future researchers. More often than Traditionals, Independents described interpersonal networks in which the artistic dimensions of media fare were discussed. This suggests that the personal information spheres may vary across the two communities. That is, there is one type of discourse that is more diverse in terms of which critical skills are acceptable, contrasted with another that is more restrictive and didactic. In addressing the issue of media-related conflicts, parents, church leaders, counselors, and so on may want to examine these networks more closely to better understand how media use is related to the social contexts of everyday experience.

Another variable that might account for the diverse ways these religious audiences interpret the media centers on gender differences. The BYU sample suggests that gender partially accounts for the different groups. Specifically, female students were more likely to adopt a rules-based approach to choosing movies, relying heavily on guidelines from church leaders. The Mormon Church encourages domestic roles for women and stresses child rearing as a priority for young adult women. New studies are needed to learn more about the relationship between Mormon gender roles and media use.

This research may also have implications in other situations in which institutions attempt to influence their members about the issue of media effects. Political parties, health organizations, extended families, and so on have at times suggested ways of thinking about the media to their members. In fact, there are few instances in contemporary society when audience members feel no pressure to conform to an institutional view of the media. The data presented here suggest that a model of mass communication research that avoids a homogeneous conceptualization of the religious audience may be more fruitful when considering the question of media-related conflict.

REFERENCES

Anderson, J. A., & Meyer, T. P. (1988). *Mediated communication: A social action perspective.* Newbury Park, CA: Sage.

Ballard, M. R. (1989, May). The effects of television. *Ensign*, pp. 78-81.

Benson, E. T. (1986, May). To the youth of the noble birthright. *Ensign*, pp. 43-46.

Browning, L. D. (1978). A grounded organizational communication theory derived from qualitative data. *Communication Monographs, 45*, 93-107.

Fish, S. (1980). *Is there a text in this class?* Cambridge, MA: Harvard University Press.

Fiske, J. (1987). *Television culture.* London: Methuen.

Hinckley, G. B. (1975, November). Opposing evil. *Ensign*, pp. 38-40.

Lindlof, T. R. (1988). Media audiences as interpretive communities. In J. A. Anderson (Ed.), *Communication yearbook 11* (pp. 81-107). Newbury Park, CA: Sage.

Lindlof, T. R., Coyle, K., & Grodin, D. (in press). Is there a text in this audience? Science fiction and interpretive schism. In C. Harris & A. Alexander (Eds.), *Theorizing fandom: Fans, subcultures, and identity.* Creskill, NJ: Hampton.

Making the most of TV. (1990, October). *Ensign*, pp. 70-71.

Morley, D. (1988). Changing paradigms in audience studies. In E. Seiter, H. Borchers, G. Kreutzner, & E. M. Warth (Eds.), *Remote control: Television, audiences, and cultural power* (pp. 16-43). New York: Routledge.

Peterson, H. B. (1993, November). Touch not the evil gift, nor the unclean thing. *Ensign*, pp. 42-44.

Radway, J. A. (1984). *Reading the romance: Women, patriarchy, and popular literature.* Chapel Hill: University of North Carolina Press.

Schaefermeyer, W. A. (1991, December). Can I watch a movie? *Ensign,* pp. 29-32.

Stout, D. A. (1994). Resolving conflicts of worldviews: LDS women and television. *AMCAP Journal, 20*(1), 61-79.

Tucker, L. A. (1988, February). What's on TV tonight? *Ensign,* pp. 18-22.

PART V

The Future

*Religion and the Changing
Information Environment*

18

Religion and the
Information Society

JORGE REINA SCHEMENT
HESTER C. STEPHENSON

"The fact of the matter is that dialogue between the fields of theology and communication is already taking place simply because it is unavoidable. In public policy decisions regarding the evolving 'Information Society' the debate involves questions of the future of national cultures, and public figures seek to base their arguments on philosophical or theological principles. Within the churches, too, major questions such as the appropriateness of the 'electronic church' almost immediately become theological issues." (Soukup, 1991, p. 7)

—Robert A. White, S.J., Centre for the
Study of Communication and Culture

"We have to use this technology so it won't further isolate children and families within their own little world. . . . We have to show that individuals have a responsibility to a group larger than themselves, that we have an interdependence. We have a real lack of that. We need something to enrich the soul, human spirit or community." (Bollier, 1995, p. 6)

—Governor Gaston Caperton of West Virginia

In the late 20th century, Americans increasingly worship in electronic churches, participate in megacongregations, and seek solace in charismatic Evangelicalism.[1] That Americans are increasingly comfortable with these emerging church forms reflects the importance of new information technologies within the U.S. culture of worship. Yet just as any technology arises out of the values of its creators, so too do new mediated forms of worship arise out of understandings of church, rite, and spirituality. In this chapter, we weave together the connections between the information society and religion, particularly Protestantism, by exploring the historic and contemporary threads that link the information society to Judeo-Christian institutions and beliefs.[2] We first review the tendencies and tensions of the information society and then discuss emerging forms of religious practice. At the chapter's end, we speculate on consequences.

THE INFORMATION SOCIETY

Most Americans use the phrase "information society" to explain the changing technological terrain of their homes and offices. Even journalists and social observers tally up long lists of devices that include automatic teller machines, satellites, and personal computers as characteristic symbols of the new age. Although we might fixate on information technologies, the domain of the information society extends far beyond the sphere of the technological and its depth plumbs down to the very roots of culture. The following attributes briefly summarize the far-reaching transformation that unites the abstractions "information" and "society" into a cohesive whole.[3]

Underlying Forces: The Driving Catalysts and the Defining Contexts

Capitalism and Industrialization. These are the primary forces that converged and caused a transformation in the production and distribution of information—in technology, in the economy, and in the workforce.

Evolution and Continuity. The information society is one evolutionary development of industrial capitalism. Changes that we observe in information work, in media environments, and in technological innovation took place over a long period of time, characterized by continuity.

Dominant Tendencies:
The Trends That Shape Awareness

The Idea of Information. The fundamental condition that makes the information age seem understandable is the ease with which people think of information as a thing. This conceptualization facilitates the exploitation of information as a commodity—the basis of the information economy—and provides the language with which we make sense of the information society.

The Information Economy. Information holds a leading role in U.S. economic life as an item of production and consumption. The status of the United States within the world's economic system now depends on its ability to compete in markets for information and information technologies.

Information Work. The majority of adults now work in occupations whose primary tasks involve manipulating information in some form.

Interconnectedness. People continue to maintain a small number of primary intimate relationships, but the number of secondary public relationships has vastly increased as individuals seek to accomplish personal and work-related tasks by relying on impersonal relationships—mostly mediated through some form of communication technology.

Media Environments. Throughout the 20th century, Americans have contrived habitats capable of receiving huge quantities of messages. Today, these media environments constitute an indispensable part of life in the information society—so much so that they now typify U.S. households.

Information Technologies. Information technologies are to the flesh of the information society as capitalism and industrialism are to the spirit. So pervasive are they that numerous observers view the development of the information society as a study in technological growth.[4]

Major Tensions: The Fault Lines
That Precipitate Dispute and Debate

The Social Value of Information. Whether to rely on the forces of the market or to depend on government for the proper allocation of information is the most basic question of information policy. Institutionalized at the very inception of the republic, this tension persists because of conflicting traditions.

Privacy. As more institutions take on the functions of gathering information about individuals, the construction of privacy has expanded to include a concern for loss of control over personal information.

Political Discourse. Electoral campaigns are now controlled by big media organizations and a nucleus of politicians and consultants. In response, citizens either abstain and become apathetic, narrow their focus to single issues and simplified images, or in some cases gravitate to virtual communities by opting to exploit small media for local political purposes.

Literacy. Recent declines in literacy rates confer an unexpected urgency to the central concerns of the information age. At a time when reading and writing have reemerged as fundamental skills, lower literacy levels threaten the knowledge base and our competitiveness as a global economy.

The Logic of Images. Constrained by the vast scale of U.S. society, individuals increasingly experience important realities through images they receive from the media. Americans depend on mediated images to learn about the people, institutions, and events that affect their lives—even within their own communities. Yet increasingly, institutions and public figures consider improving their images to be the solution to problems of substance.

Information Poverty. To lack information often means to lack power. Those at the margins of society often lack access to information sources that might provide new opportunities or a greater voice in public discourse.

Marginalized Voices. Voices in the information age remain marginalized by gender and ethnicity. Predictions that the growth of information occupations would diminish the gender gap by raising the status of jobs traditionally held by women have not been realized. Expectations of equality failed to anticipate that women and minority professionals would face difficulty finding work in central institutions, such as universities and banks. Nor did these expectations predict the existence or establishment of glass or stained-glass ceilings.

African Americans and Latinos make up 20% of the population of the United States.[5] In a nation marked by rich ethnic diversity, African Americans and Latinos will have significant impact on the information society, by virtue of their changing numbers in media markets. Minorities, particularly African Americans, are increasing their numbers within the mainstream media. Although these advances in visibility convey the impression that minorities are entering communication industries in large numbers, imbalance persists. Though they are readily identifiable as media consumers, African Americans and Latinos have yet to convert their newfound visibility into success as media producers. Questions of equality and justice challenge the information society.

Keys to Understanding

The information society depends on recognizing elements of both change and continuity. U.S. industry is no longer hog butcher to the world, because it has changed or, more properly, evolved away from its earlier form. Instead, it is now educator, banker, entertainer, and data processor to the world, for reasons of continuity—because of the persistence of the profit motive and the industrial character of these activities. And because the information society extends across the entire fabric of social interaction, it touches the entire culture. This information society has been taking shape throughout the 20th century, in interaction with social forces such as religious institutions and the specific belief systems of individuals.

ROOTS

The roots that intertwine modern Christian religions and the information society can be traced to the invention of the printing press and the subsequent rise of the idea of information. Eisenstein (1979, 1986) recognized the shift from script to print as one of the few true communications revolutions that enabled three major movements: the Reformation, the Renaissance, and the scientific revolution. The growing availability of texts and the new interactions of occupations such as printers and scholars to create such texts led to changed perceptions of learning, a heightened sense of individualism, a popular appreciation for the Bible, and a marketplace of ideas.

Those connections of Protestantism and capitalism undergird the modern era and its progeny, the information society. When Max Weber (1958) first explored the relationship, he located the impetus for contemporary capitalism within the religious beliefs of Protestantism, particularly Calvinism. The Calvinist idea of work as a calling and as an expression of faith gave capitalism a "spirit." Calvinists and their like-minded brethren elevated the spirit to the level of a cardinal virtue by redefining wealth as the product of diligent work and thrift pursued for God's greater glory, instead of the medieval association of wealth with the contemptible accumulation of worldly goods.[6]

Even so, the success of ideas from such sources as Calvin, Luther, and Zwingli depended on the availability of printed texts. Although the newly available content catalyzed the religions of the book, the invention of printing itself set in motion forces such as the book trade and popular literacy whose consequences for reshaping European society extended beyond Protestantism and capitalism.[7] Indeed, Weber himself only hinted at the influence of literacy and printing, though he searched for the spirit of capitalism among the writings of a famous printer—Benjamin Franklin. The popularization of Bible reading encouraged the literacy necessary for the later expansion of the white-collar workforce.[8] Long narrative poems, such as *Paradise Lost* (Milton, 1667), evolved into the modern novel creating the basic unit of exchange in the world's literary marketplaces. Religious collections of universal knowledge, such as Thomas Aquinas's (1265-1273/1912-1936) *Summa Theologica*, gave way to itemized secular compendia, such as Diderot's *Encyclopédie*, and, in turn, the modern idea of bits of information.[9] Thus, today, we should experience no surprise at finding information technology in the service of religious entrepreneurs or at finding the exploitation of religious symbols for purposes of secular entertainment. Since Gutenberg first printed his edition of the 42-line Mazarin Bible for profit, the two sides have intertwined with persistently unanticipated repercussions.[10]

SOME ASSOCIATED TENDENCIES

The Idea of Information and the Idea of Religion

Medieval Christian Europe imagined the cosmology of the universe as an organic unity, a great chain of being, whose purpose was to glorify God (Lovejoy, 1936). To lead an integrated life, submission to the knowledge and time of the religious community was necessary.

In turn, the goal of preparing for salvation reinforced an attitude of sacredness toward manuscripts and books (McArthur, 1986). For example, under the rule of Saint Benedict, monks aimed at forming a prayerful atmosphere within their communities. To do so, they created a special place for reading within the life of the monastery and generated a demand for books to be copied and stored (Benedictus, 547/1975). Whereas individuals pursuing knowledge for the greater glory of God might seek a book from a monastery library, Benedictines and other orders of monks established an attitude toward books, reading, and information that stressed community and authority (and by doing so founded many of Europe's great libraries) (Putnam, 1896/1962). Thus, along with the book came the monastery's assumptions. An indication of this attitude is reflected in the common word for library in the monasteries of the middle ages— books were kept in the armarium, literally the bookchest, and the armarius held the keys, preventing unauthorized use (Johnson, 1970).

The rule also demanded strict attention to time so as to satisfactorily discharge the work of God and the prayers due to God. For members of the monastic community to divide their days between prayer, reading, copying books, and manual labor, they needed a means to divide up their day; that is, they needed information about time. Consequently, the first mechanical clocks in Europe were invented by monks and communicated the passing of the canonical hours to all of the surrounding peasantry by manual ringing of the monastery bell.[11] (Consequently, we still associate church services with bells ringing out time.) And as with the labor of copying books, monks measured time for one purpose only, "To love the Lord God with all our heart, soul, and strength" (Benedictus, 547/1975, p. 52).

The information contained in books and clocks served one great purpose, subsuming all other possibilities. Within such a paradigm, monks and other literate Christians could not easily venture beyond the limits of the religious community, much less consider the value of reading a book for one's individual pleasure (Hampson, 1968). Custom and law dictated that the application of information from books and clocks must not detract from the greater glory of God, making the distinction between secular and religious meaningless.

By contrast, modern social organization stresses the individual, emphasizes distinct spheres of life, elevates the secular, and exploits the idea of information to maintain the partitions. The ingrained division between public and private life, within which modern individuals perceive daily life, is reinforced by the idea of information with its emphasis on discrete units and sources. The notions that we should go to school for information about history, turn to political advertising for information about elections, enroll in management courses for information about organizational dynamics, and attend church services for information about morality illustrate the modern compartmentalization of knowledge. That we read self-help books to learn how to keep our marriages together, listen to talk radio to bolster our political beliefs, view behavioral video-tapes to help us maximize our productivity, and read the Bible to help us achieve salvation also point to the segmentation within which we lead our lives. Thus, the idea of information has enabled an idea of religion that is restrictive—indeed, the adage "religion and politics don't mix" captures the sentiment. In this climate, religious ideas struggle to be heard amid torrents of secular information.

Beliefs in opposition to this tendency do exist; they may, perhaps, be gaining ground. Nevertheless, it is important to appreciate the role of the idea of information in constricting the perceived relevance of religious knowledge and in encouraging the modern idea of religion as a partitioned sphere of daily life. When individuals shop around for a religion as if it were a product to be consumed, they further this perception. Similarly, the development of new religious products—radio and television programming, Internet and satellite religious connections—places religion on the same plane with commercial products. In 1994, *Chant*, a CD featuring the voices of Benedictine monks in musical prayer, sold 6 million copies worldwide, reaching number three on the pop charts in the United States (Thigpen, 1995).

Because religion has come to be viewed as a distinct body of ideas jostling for attention among other equally compelling sources, it is not surprising to find an unconscious melding of the modern idea of religion and the idea of information. After all, each reinforces the other. What is surprising is the power of the mixture. That mixture, transparent and pervasive, will set the context for other tendencies and tensions as they progressively define the information age.[12]

Institutionalized Religion and the Information Economy

Capitalism stands at the root of the drive to produce and market information. At all levels, from industries to individual consumers, demand rises for information to coordinate complex activities and as a consumption good in its own right. The tendency has been for the growth and elaboration of information markets, so much so that the information sector ranks first among the sectors of the U.S. economy. The information economy, then, has come to be seen as a place in which messages count as distinct goods and consumers purchase information within a maze of direct and indirect pricing schemes. In such a world, it is difficult to differentiate a church's messages from those of other "vendors." Consequently, from Weber to the present, social theorists continue to seek a deeper under-standing of the relationship between religion and capitalism (Neuhaus, 1992; Novak, 1993). Pope John Paul II offers his view of the relationship in the 1991 encyclical *Centesimus Annus*, in which he proposes that the capitalist ethos, " 'rightly understood,' " is rooted not only in Protestantism but also in Judaism and Catholi-cism (Novak, 1993, p. 114).

If the prospect grows for a more intimate association between the two spheres, that may be a cause for concern or at least ambivalence. Nevertheless, churches are often viewed as businesses that partici-pate in the market economy and their followers viewed as consum-ers. Once portrayed as a devotee or pilgrim, the religious adherent now assumes the role of a "consumer" of religious messages who may shop at a variety of sects and churches for an acceptable or comfortable worldview. Moreover, for the consumer, the process of choosing a church may be experienced as bargaining, while minis-ters attend seminars on marketing techniques to attract clients to their product (Niebuhr, 1995a). Though some may interpret the tension between sects and churches as representing conflicting hu-man desires for "otherworldly" beliefs, few can doubt that churches experience competitive pressures comparable to those experienced in other information markets.

The contribution to the information economy of the nation's religious activities is probably significant, but it is impossible to estimate with any accuracy. The patterns of institutional behavior— the competitiveness, the marketing strategies, the management of image, the focus groups—however, are easier to observe. Their impact on the culture of the information society may be more direct.

Religious Work and Information Work

Information workers, those whose main task involves information processing or manipulation in any form, total more than all industrial, service, and agricultural workers combined in the U.S. labor force (Schement, 1990). Because all information workers manipulate symbols for consumption by others, the parallel to religious work is obvious; the lay worker and the religious worker perform similar tasks. Information workers possess verbal and literary skills once reserved for the clergy. Literacy skills necessary for personal interaction with religious texts are now the fundamental skills for all information work tasks. In addition, religious leaders have taken on roles comparable to those of idea experts in secular fields such as business, science, and technology. Like all experts, religious leaders attend professional schools at which the skills needed to perform institutional religious work are taught. If one ignores the greater meaning of the content of religious work and focuses on the daily tasks, the distinctions between secular and religious information workers blur completely.

It, therefore, seems likely that haziness at the boundaries imposes on religious work one of the growing malaises of information work. Because religious workers are also information workers, the alienation possible in information work is likely to be experienced in religious work as well. Once the aura of working for God wears off, the religious workers will see little difference between their tasks and those of other information workers. The ease with which religious work skills transfer to secular information work diminishes the uniqueness of the calling, especially when compounded by the decline in status and special identity associated with religious work. Workers in both spheres may easily view themselves as commodities, and when religious workers find themselves embedded in large organizations, they also may become estranged from a sense of personal ownership of the product.[13]

Media Environments

At home and at leisure, individuals constantly consume information, often via several channels simultaneously. Middle-class homes resemble multiplex theaters. The amount of personal media devices in each home is far greater than the number of people.[14] By adding to their household media environments throughout the 20th century, Americans have created a culture of information consumption even if they cannot claim that they are better informed. What is clear is that media environments are pervasive and inescapable. Religious messages that previously held a monopoly on attention by virtue of their special channels now blend in with secular messages because of the use of common marketing techniques and product formats. The result is that religious messages must contend with a blizzard of competing secular messages to be heard.

Organized religion has always depended on media in some form. One need only consider the prominent place given to pulpits, tapestries, and stained-glass windows in medieval churches to get a sense of the house of worship as a multimedia environment. Throughout U.S. history, religious entrepreneurs have explored the potential synergy between information technologies and the evangelical mission. The media-centered impulse of Evangelicals during the second Great Awakening of the 19th century was based on the fusion of a theology emphasizing proclamation and the fascination with new technologies typical of Americans (Schultze, 1987). In the 20th century, print-based media have given way to electronic media as preferred channels for disseminating the Word. Like the connection between Protestantism and printing, the movement from printed text and revival meetings to radio sermons and televised services has been gradual and persistent, with the evangelical and fundamentalist wing of the Protestant movement leading the way.

That the evangelical tradition of using media has shaped the contemporary electronic church in its many formats can be observed in the achievement by the Reverend Billy Graham of worldwide satellite hookup revival meetings called "World Mission." In 1995, Graham beamed his message from Puerto Rico to satellite dishes in 165 countries and to 10 million people from Rwanda to Latin America and Oceania (Landers, 1995). In fact, the realities of the information society are so pervasive, they touch even the technologically conservative Catholic hierarchy. The pope's visit to the United States in 1993 included a televised outdoor mass for the Feast of the

Assumption; more recently, John Cardinal O'Connor of New York was featured on the evening news for hosting on-line question-and-answer sessions on a national computer network.[15] That the work of churches is fundamentally about communication is underscored by televised masses and a cardinal's interactive electronic ministerings.

In the information society, work, leisure, production, distribution, and the political system revolve around the importance of symbols and their transmission. Religion with its symbolic core can gain new energy from this new environment. Yet religious expressions must also compete with the flood of secular messages. So, although innovators find new uses for information technologies in the service of evangelism, religious messages themselves increasingly resemble the forms of secular messages. Thus, each tendency of the information society brings an opportunity and challenge to the evangelical impulse.

Religion in the information society, however, cannot be understood solely in terms of characteristics. The tensions that arise among the members of the information society contribute dynamics that add complexity to the picture. These are the tensions that challenge morality.

ENDEMIC TENSIONS

The tendencies that now dominate the information society have become patterns in U.S. life. Although the tendencies give direction even as they reweave the social fabric, the tensions strain the cloth of society. They are not problems, for they cannot be "solved." Instead, they constitute unavoidable frictions that will be reflected in the private sphere, the public sphere, and religion. It would, moreover, be an error to presume that the information society with its tensions exists entirely within a secular sphere. Eliade (1959) points out that the profane region is never entirely free of the sacred. Religion and the public sphere interact, as evidenced by the powerful presence of the Protestant movement in the institutions of education, media, and government.[16] The essential tensions are not only informed by the conflict of a market or government perspective but also derived from conflicting worldviews of religions. Ultimately, the balances achieved for the tensions outlined in the next sections will define what individuals consider to be fair and just.

Privacy

Privacy once meant the right to be left alone, its religious dimension being the solitude of a person in the presence of God. There existed an expected balance between a person's secret intimacy with God, often expressed in the home, and engagement with one's community through the congregation. In this vision, privacy represents one anchor in a person's integrated life, the other being participation in the public sphere.

Throughout the 20th century, the private sphere has advanced, whereas the public sphere has retreated. For the practice of religion, this has meant a shift in the balance between the two spiritual arenas, especially because Americans tend to define the public sphere in secular terms. For the most part, Americans hesitate to disclose their religious fervor in the workplace or in the community beyond a perfunctory acknowledgment of attendance at a particular church. The family that regularly says grace before meals is not likely to do so when eating out. In the home, religious expression can still be found, whether through the ritual gatherings of Jews, the icons typical of Catholic and orthodox practice, or the Protestant preference for behaviors such as bedtime prayers. Given the traditional distinction between the two spheres, the private offers a refuge from worldliness and fragmentation.

Ironically, the growing importance of the private sphere has been encouraged by the reinvention of the home into a window on the world fueled by consumer media and devices for processing information. The home as media center now functions as the locale for learning about current events, thereby replacing older public forums, such as the village commons and the corner saloon. Moreover, as leisure has moved from public institutions to the privacy of the home, so too has the focus of the media environment. From the spectacular introduction of radio in the 1920s to the spread of the personal computer in the 1990s, Americans require more and more home-based media to meet the demands of individualism and the pressures of fragmentation. Religious media—books, musical recordings, videos, and satellite revival meetings—suggest a parallel burgeoning of the private pursuit of religious experience. The wider variety of media products supports shopping, leisure, and work. The redefinition of the home as a refuge and as a window has also created the opportunity for an unprecedented intersection between religion and consumption.

There is no doubt that solitude—an essential condition for communing with God in many faiths—can be achieved in church, in public, or at home. The reinvention of domestic space has led to a subtle shift. Transforming the home into a media center has replaced solitude with privacy.

Politics and Logic of Images

The tension between politics and religion is an old one in U.S. culture, especially for Protestants. The self-presentation of Americans as a religious people can be found in the first paragraph of the Declaration of Independence, where the revolutionaries armed themselves with divine justification. But whereas the signatories to the Declaration stood united in the uprightness of their moral purpose, they were less confident of the good intentions of the many religious institutions in their midst; the fear of tyranny exacted by an official state church bellows from the first clause of the First Amendment of the Constitution.[17] In the ensuing 200 years, enduring phrases, such as "God bless America," "In God we trust," and "One nation under God," reveal the central role of religious beliefs in the political culture of the United States. Their persistence has also produced a volatile mixture. Religious condemnation—and support —for state-sanctioned slavery dominated public debate in the first half of the 19th century. In our own century, the morality of the Civil Rights movement, the Vietnam War, school prayer, family values, and abortion has contributed to the ongoing interpretation, and reinterpretation, of the First Amendment.

The information society inserts a twist to this constant of U.S. culture. The battle over religion, morality, and the duties of the state was once played out in the pulpit, the revival meeting, and on the Chautauqua circuit. With the enlargement of the private sphere, however, the battle more than ever takes place in the media. Religious talk shows, broadcast rites, and video sermons in the interest of political agendas reach millions who need not leave their homes to participate. Political positions are taken by religious leaders who use the mediated pulpit to promote a particular moral blueprint. Public demonstrations, such as those at abortion clinics, aim to attract media attention and, thereby, penetrate the homes (and consciences) of potential supporters. The logic of images frames the entire debate, even (perhaps especially) where scandals are concerned; images of "fallen" ministers are presented, destroyed, and reconstructed for audiences. In the information society, public debate and religion takes place in the home. The merging of these two overlapping orbits foreshadows the growing intrusion of religious issues into public political life.

Literacy

Religions of the Book have long depended on literacy as discipline. The invention of printing made available biblical texts to common people and broke the 1,000-year-old monopoly of interpretation held by priests. It was the drive for mass literacy, however, that completed the sociotechnical revolution begun by Gutenberg (Eisenstein, 1979, 1986). Protestants sought to convert each adherent into a self-contained interpreter of the Word and, in so doing, fundamentally altered the social terrain of Europe.

Literacy represents more than a technique for accessing recorded characters; it is also a way of thinking tied to the interpretation of symbols presented in a linear format. Literacy converted words from sounds into physical artifacts. Because writing allowed written messages to be separated from their originators by virtue of their independent existence as artifacts, literacy converted the Bible from a tradition into a fixed text. Writing conquered time and space, allowing geographically dispersed groups to maintain organization around a common set of documents; early church councils sought to fix wordings of texts to preserve unity of doctrine. Literacy imposed rigidity on speech by elevating the written form to higher status than the spoken form; the sermon became an instrument to augment the Bible.[17] Thus, as long as print and reading dominated religious instruction and practice, the thought processes associated with literacy shaped attitudes toward the proper expression of religion, but never completely.

In the 19th century, when even the Catholic Church with its reliance on tradition and the cycle of feasts moved toward a literate laity, currents of orality and emotional expression reemerged among U.S. evangelical Protestants. Methodist and Baptist revival and camp meetings spread throughout the country, attracting huge crowds for several days of nonstop preaching, exhorting by both men and women, music, swooning, jerking, and dancing (Finke & Stark, 1992). Indeed, in all Western religions, as in Western culture, there exists a balance between orality and literacy; that is, both forms of expression must be available.

The age of multiple communication technologies creates a basis for a reshift in the balance. Marshall McLuhan (1958, 1962, 1964, 1968; McLuhan & Fiore, 1967) caught a glimmer in the 1950s. He then proposed that media function as extensions of the senses and so determine the ways in which a society functions, thus profoundly affecting people's thought processes and their organization of social life.

His interpretations of the impact of information technologies carry a spiritual quality as, for example, in his suggestion that radio offers "a world of unspoken communication between writer-speaker and the listener . . . a private experience . . . charged with the resonating echoes of tribal horns and antique drums" (McLuhan, 1964, p. 261). He is emphatic in his assertion that information technologies will push humanity toward a single consciousness, the global village (McLuhan, 1964, p. 67).[18] Though the most extreme of social theorists, McLuhan is not alone in suggesting that the world created by the adoption of so many information technologies will result in a decline in traditional literacy and a resurgence of orality.[19] The implications for religious organization go far beyond reading the Book.

The religions of the Word are on the verge of being reconquered by a new kind of orality, in which multimedia environments will frame the religious experience. Whereas medieval megachurches, such as the Cathedral at Chartres, provided religious information to its believers through icons and symbols, gargoyles and stained-glass windows, and the physical, theatrical ritual of the mass, new megachurches, such as Willow Creek in Illinois, provide religious information through the electronic media of music and video and theatrical presentations on moral issues, all of which can be televised. Bible reading and study are relegated to advanced, committed believers (Niebuhr, 1995b). Ironically, the decline in focus on print literacy is leading to the return of the theatrical, ritual characteristics of the original megachurches.

Of the consequences of this tension, we have only clues and questions. What role will religious institutions play in the development of the new literacy? As literacy declines or changes, will religions of the Book move to new media formats and new ways of understanding religious beliefs? And will the shift away from print culture to a new, visual, "virtual reality" culture undo the foundation from which Protestant Christianity grew?

Community

The resurgence of enthusiasm for spirituality and religion may be traced in part to the decline in community brought about by the fragmenting tendencies of the information society. The more people take advantage of the increased interconnectedness made possible by information technologies, the more they depend on secondary relationships for their daily interactions, and the more they feel disconnected from their immediate surroundings. Still, the desire for community remains strong and, along with it, for membership in religious congregations as one solution.

Traditional communities, that is, those conceived of as geographical locations, find themselves challenged by the information society. As more and more Americans experience fewer primary relationships either at work or where they live, the hometown as community becomes more an ideal than a reality. Nevertheless, the new conditions are met with ambivalence. Americans desire the coziness and familiarity of Mark Twain's (1874) Hannibal, Missouri, or of Meredith Willson's (1958) town square in *The Music Man*. At the same time, they dislike the stifling small-mindedness and quickness to judge of Sinclair Lewis's (1920) *Main Street*, or Sherwood Anderson's (1919) *Winesburg, Ohio*.[20] And for those who have ever lived on the wrong side of the tracks, the small-town ideal is tinged with resentment. The community as a cohesive unit, especially the small-town variety, has been under attack for most of the century. First, the telephone, allied with the automobile, allowed Americans to shed the constraints of small-town life while still maintaining connections to family and friends. Then, radio and television, in their successive incarnations, broke the monopoly of the local gathering place for up-to-the-minute news. Now, new interactive technologies revolving around computer networks further extrapolate this trend by creating the basis for new virtual communities.

Virtual communities supply one kind of connectedness through electronic technology. These "network communities" of individuals bound by common interests transcend the limits of time and space found in face-to-face personal encounters and, therefore, in all geographic communities. Primary relationships, necessary to the ideal community, no longer dominate life as we live far from the family and friends who make up our personal communities. Network members, even though they lack the mundane, physical, and emotional dimensions of primary interpersonal relationships, create dispersed communities that provide opportunities for equality, fantasy, and autonomy, while challenging expectations of interdependence and responsibility. Beyond the virtual communities of hackers and Internet aficionados, similar telenetworks meet our daily needs. Home shopping and telecommuting limit our interactions to strangers or secondary relationships but extend our capacities as consumers and workers. They work because the progressive fragmentation of society experienced during the 20th century has not dimmed individuals' desire for interconnectedness and the reassurance of community. Yet though they meet the needs of their members, the emergence of virtual communities raises questions of a broader nature. How is community to be achieved among isolated individuals? What binds virtual communities together? And in line with Governor Caperton's concern, can virtual communities by themselves reverse the larger tendency toward social fragmentation?

Given that we have no clear answers to these questions, the continued convergence of religion and technology is likely to result in religious expressions within the medium of virtual communities. After all, the fragmentation that has led to decline in neighborhood structures has not diminished the desire for connection that may find expression within the contexts of new information technologies. Americans may increasingly imagine the religious experience as a personally isolated communion between the individual and God, join electronic congregations in which the members know little about each other, and adopt a kind of religious practice that is centered in the home. When this version of Christianity becomes a major presence in the culture, it will represent a new ideal of community, whereas old communities, of the geographically centered kind, will have lost one of the ties that bind.

Marginalized Voices

In the search for equality in the information society, feminist theorists both from within and outside of Judeo-Christian tradition have struggled with implications of mainline religious belief systems for women. The language and image of God as male only has been analyzed as the expression, or perhaps the origin, of patriarchal culture. Achtemeier (1993) writing in *Christianity Today* explains why God cannot be understood as mother from the evangelical viewpoint. Although language changes have made little impact on fundamentalist and evangelical groups, or the electronic church, the movement to alter the male-only conception of God has had an impact on mainline denominations through its acceptance of women as ministers. Feminists such as Mary Daly (1968, 1973), Rosemary R. Ruether (1975, 1992), and Tivka Frymer-Kensky (1992) propose that this very change in our understanding of divinity will eventually provide the key to women's equality. Aburdene and Naisbitt (1992) point to feminist theology and goddess worship as some of the most powerful trends currently influencing women's lives. Over the past 20 years, women have begun attending theology schools; they now account for nearly half of the students in Yale Divinity School. The search for gender equality has led to a fundamental questioning of our understanding of God and religious ideas.

Latinos represent another important challenge to equality in the information society because they contain a large percentage of Spanish speakers. Motivated to improve their levels of economic development and political participation, Latinos will likely press for greater access to information resources in Spanish. Moreover, the logic of an open democracy will encourage them to do so. Yet such efforts are sure to trigger deep resistance by Americans who fear the institutionalization of any language other than English. This is sure to result in renewed conflict over a national language, with calls to enforce the use of English becoming more strident.

As metaphors for the culture of the United States change from a melting pot to a patchwork quilt, the dual tension of individual and community is revealed and language takes center stage. Again the question of equality lies in the balance. Two religious approaches to this tension arising from feminist, Latino, and African American communities include political theology and Pentecostal movements, the first depending on cultural analysis to create change and the other depending on the experience of the mystical—speaking in tongues, healings, physical and emotional expressions—to challenge understandings.

Women and minorities in the information society will be affected by factors deeply rooted in racism, economics, and the patriarchal culture. The realignment of forces brought about by the information society will bring consumption, employment, and language to center stage. Religious belief systems play a crucial role in resolving these issues of the information society.

UNDERCURRENTS

The act of writing this chapter taught us that the impact of the information society on the practice of religion will produce a most complex range of possibilities beyond any simple predictions. At best, the dynamics we identify should be taken as markers or as a context within which to interpret old and new religious practices. Still, the tendencies and tensions, along with their derivations, are pervasive and, therefore, deserve contemplation if one is to attempt to understand the following changes facing religions in the United States today:

1. As information comes to be considered a thing, so too will religion. The facility with which information can be converted into a commodity also encourages the brokering of religious symbols in the marketplace, resulting in fuzzy boundaries. Americans will consume spirituality in the same settings in which they consume entertainment.

2. The reinvention of domestic space has remade the home into a media center. The old public exposure to the norms of the congregation has been left behind for the liberation of the privacy of one's home. Where the faithful once sought solitude, they now claim privacy.

3. Americans are busy constructing virtual communities, both within and beyond the Internet. The power of the home as media center assists in this quest, and the new attitude toward religious privacy encourages the practice of religion apart from traditional geographically oriented communities. Certainly, the mainstream religions, with their dependence on a centralized hierarchy to govern and socialize the members, will adapt. But many will do so by bringing together mostly anonymous congregations. Still, the yen for intimate community continues unabated.

4. Religions of the book must reexamine their skill base, as traditional literacy declines and new forms of electronic literacy establish themselves. That is, along with the emergence of megachurches and electronic congregations will come the adoption of presentation rituals that emphasize the visual and the oral.

5. The line between media entertainment and media religion will continue to blur, as the consumption of religion and the consumption of secular entertainment take place in the same settings. Individuals accustomed to meeting so many needs via the same channels are thus likely to further blur the separation between religious belief and political conviction.

From this intertwining of religion and the information society, we pose three lasting questions. How will the tendencies and tensions of the information age lead people to imagine their God differently? In what ways will these interactions alter religious practice? Will new religious sects grow from the dynamics of the information society?

The United States is too large a country to be thought of as a single society; one-quarter billion people do not subscribe to a single set of values, and this has always been especially true for people's religious practices. Yet the "societies" that make up the United States evolve along parallel paths. Indeed, the tendencies of the information age comprise some of the paths that are reshaping all of those societies, whereas the tensions emerge out of the struggles to negotiate the consequences. It is within this ferment that Americans are choosing new settings for religious expression. As they do, the most ancient and fundamental assertion of humans as self-conscious beings will undergo one more reiteration—shedding old conventions, adopting new outlooks.

NOTES

1. The rise and growth of the evangelical movement, the electronic church, and megachurches in the United States have been documented in the popular and academic press in numerous polls, surveys, and historical discussions. See, for example, Dorgan (1993), Elvy (1986), Erickson (1992), Finke and Stark (1992), Fishwick (1995), Hoover (1988), Niebuhr (1995b), Schultze (1990), Sheler (1994), and Sweet (1993).

2. Our understanding of religion is a sociological one, and we are indebted to Peter Berger's (1967) definition of religion as a world-constructing, world-maintaining enterprise by which a sacred cosmos is established. Like Berger, we recognize the biblical tradition and monotheism that bind Judaism, Catholicism, and Protestantism together historically and create the dominant Judeo-Christian tradition in the United States.

Protestantism is the dominant religious perspective in the United States and is therefore our main focus. Finke and Stark (1992), Fishwick (1995), Hammond (1992), Hoover (1988), Marty (1992), Schultze (1990), and Sweet (1993) trace the complicated roots of Protestantism religious trends and the growth of conservative, Evangelical churches in the United States. In light of this complex history, it becomes difficult to define religious groups by such constantly evolving terms as *Fundamentalist, Evangelical, neo-Evangelical, conservative, liberal,* or *mainline* denominations. In this chapter, we will not attempt to retrace the steps leading to such terminology. Fundamentalism will be viewed as the more conservative, antimodernist wing of the evangelical movement. Following Hoover (1988), the term *evangelical* will for our purposes incorporate the neo-evangelical movement personified most prominently by Billy Graham and associated with the politically conservative, charismatic, Pentecostal belief systems frequently espoused in evangelical religious media.

3. The theory of an information society presented here is fully developed in Schement and Curtis (1992) and is derived from the work of Bell (1976), Boorstin (1961), and McLuhan (1964), who took information and communication as central themes and shaped the popular images and scholarly interpretations that have come to dominate thinking about the information society.

4. The willingness to see social change as a result of developments in technology commits the fallacy of technological determinism, because it fails to recognize the roles played by social forces and personal choices. See, for example, David (1986), Heilbroner (1967), and Winner (1977).

5. See U.S. Bureau of the Census (1991), Tables 11 and 45.

6. Remember that Jesus proclaimed in the New Testament, "It is easier for a camel to go through the eye of a needle than for a rich man to enter the kingdom of God" (Matthew 19:24, NAB).

7. After 500 years, the consequences of mass literacy and printing are still being comprehended. For a sense of the extent of this long transformation, see, for example, Altick (1957), Darnton (1979, 1984), Eisenstein (1979), Febvre and Martin (1976), Goody (1986), and Putnam (1896/1962).

8. While pursuing research on a Fulbright fellowship to Finland in 1986, Schement observed the link between the establishment of literacy through Protestantism and the growth of an information workforce. In 19th-century Finland, women were encouraged to learn to read the Bible as the protectors of Protestant tradition in the face of the encroachment of Russian Orthodox Catholi- cism. In the second half of the 20th century, the existence of a solid base of mass literacy enabled women to leave the farms and go directly into office work, thus empowering Finland's dramatic industrialization of the 1950s and 1960s.

9. Diderot's radical reorganization of knowledge is not readily available today, but Aquinas's can be read in an excellent translation (see Aquinas, 1265-1273/ 1912-1936).

10. Probably the best extant copy in North America of Gutenberg's Bible can be found in the collection of the Huntington Library, Los Angeles, California. The University of Texas at Austin also possesses a copy; however, this copy is a composite of two previously partial volumes.

11. The word "clock" reflects its monastic origins and is derived from the German word *glocke*, which means bell. See Boorstin (1985, pp. 36-39), Landes (1983, pp. 62-66), and Mumford (1934/1962, pp. 12-14). Rouget (1980/1985) identifies various ancient and contemporary spiritual and religious worldviews in which bells are identified with a voice or sound of divinity.

12. This idea of information as thing is so recent that we are just beginning to understand its cultural and historical roots and examine its taken-for-granted status as a social construction. Kenneth Gergen (1991) provides a social constructionist perspective on the modernist and romantic worldviews contributing to the emerging postmodern perspective. Gergen points out that the modernist view of the rational, unitary, "machine-like" individual is derived from the same Enlightenment period that created the dictionary and encyclopedia leading to the idea of information as a product or thing.

James Carey (1988), a communication theorist, uses the social constructionist view to identify two understandings of communication at work in U.S. culture, the dominant transmission view and the older, ritual view. The transmission view is concerned with the technology of communication and the information to be derived from the messages. It is expressed in metaphors of transportation, in the language of technology and electricity, and in the modern social science model of humans. Carey offers the broader ritual view of communication that recognizes the role communication plays in providing information but also in confirming our identities and our connection to the larger community. Communication produces the social bonds that make life possible and humans exist in relation not in the isolation of the individualist perspective.

These social constructivist views question our understanding of information and religion as thinglike and point to the modernist assumptions informing such an understanding.

13. Finke and Stark (1992) document the decrease in religious workers in the Catholic Church from 1955 to 1990. Julia Lieblich (1992) takes a case study approach to the complexity of religious callings in the contemporary world. Reconciliations with some aspect of capitalism, for example, the excesses of capitalists and financial manipulators, may not prove easy for religions to achieve. Engels (1845/1987) and Marx (1886/1906) long ago pointed out negative effects of industrial capitalism such as alienation. See also John Paul II (1981) on human work.

14. For example, on the average, U.S. homes contain two television sets and five radios but fewer than three people. See U.S. Bureau of the Census (1991), Table 919.

15. The pope's Feast of the Assumption Mass was carried on the NBC network, August 15, 1993, live from a park in Colorado holding more than 500,000 celebrants.

16. Hutchison (1989) refers to the Protestant influence in the institutions of the 18th- and 19th-century United States as a "taken for granted hegemony within American society" and documents the impact of religious diversity in the 20th century as the transition is made from "Protestant America to pluralist America" (p. vii).

17. From the Declaration of Independence: "When in the Course of human events, it becomes necessary for one people to dissolve the political bands which have connected them with another, and to assume among the Powers of the earth, the separate and equal station to which the Laws of Nature and of Nature's God entitle them, a decent respect to the opinions of mankind requires that they should declare the causes which impel them to the separation." And further on: "that all men are created equal, that they are endowed by their Creator with certain unalienable Rights, that among these are Life, Liberty and the pursuit of Happiness." The First Amendment reads as follows (Note the order of the clauses for a clue to the concerns of the drafters.): "Congress shall make no law respecting an establishment of religion, or prohibiting the free exercise thereof; or abridging the freedom of speech, or of the press; or the right of the people peaceably to assemble, and to petition the Government for a redress of grievances."

18. The shift from oral to literate culture is of enormous importance to any understanding of the roots of the information society. For a fuller discussion of the successive impacts of the invention of writing, see Clanchy (1979), Couch (1989), Dalby (1986), Gelb (1952), Goody (1986, 1987), Havelock (1976, 1982), LePan (1989), Lord (1964), Ong (1982), and Ullman (1932/1969).

19. Most scholars agree that McLuhan derived his ideas from those of his mentor, Harold Innis. Innis was a graduate of the University of Chicago where he studied under Robert Ezra Park and was influenced by the work of Siegfried Giedion. Park's and Giedion's views on technology strongly influenced Innis, contributing to the element of technological determinism in his writings and later in McLuhan's. See Giedion (1948), Innis (1950, 1951), and Park (1916).

20. See, for example, new forms of literacy and orality described in Davidson (1989), Howell (1989), Klapp (1986), Ong (1982), Postman (1985), and Zill and Winglee (1990).

21. It should be noted that Carol Kennicott eventually makes her peace with the townspeople of Gopher Prairie in *Main Street* (Lewis, 1990). George Willard is

Winesburg's confidant and the ear to many tales of hope and failure in *Winesburg, Ohio* (Anderson, 1919). For another example of this genre, see Howe (1882) *The Story of a Country Town*, in which Ned Westlock and his family struggle to improve themselves against misfortune and the disapproval of the townsfolk of Twin Mounds. Kenneth Gergen (1991) begins his discussion of the rise of postmodernism and accompanying technological changes with a lament for the small-town community of his childhood.

REFERENCES

Aburdene, P., & Naisbitt, J. (1992). *Megatrends for women*. New York: Villard Books.

Achtemeier, E. (1993, August 16). Why God is not mother. *Christianity Today, 37*(9), 16-23.

Altick, R. D. (1957). *The English common reader: A social history of the mass reading public*. Chicago: University of Chicago Press.

Anderson, S. (1919). *Winesburg, Ohio: A group of tales of Ohio small-town life*. New York: Modern Library.

Aquinas, T. (1912-1936). *The summa theologica* (L. Shapcote, Trans.). London: Burns, Oates. (Original work written 1265-1273)

Bell, D. (1976). *The coming of post-industrial society*. New York: Basic Books.

Benedictus. (1975). *The rule of Saint Benedict* (A. C. Meisel & M. L. del Mastro, Trans.). New York: Image Books. (Original work published 547)

Berger, P. L. (1967). *The sacred canopy: Elements of a sociological theory of religion*. New York: Doubleday.

Bollier, D. (1995, August). The future of community and personal identity in the coming electronic culture. In *A report of the third annual Aspen Institute Roundtable on Information Technology* (pp. 1-38). Washington, DC: Aspen Institute, Communications and Society Program.

Boorstin, D. J. (1961). *The image: A guide to pseudo-events in America*. New York: Athaneum.

Boorstin, D. J. (1985). *The discoverers*. New York: Vintage.

Carey, J. W. (1988). *Communication as culture*. New York: Routledge.

Clanchy, M. T. (1979). *From memory to written record: England 1066-1307*. Cambridge, MA: Harvard University Press.

Couch, C. J. (1989). Oral technologies: A cornerstone of ancient civilizations? *Sociological Quarterly, 30*(4), 587-602.

Dalby, A. (1986). The Sumerian catalogs. *Journal of Library History, 21*(3), 475-487.

Daly, M. (1968). *The church and the second sex*. New York: Harper & Row.

Daly, M. (1973). *Beyond God the father: Toward a philosophy of women's liberation*. Boston: Beacon.

Darnton, R. (1979). *The business of Enlightenment: A publishing history of the Encyclopédie 1775-1800*. Cambridge, MA: Belknap Press.

Darnton, R. (1984). *The great cat massacre and other episodes in French cultural history*. New York: Vintage Books.

David, P. A. (1986). Understanding the economics of QWERTY: The necessity of history. In W. N. Parker (Ed.), *Economic history and the modern economist* (pp. 30-49). New York: Basil Blackwell.

Davidson, C. N. (Ed.). (1989). *Reading in America: Literature and social history*. Baltimore, MD: Johns Hopkins University Press.

Dorgan, H. (1993). *The airwaves of Zion: Radio and religion in Appalachia*. Knoxville: University of Tennessee Press.

Eisenstein, E. L. (1979). *The printing press as an agent of change: Communications and cultural transformations in early modern Europe*. Cambridge, UK: Cambridge University Press.

Eisenstein, E. L. (1986). Print culture and Enlightenment thought. In *Hanes Foundation for the study of the origin and development of the book* (The sixth Hanes lecture). [Rare book collection/University library]. Chapel Hill: University of North Carolina.

Eliade, M. (1959). *The sacred and the profane: The nature of religion* (W. R. Trask, Trans.). New York: Harcourt, Brace and World.

Elvy, P. (1986). *Buying time: The foundations of the electronic church*. Essex, UK: McCrimmon.

Engels, E. (1987). *The conditions of the working class in England* (F. Wischnewetzky, Trans.). Harmondsworth, UK: Penguin. (Original work published 1845)

Erickson, H. (1992). *Religious radio and television in the United States, 1921-1991: The programs and personalities*. Jefferson, NC: McFarland and Company.

Febvre, L., & Martin, H.-J. (1976). *The coming of the book: The impact of printing, 1450-1800* (D. Gerard, Trans.). London, UK: N.L.B.

Finke, R., & Stark, R. (1992). *The churching of America, 1776-1990: Winners and losers in our religious economy*. New Brunswick, NJ: Rutgers University Press.

Fishwick, M. W. (1995). *Great awakenings: Popular religion and popular culture*. New York: Haworth.

Frymer-Kensky, T. (1992). *In the wake of the goddesses: Women, culture, and the biblical transformation of pagan myth*. New York: Free Press.

Gelb, I. J. (1952). *A study of writing*. Chicago: University of Chicago Press.

Gergen, K. J. (1991). *The saturated self: Dilemmas of identity in contemporary life*. New York: Basic Books.

Giedion, S. (1948). *Mechanization takes command: A contribution to anonymous history*. New York: Norton.

Goody, J. (1986). *The logic of writing and the organization of society: Literacy, family, culture and the state*. Cambridge, UK: Cambridge University Press.

Goody, J. (1987). *The interface between the written and the oral: Literacy, family, culture and the state*. Cambridge, UK: Cambridge University Press.

Hammond, P. E. (1992). *The Protestant presence in twentieth-century America: Religion and political culture*. Albany: State University of New York Press.

Hampson, N. (1968). *The Enlightenment*. Harmondsworth, Middlesex: Penguin.

Havelock, E. A. (1976). *Origins of Western literacy* (Monograph Series No. 14). Toronto: Ontario Institute for Studies in Education.

Havelock, E. A. (1982). *The literate revolution in Greece and its cultural consequences*. Princeton, NJ: Princeton University Press.

Heilbroner, R. L. (1967). Do machines make history? *Technology and Culture, 8*(3), 335-345.

Hoover, S. M. (1988). *Mass media religion: The social sources of the electronic church*. Newbury Park, CA: Sage.

Howe, E. W. (1882). *The story of a country town*. New York: Blue Ribbon Books.

Howell, R. P. (Ed.). (1989). *Beyond literacy: The second Gutenberg revolution.* San Francisco: Saybrook.

Hutchison, W. R. (Ed.). (1989). *Between the times: The travail of the Protestant establishment in America, 1900-1960.* Cambridge, UK: Cambridge University Press.

Innis, H. A. (1950). *Empire and communication.* Toronto, Canada: University of Toronto.

Innis, H. A. (1951). *The bias of communication.* Toronto, Canada: University of Toronto.

John Paul II. (1981). *On human work: Laborem exercens.* In C. Carlen (comp.), *The Papal Encyclicals* (vol. 5 pp.. 299-325). Wilmington, NC: McGrath Publishing.

Johnson, E. D. (1970). *History of libraries in the Western world.* Metuchen, NJ: Scarecrow Press.

Klapp, O. E. (1986). *Overload and boredom: Essays on the quality of life in the information society.* New York: Greenwood.

Landers, P. (1995, February 26). Billy Graham: Beyond the next crusade. *Miami Herald,* pp. E5-E7.

Landes, D. S. (1983). *Revolution in time.* Cambridge, MA: Harvard University Press.

LePan, D. (1989). *The cognitive revolution in Western culture: The birth of expectation.* London, UK: Macmillan.

Lewis, S. (1920). *Main street.* New York: Harcourt Brace.

Lieblich, J. (1992). *Sisters: Lives of devotion and defiance.* New York: Ballantine.

Lord, A. B. (1964). *The singer of tales.* Cambridge, MA: Harvard University Press.

Lovejoy, A. O. (1936). *The great chain of being.* Cambridge, MA: Harvard University Press.

Marty, M. E. (Ed.). (1992). *Trends in American religion and Protestant world.* New York: K. G. Saur.

Marx, K. (1906). *Capital: A critique of political economy.* New York: Modern Library. (Original work published 1886)

McArthur, T. (1986). *Worlds of reference: Lexicography, learning and language from the clay tablet to the computer.* Cambridge, UK: Cambridge University Press.

McLuhan, M. (1958). Media alchemy in art and society. *Journal of Communication, 8,* 63-67.

McLuhan, M. (1962). *The Gutenberg galaxy: The making of typographic man.* New York: New American Library.

McLuhan, M. (1964). *Understanding media: The extensions of man.* New York: New American Library.

McLuhan, M. (1968). *War and peace in the global village.* New York: Bantam.

McLuhan, M., & Fiore, Q. (1967). *The medium is the massage.* New York: Bantam.

Milton, J. (1667). *Paradise lost: A poem written in ten books.* London, UK: Samuel Simmons.

Mumford, L. (1962). *Technics and civilization.* New York: Harcourt, Brace and World. (Original work published 1934)

Neuhaus, R. J. (1992). *Doing well and doing good: The challenge to the Christian capitalist.* New York: Doubleday.

Niebuhr, G. (1995a, April 18). The minister as marketer: Learning from business. *New York Times,* pp. A1, A20.

Niebuhr, G. (1995b, April 16). Where religion gets a big dose of shopping-mall culture. *New York Times,* pp. A1, A14.

Novak, M. (1993). *The Catholic ethic and the spirit of capitalism.* New York: Free Press.

Ong, W. J. (1982). *Orality and literacy: The technologizing of the word.* London, UK: Methuen.

Park, R. E. (1916). The city: Suggestions for the investigation of human behavior in the urban environment. *American Journal of Sociology, 20,* 577-612.

Postman, N. (1985). *Amusing ourselves to death: Public discourse in the age of show business.* New York: Penguin.

Putnam, G. H. (1962). *Books and their makers during the middle ages.* New York: Hillary House. (Original work published 1896)

Rouget, G. (1985). *Music and trance: A theory of the relations between music and possession* (B. Biebuyck & G. Rouget, Trans.). Chicago: University of Chicago Press. (Original work published 1980)

Ruether, R. R. (1975). *New woman, new earth: Sexist ideologies and human liberation.* New York: Seabury.

Ruether, R. R. (1992). *Gaia & God: An ecofeminist theology of earth healing.* San Francisco: Harper.

Schement, J. R. (1990). Porat, Bell, and the information society reconsidered: The growth of information work in the early twentieth century. *Information Processing and Management, 26*(4), 449-465.

Schement, J. R., & Curtis, T. (1995). *Tendencies and tensions of the information age.* New Brunswick, NJ: Transaction.

Schultze, Q. J. (1987). The mythos of the electronic church. *Critical Studies in Mass Communication, 4,* 245-261.

Schultze, Q. J. (Ed.). (1990). *American Evangelicals and the mass media: Perspectives on the relationship between American Evangelicals and the mass media.* Grand Rapids, MI: Academie.

Sheler, J. L. (1994, April 4). Spiritual America. *U.S. News & World Report, 16*(13), 48-59.

Soukup, P. A. (1991). *Communication and theology: Introduction and review of the literature.* London: World Association for Christian Communication.

Sweet, L. I. (1993). *Communication and change in American religious history.* Grand Rapids, MI: Eerdmans.

Thigpen, D. E. (1995, May 22). Leaving little to chants. *Time, 45*(21), 72.

Twain, M. (1874). *Life on the Mississippi.* New York: Harper & Brothers.

Ullman, B. L. (1969). *Ancient writing and its influence.* Cambridge: MIT Press. (Original work published 1932)

U.S. Bureau of the Census. (1990). *Statistical abstracts of the United States: 1990.* Washington, DC: Government Printing Office.

U.S. Bureau of the Census. (1991). *Statistical abstracts of the United States: 1991.* Washington, DC: Government Printing Office.

Weber, M. (1958). *The Protestant ethic and the spirit of capitalism* (T. Parsons, Trans.). New York: Scribner.

Willson, M. (1958). *Libretto for Meredith Willson's The music man.* New York: Music Theatre International.

Winner, L. (1977). *Autonomous technology: Technics-out-of-control as a theme in political thought.* Cambridge: MIT Press.

Zill, N., & Winglee, M. (1990). *Who reads literature? The future of the United States as a nation of readers.* Washington, DC: Seven Locks Press.

About the Contributors

Margaret Lamberts Bendroth is a lecturer at Andover-Newton Theological Seminary in Newton Centre, Massachusetts. She is the author of *Fundamentalism and Gender, 1875 to the Present*. Her writings on gender, Evangelicalism, and Fundamentalism have appeared in a number of scholarly publications, including *Evangelicalism and Modern America* and *Church History*.

Judith M. Buddenbaum is Associate Professor in the Department of Technical Journalism at Colorado State University. She has worked as a religion reporter and has conducted media research for the Lutheran World Federation, Geneva, Switzerland. Her research on religion and the mass media has been published in *Journalism History*, *Journalism Quarterly*, *Newspaper Research Journal* and as book chapters.

Cheryl Renée Gooch is Associate Professor at the University of North Dakota. Her research interests in international, intercultural, and popular communication devolve, in part, from her work as a reporter for both print and broadcast media. She has published numerous journal articles and book chapters. Recent works include

"Gangster Rap: Message Music or Mayhem for Profit?" in *Media Development* and "The Centrality of Endrogenous and Participatory Approaches to Communication Planning: A Case Study of Television Programming Policy in Barbados" published in *Gazette*.

Stewart M. Hoover is Associate Professor in the School of Journalism and Mass Communication and Professor Adjoint of Religious Studies and American Studies at the University of Colorado, Boulder, where he is also an associate of the Center for Mass Media Research. He is the author of *Mass Media Religion* and *Legacies of Misunderstanding and Mistrust* and coeditor of *Religious Television: Controversies and Conclusions* and *Rallies, Rituals, and Resistance: Rethinking Media, Religion, and Culture*.

Sharon Hartin Iorio is Professor in the Elliott School of Communication, Wichita State University, Wichita, Kansas. Her areas of funded research and refereed publication are social-historical studies of communication cultures, media information flow and political issue development, and communication curriculum development at secondary and postsecondary levels. Currently, she is developing a book on communication among Mennonite people during the 20th century. She has published in a number of scholarly journals such as *Journalism Quarterly*, *Journalism and Mass Communication Educator*, and the *Journal of the Association for Communication Administration*.

Ted G. Jelen is Professor of Political Science at Illinois Benedictine College in Lisle, Illinois. He has written, edited, and coauthored several books and numerous articles on religion and politics, the politics of abortion, and feminism. He is currently at work on a piece of normative political theory tentatively titled, *Christianity and Citizenship: Theoretical Perspectives on the Relationship Between Religion and Politics*.

Thomas R. Lindlof is Associate Professor of Telecommunications at the University of Kentucky. His research interests include mediated communication processes, cultural analysis of audiences, and qualitative methodology. His books include *Natural Audiences, Qualitative*

Communication Research Methods, and *Constructing the Self in a Mediated World* (with Debra Grodin).

Dennis G. Martin is Professor of Communications at Brigham Young University. His research interests include advertising, cultural anthropology, and the history of advertising. His books include *Strategic Advertising Campaigns* (with Don Schultz) and *Media Flight Plan.*

Sam G. McFarland is Professor of Psychology at Western Kentucky University, a Fellow of the Society for the Scientific Study of Religion, and a member of the Governing Council of the International Society for Political Psychology. His research interests include the psychology of religion, prejudice, ethnocentrism, the authoritarian personality, and moral reasoning. Most recently, he has studied Russian authoritarianism, with comparisons to authoritarianism in the United States; this work may be found in *Journal of Personality and Social Psychology* (December 1992); *Strengths and Weaknesses: The Authoritarian Personality Today* (Stone, Lederer, & Christie, 1993); and *Personality and Social Psychology Bulletin* (February 1996).

Tony Rimmer is Professor in the Department of Communications, California State University, Fullerton. He was formerly a TV producer. He is interested in the role of mass media in political life.

Jorge Reina Schement is Associate Professor at Rutgers University in the School of Communication, Information and Library Studies, as well as in the Department of Puerto Rican and Hispanic Caribbean Studies. In 1994, he served at the invitation of the chairman of the Federal Communication Commission, as director of the F.C.C.'s Information Policy Project. He is the coauthor and coeditor of many books and articles on the information age, including the recently published *Tendencies and Tensions of the Information Age.*

Quentin J. Schultze is Professor of Communication Arts and Sciences at Calvin College in Grand Rapids, Michigan. He is a former president of the Religious Speech Association and has authored or coauthored ten books, including *American Evangelicals and the Mass Media* and *American Culture: The Business of Popular Religion*. He has also written dozens of scholarly articles in communication and sociology journals as well as more than 100 articles for popular and religious periodicals. He speaks widely on media-related topics and has been quoted in nearly all of the major broadcast and print news media.

David W. Scott recently earned his M.A. in Communications at Brigham Young University. He is now an account representative for W.H. Freeman, a major textbook publisher. He writes about Mormon culture with specific attention to the role of mass media in Mormon life. Recently, he made a public presentation of his research at the annual convention of the Society for the Scientific Study of Religion (SSSR).

Hester C. Stephenson is a doctoral candidate at Rutgers University, School of Communication, Information and Library Studies and was invited by Professor Jorge Schement to coauthor their chapter in this book. Her interest in radical feminism and contemporary expressions of spirituality began a conversation and collaboration on a topic of concern for both authors from which this chapter emerged.

Daniel A. Stout is Assistant Professor of Communications at Brigham Young University. His writings on media issues appear in *Information and Behavior,* the *Southern Speech Communication Journal, Public Relations Review,* and the *Newspaper Research Journal.* Recent articles focus on mass media and the sociology of Mormonism.

JoAnn Myer Valenti is Professor of Communications at Brigham Young University and has been an educator for more than 15 years. She is corecipient of the Olive Branch Award for outstanding reporting on the nuclear arms issue in 1987. Her work appears in numerous publications, including *Public Understanding of Science, Health Education Quarterly, Public Relations Research Annual,* and contributed chapters in *Media Ethics: Issues and Cases* and *Women Transforming Communication* (in press).